8/6/05

To Jerry

Th

abou. Trusting Faith!

Counting
on a
Miracle

Clifford J. Fazzolari

CLIFFORD J. FAZZOLARI

CYNTOMedia
CORPORATION

Pittsburgh, PA

ISBN #1-58501-085-5

Non-Fiction
© Copyright 2004 Clifford Fazzolari
All Rights Reserved
First Printing — 2004
Library of Congress #2004106635

Request for information should be addressed to:

SterlingHouse Publisher, Inc.
7436 Washington Avenue
Pittsburgh, PA 15218
www.sterlinghousepublisher.com

CeShore is an imprint of SterlingHouse Publisher, Inc.

SterlingHouse Publisher, Inc. is a company
of the CyntoMedia Corporation.

Art Director: Matthew J. Lorenz
Cover Design: Matthew J. Lorenz
Typesetting & Layout Design: Beth Buckholtz
Illustration/Cover Art: Matthew J. Lorenz

Printed in the United States of America

Dedication

Counting on a Miracle
is dedicated to the memory of
Heather Cataldo
and to the wonderful people at
The Women & Children's Hospital of Buffalo.

Introduction

Counting on a Miracle: A Story of a Child's Care at the Children's Hospital of Buffalo is the compelling story of a family's response to one of its greatest threats: the illness of a child. It is written by a father who shares the fears, hopes, and spiritual resources a family uses to cope with a child's illness. While it is a unique story, it is also a common story we have observed as doctors in a children's hospital. Each family we care for depends upon a unique blend of family, friends, humor, and spirituality to cope with the fear, anxiety, and despair they may confront during the care of their child.

Counting on a Miracle is a story with value for families of sick children and the doctors, nurses, and hospitals that care for them. Families will see an example of how the combination of spirituality and family strength helped the Fazzolaris grow during Jacob's illness. Medical professionals will benefit from an inside look at the fear, loss of independence, and uncertainty that a family faces during a long illness.

We are grateful for Mr. Fazzolari's poignant account of Jacob's illness and are grateful to be entrusted with the health and well-being of so many children like Jacob. In the final analysis, this is a story of hope and trust, and we are proud to be a part of it.

Michael G. Caty, M.D.

Marc A. Levitt, M.D.

———Acknowledgements———

The writing of this story has been a spiritual journey of epic proportions. It has also been an educational process, as my appreciation of the medical community was especially heightened. We are forever grateful to the talented men and women of The Children's Hospital of Buffalo.

I would especially like to thank Doctor Marc Levitt, Doctor Michael Caty, Doctor Joy Graf, Pediatric Nurse Practitioner Karen Iacono, Doctor Doron Feldman, Doctor Bradley Fuhrman, Doctor James Foster, and OR Nurses Rosemary Silvashy, Helen Noblett, and Patricia Long and the entire staff of physicians and technicians that saved Jake's life. A special thanks to the ICU staff, including, but not limited to, Jeff Klempf, Ken Smith, and Ellen Eckhardt. Thanks to Janine and Neal Cross for years of friendship and talking us through it. To Sue Mazurchuk, Jake's all-time favorite nurse — you're a special person. A hearty thanks to photographer Brian Smistek for his outstanding work.

Our spiritual journeys were started by John and Lynda Fazzolari and John and Carolyn Foutz — everything we needed to find inside was there because of you — we love you, Moms and Dads.

Our siblings were simply marvelous and there's so much to be thankful for — just know that we depended on you, and you didn't let us down. Each and every one of you is special to us and each night our boys pray for you and your family. Thank you: Corinne and Chuck Leone, John and Dana Fazzolari and Andrea and Nicole, Jim and Lisa Fazzolari and Adam and James, Jeff and Lynn Fazzolari and John and Farrah, Mike and Carrie Peterson and Paige, Mike and Lori O'Neill and Briana, Ryan and Cory, John Foutz Sara, Laura, and Toni, Jim and Carilee Shea Jennie and Katie.

We have so many people to thank that we wondered if we should just offer a general word or acknowledgement, but you all deserve individual thanks and you are listed in no special order of importance — you are all equally loved and we include your families in our prayers. So, here goes:

Thank you, Grandma Edna and Grandma Schryver, Scott Danahy Naylon, Holy Spirit Church of North Collins, Our Lady of the Sacred Heart, The 1st Congregational Church of North Collins, Mike and Denise Palmer, Janice Catalano, the Schryver family, Tony and Yvonne Conza, Al and Jen DeCarlo, John and Mary Cataldo, Tom and Patrice Rybak, Joe and Amy Mathis, the Popple Family, the Smith family, Terri Prime, the Weiser Family, Dan Pisa, Chris and Andrea Heinold, Chris and Tina Miller and Alexis and Tori, Jeff and Kathy Renaldo, John Andolina, the Hemer Family, the Gier

Family, Bob and Pat Overhoff, Jim and Lori Goss, Mike LiVecchi and Carla Ayers, the Switala Family, the Gallego Family, James and Cheri Fazzolari, Carol and Mike Wittmeyer, Chuck and Karen Renaldo, Frank and Lisa Zocco, Jeff and Debbie Taylor, Cindy Anton, Kathy Ruh, Christopher Colantino, the Colantino Family, Bob and Tracy Brunner, Aaron DeCarlo, Kevin and Mary O'Neill, Pete Wade, Kim and Maria Patterson, Tim Janus, the McGrath Family, the Bantle family, the George Family, the Meads, the Partridges, the Haas Family, the Montaldi Family, the Stoklosa Family, Irma Dole, Mrs. Matte and Mrs. Karns of Our Lady of the Sacred Heart, and Mary Flanigen.

I sincerely hope that I did not leave anyone off the list. If I did, please take solace in Jake's new amended prayer:

God Bless Mommy and Daddy, Matt, Jake, and Sam, Max, Shadow, and Nobody, Grandma and Grandpa Foutz, Grandma Spiffy and Poppa John, aunts, uncles, and cousins. Make me be a good boy, God, and thank you for making me better. Thank you for all the people who helped me when I was sick. Amen.

Chapter One

Saturday — October 6, 2001

I heard the first cry at a little after five. My mind shifted to thoughts of rage. It was Saturday morning, for God's sake. I had worked hard all week. I deserved to sleep past five on a Saturday. I hesitated, hoping my fifteen-month-old son, Sam, hadn't really cried out. Maybe I had imagined it. Max, my golden lab, danced at the end of the bed, trying to nuzzle me out with his nose.

"Lie down!" I yelled.

But Max heard the second cry and, like it or not, I knew we were up for the day. I followed Max out of the bedroom and down the stairs just in time to hear Sam's third cry. At least Matthew wasn't home. My eight-year-old stepson was staying with his dad. But I didn't need four-year-old Jake to hear Sam's cries, either.

I slid open the door to Sam's bedroom and found him lying completely askew in his crib. His wailing cry was replaced with an ear-to-ear smile that lost some of its effectiveness this early in the morning. Now, Sam was a fairly low-maintenance baby. He only seemed to wake up early when Kathy was on the 4:30 to 12:30 shift.

I offered Sam a bottle, and he casually tossed it over the side of the crib.

"It ain't time to wake up yet." I had a feeling I was talking more to myself than to him. Sam responded with an earnest gaze from those big, brown eyes that made my heart stand still. Although the room was still half-dark, I imagined the smile behind those eyes. I made another half-hearted attempt to hand him the bottle, and he pitched it back over the side. "Come on, please." I plucked him out of the crib and — I couldn't help it — kissed him on the left cheek.

On the way out of Sam's room, we peeked in on Jake. The last thing I needed was to have both of them directing me around the house. Besides, Jake was an absolute terror some days, and I didn't have the energy to handle him. On the way out of the room, I heard Jake's labored breathing. He was an asthmatic with a touch of a cold, and even asleep he sounded horrible. As Sam and I made our way down the hallway, I stumbled over Max and almost flew headlong into the wall. Sam laughed, Max yelped, and I growled at the dog.

I put Sam in the walker, handed him the bottle (which he took now that he was out of the crib) and parked him in front of the television set. I started his favorite tape and rushed up the stairs. I figured that I had about three minutes to take a shower. Not quite enough time, but I knew that if I didn't run some water over my head, I'd be an absolute wreck. I left the bathroom door open and, under a shower of warm water, I seethed.

We had to have the world's worst schedule. Kathy worked ten straight days at the 4:30 to 12:30 shift, and I normally went Monday through Friday from seven to five. I also had an office in the house where I'd tie up loose ends and work on my writing career. I was in the middle of negotiating the contract for my fifth book.

"This sucks," I said to the rising steam.

I heard Sam cry out and, for good measure, our black lab, Shadow, barked to get out of the dog crate that we kept her in. I dressed on the way down the stairs, a leg and an arm at a time. My heart was already racing.

"Let the games begin," I said.

I fed the dogs and let them out into the fenced-in backyard. Then I put the gate up to restrict access to the stairs, returned to the living room and pulled Sam out of the walker. He smiled at me, and despite myself, I smiled back. He pointed at a half-dead balloon in a corner of the room, and I nodded along with him. There was no doubt that I loved my children more than anything else that this life had to offer, but honestly, I loved them a little less before six in the morning.

A couple of singing rhinos danced across my television screen. "It's going to be a rhino-rrific day," the obnoxious narrator's voice cried.

Sam crawled across the floor and sat a couple of feet away from the screen. The voice of the singing rhino went through me like a sharp razor. I had a passing thought about a cup of coffee, but I leaned in and kissed Sam instead. He slapped me good-naturedly on the side of the head. I telephoned Kathy at her office to let her know that Sam hadn't slept to seven as she had promised. Kathy was always concerned, and it upset her almost as much as it did me.

"I'm sorry he got you up," she said. "How's he doing?"

"Rhino-freaking-rrific," I said.

I spent the next two hours running from child to child. Neither Sam nor Jake would sit still for too long, and there were diapers to change and toast to butter. Thankfully, Kathy works just five minutes away, at Bethlehem Steel as a clerk, and she always plans her hour lunch to coincide with the moment when I am about to break down. I was reaching that moment. I glanced at the clock, and Jake noticed the movement of my eyes.

"What time is Mom coming home?" he asked. His voice was unbelievably raspy, and it caused me a split-second of concern.

"You don't sound too good," I said.

"I have a cold just like you," he answered.

Jake's most noticeable features are his big, brown eyes and very pronounced dimples in his cheeks. The brown eyes come from me, and the dimples are compliments of Kathy.

"Maybe we should do a breathing treatment," I said.

"I'm okay," Jake answered.

"You sound like a big monster," I said.

Jake feigned anger. He came at me, and I wrapped him in my arms. Sam crawled over to us and joined in the melee. We were in the middle of the wrestling match when we heard the downstairs door open and close.

"Mom's home," Jake growled.

The dogs were locked in the front room, and hopefully Shadow hadn't chewed anything to pieces. The washing machine was in its spin cycle, the dishes were washed, and the kitchen counter was clear.

"Hey, babe! How'd it go?" Kathy asked.

I rolled my eyes and sighed heavily. I couldn't put into words how good it felt to see her, but I couldn't put much into words at all at that point.

Kathy brushed by our little wrestling match and stepped into the kitchen. I heard her plastic coffee mug hit the sink, and she opened the cupboard door to retrieve Sam's cereal. Jake and Sam eased their hold on me, and we all headed for the kitchen.

"You look tired." Kathy said. She put a bowl in the microwave and set the time for thirty seconds. She offered her biggest apologetic smile, but I decided to milk it for all that I was worth.

"I'm miserable," I said. "I got a cold, and four hours of sleep a night just doesn't cut it." I grabbed the sports page and headed for the chair at the front of the kitchen table. Sam scooted across the floor; Jake screamed for Kathy; the dogs barked in the downstairs room. I held in my own personal scream.

"Jake sounds awful," I said. "He's hacking and coughing and gasping for air."

"I'm calling the doctor. He got the steroid. It doesn't seem to be working," Kathy said.

"I'm all right," Jake said.

We'd been through it a million times. Just over two years ago, Jake had been diagnosed with exercise-induced asthma. His breathing was always roughest when he caught a cold. I didn't give it a second thought, even though it seemed as if he was always on the verge of a cold.

"I've got to get something to eat before you go back to work," I said. I glanced at an article about the Yankees for a moment. I folded the paper and pushed it across the kitchen table. "I'm going to play with the dogs for a minute. I have to fold the laundry too."

I have a habit of not looking Kathy in the eye when I'm agitated, and I looked away as I made my way past her. She was stirring Sam's cereal, but she put the bowl on top of the microwave and grabbed me by the left arm. "Don't I get a kiss?" she asked.

4   CLIFFORD FAZZOLARI

"You're pushing your luck," I said, but I couldn't resist. I held her for nearly a full minute.

"I'll be home by 12:35," she said, "and we can all take a nap."

"Not me," I said. "I promised my father I'd help him make Italian sausage."

Kathy frowned deeply and offered me a sympathetic pat on the back. "You're going to the football game tomorrow, too, right?"

"Don't remind me," I said.

The hour that Kathy was home went by in what seemed like thirty seconds. She put the breathing machine on for Jake as I flopped down on the couch.

"Jake has to hold that in his mouth for ten minutes," she said. "Sam's fed and changed, and I'll be home before you know it." She kissed me on the cheek and brushed by me out the door. I wanted to follow her to freedom, but I simply rubbed my eyes. I just had to suck it up.

We watched the rhino tape at least three more times. Jake's breathing treatment didn't do much to help his congested lungs, but I figured that he just needed more rest. I battled my way to 12:30, and I lowered Sam into the crib just a few minutes before Kathy came through the door to end her work day. She walked in as I walked out, headed to North Collins and my parents' home to make the Italian sausage.

"Maybe you should skip it," Kathy said. "You really could use a nap."

"I promised I'd go. I haven't seen Mom and Dad. It'll give me a chance to visit."

Kathy leaned in once more, and I kissed her quickly. "Thanks for keeping the kids alive."

"We do have to take Jake to the doctor," I said.

"It's set for Monday," Kathy said.

I made the half-hour drive to my parents' home. I honestly didn't have a coherent thought in my head. I was too tired to think. The sky was cloudy and gray, and there was just enough rain to force me to turn on the wipers every thirty seconds. Even the usually peaceful drive was irritating.

My father was waiting, and we worked for a couple of hours stuffing ground pork into sausage casings. Dad's eyes were droopy too. "Maybe we can finish this tomorrow. I need a nap."

"I can't come out tomorrow," I said. "Kathy has to work again, and I'm going to the football game to watch the Bills get their asses kicked."

Dad laughed. "You couldn't pay me to go sit out there. It's supposed to snow tomorrow."

"Wonderful," I said. "The Bills have lost two straight, the ticket is going to cost me fifty bucks, and it's going to snow on my head."

He put the rest of the pork back into the refrigerator. "I'll get one of your brothers to finish this with me. I'm going to bed."

I followed my father up the cellar stairs. Everything about the house was still familiar although I had left nearly twenty years ago. My mother was putting dishes away, and she took a break to sit across the kitchen table from me.

"What's going on?" she asked.

"Kathy worked today. I'm so tired. I hate when she works the weekend."

"How are the boys?" she asked.

All of the grandchildren were pictured on the wall behind her. It's impossible to sit at the table and not look at them. I focused on the picture of a smiling Jake.

"Jake's sick," I said. "His voice is hoarse. He sounds like one of the monsters in his cartoons."

"I worry about him," Mom said. "He's never sounded right."

"It's that stupid asthma," I said.

"I wonder if that doctor knows what he's doing," Mom said. Her forehead creased with worry.

"Kathy takes him in every other week it seems," I said. "Asthma is a nasty condition, I guess."

I wanted to spend more time just chatting with Mom, but I had to think about getting home. We gossiped about the news of the town, and when at last it was time to leave I took a couple of packages of sausage and headed toward the door.

"Kiss the boys for me," Mom said.

The boys had slept for a couple of hours, but if the dark circles under her eyes were any indication, Kathy's nap hadn't gone so well. She was washing out Sam's bottle, and she turned to me as I stepped into the kitchen. Kathy held her arms open, so I hugged her. Within seconds, the purple dinosaur's idiotic voice filled the room and Jake called out for Kathy.

"Well, it was fun for a second," I said.

I began preparing dinner as Kathy sat on the floor of the living room with the boys. She catered to their every whim and even sang along with the portly T-rex. These were the family roles we'd chosen and the ones we were most comfortable handling.

After dinner the boys headed for their rooms, and we cleared the dishes together. I rinsed the dishes and placed them in the dishwasher, and she wiped down the table and counter. We performed the same tasks after each meal.

"Do you have anything planned for tonight?" I asked.

Kathy shrugged. "Like what?" she asked. "You know me — I never plan what I'm doing. You're the one that needs to schedule every minute of the day." She was teasing me, and I took it good-naturedly. "You should try to relax a little."

"I'm wound tighter than a golf ball," I said. "I got the seed for the lawn that I'd like to throw down. Maybe Jake can help. The fresh air might do him good."

"Maybe you both need fresh air," she said with a wry smile. "You seem a little cranky."

"Geez, I wonder why. I got a whole four hours of sleep, too. Go figure."

I was treading on dangerous ground. We had agreed on the staggered schedule that had her working every other weekend. It had seemed like a good idea to have one parent or the other with the children more than just two days a week. She scolded me with her eyes, and I looked away.

"I'm just dreading that football game tomorrow. I need rest!"

"No one is forcing you to go," Kathy said. "Besides, once you see Al, Jeff, and John you'll be into it. You'll be laughing your asses off all day."

She was probably right, but things didn't seem normal to me. It had been less than a month since the country had been attacked, and the country's leaders were planning a retaliatory strike.

"They wouldn't bomb the stadium, would they?" Kathy asked.

"You're always paranoid," I said. I didn't even get the chance to finish my frown. Jake raced into the room, and a crawling Sam trailed close behind. "Are we planting the grass?" Jake asked. He coughed, sniffled, and talked in his hoarse voice.

"If you need something to worry about, worry about Jake," I said.

Kathy pinched her lower lip between her thumb and forefinger. Her pretty face was a picture of concern. "Maybe Jake should stay in."

"No! I want to help," Jake protested.

"Sure, it won't take us long," I said. I had already worked the soil, and Jake's job was to simply drop the seed. *Nothing too exerting*, I thought. I draped his jacket over his shoulders and hooked up the Velcro on his Spiderman sneakers.

We headed up the back stairs and I pulled Jake to one side as Max and Shadow raced out into the backyard.

"If we get the grass to grow, Mom will be proud of us, won't she?" Jake asked.

I didn't answer. Jake is just unbelievably compassionate. If you bought him a present, it bothered him that Matt and Sam didn't get one too. He also lives to make Kathy proud of him.

"Mom will be proud, won't she?" Jake asked again.

"Yeah, pal, don't get all worked up," I said.

I held his hand as we stepped off the concrete pad and onto the patchy grass. It was a little chillier than I thought, but when fresh air smacked me straight in the face it felt all right.

"Let's make Mom proud," I said. I headed to the garage, and he was right on my heels. I grabbed a small rake and handed it to him. He smiled. It struck me as odd that he wanted to work, yet he had always been a real focused child. When he got something in his head, it stuck there, come hell or high water.

"I love working," Jake said.

"I know you do." I handed him a small paper bag of grass seed and began to loosen the topsoil with the rake. Jake grabbed a handful of seed and threw it down. The seed was in a clump.

"Can you do it like this?" I asked. I took a handful of seed and spread it a little more evenly.

"Sure, Dad," he said. We continued the process for the next ten minutes over every bare patch in the lawn. When we had the seed down, I led him to the garage. He stood off to one side as I gathered a bright orange, plastic fence. "We have to put this in front of where we planted the grass or Shadow will ruin it," I said.

Jake actually attempted to help me carry the fence.

"I got it, buddy," I said.

He was right beside me as I pounded in each stick to hold the fence up. His mouth was beside my right ear, and his breathing became more and more labored, yet he insisted on planting the seed in an effort to make Kathy proud. In the days to come, his troubled breathing would haunt me. Every time I closed my eyes, I heard the sound of his rough breaths on that fall evening.

We returned to the garage to put our tools away. He hung his rake on a nail in the far corner. He groaned when it slipped off the nail onto the concrete floor. "Uh, Dad, can you help me?"

I bent down and retrieved the rake. He was just inches from me. I placed the rake on the nail and reached out to tickle his belly. He squirmed out of the way.

"You're a good worker," I said.

"We did great, didn't we?" Jake asked.

"Yeah, give me five, buddy."

We slapped hands, and I picked him up, over my shoulder. "We have to go to sleep early tonight," I said. "So we can get rid of these stupid colds."

Sunday — *October 7, 2001*

This time the whole, sordid early morning ritual began again at four-thirty instead of five. Sam howled in his crib as Max placed his big, fat, wet nose on my cheek in an effort to rouse me from my slumber.

My first words of the day were unprintable, as I expect my children to read this some day.

How could I possibly continue to live in this manner? I knew that we were doing it to make a better life for the children, and it wasn't like Kathy was leaving me alone to party with friends on a Friday night. How mad could I get? She was going to work, for God's sake. We wanted the children to be with one parent or the other for the maximum amount of time, but why was I the parent with them on a Sunday-freaking-morning at *four-thirty*?

Again, Sam didn't want any part of the bottle. I reluctantly pulled him out of the crib. The smile on his face didn't quite melt my heart, but it was a smile that I would need with me in the next couple of days. He pointed to the decals of the balloons on his walls around the crib, and I recited the colors of the balloons to him as though I were saying a demented prayer. "Blue, red, purple, yellow." We made it to the living room, tripping over Max all the way down the hall. I felt a little like Bill Murray in *Groundhog Day* as I slid the happy rhino tape into the VCR.

We settled in, Sam on the floor and me on the couch. While he contentedly watched the tape, I stretched out and actually thought about shutting my eyes. Just then, Shadow barked.

"It's a great day to spend time with your family," the Rhino sang.

"Welcome to my nightmare," I muttered. I felt as if I were going to explode at any minute.

I sat up on the couch. It was still pitch black outside, and it was impossible to chase away the thought that I should still be sleeping. As I panned back across the room, I saw Kathy and my engraved wedding invitation. Someone had put the words of the invitation on a plaque as a gift. I took the plaque down and read the words.

"Together with their parents, Kathy Foutz Stoklosa and Clifford Fazzolari request the honour of your presence at their marriage on Saturday, the thirty-first of May, Nineteen hundred and ninety-seven at two o'clock in the afternoon North Collins Town Park Gowanda State Road North Collins, New York."

Beside the words was a photo of Matthew and my niece, Andrea. We had decided to place their photo on the plaque because frankly they looked better than we did. I smiled at the memory of our wedding day, and I considered it in light of where I was right now.

In 1993, I met Kathy at work. She was the good-looking receptionist, and I was the company safety director and all-around whipping boy. Kathy was married at that time, and I was completely single. I was living in a small apartment on the outskirts of Buffalo, and while I was convinced that it was a decent bachelor's pad, my younger brother, Jeff, referred to it as the rat's nest. The bottom line was: I had a good job, an active social life, and a dream to publish novels.

Kathy and I spent the early days becoming friends and a lot of years later we're still building the perfect friendship. We've always shared a lot of laughs, and like most good couples, we're able to communicate without words. It wasn't the world's fastest romance, but soon enough Kathy was divorced, and on that day in May of 1997, we were married. Matthew became a part of my life, as did Kathy's ex-husband Jack. To this day, we all see eye-to-eye on the best of all worlds for Matthew.

Jake arrived, and Kathy and I bought a house to share with our children. When Sam came along, we were in a fairly decent rut. It was a rut that was something we'd dreamed about all our lives. At the outset, we did our best to develop a relationship based on love and a sense of humor.

Jake got out of bed a little before seven. I was really happy to see him, as I'd watched the rhino tape five times by then. But Jake didn't seem like himself. His cough was a lot worse, and his voice wasn't much more than a gravelly whisper. Still, I was dealing with a cold. I coughed right along with him, and Jake sat beside me on the couch. His small, white blanket was wrapped around his legs. Suddenly, my own cold didn't seem like all that big of a deal.

"Sammy's a cute baby," Jake rasped.

Sam smiled as he banged on a toy that made an especially irritating and continuous merry-go-round sound. To turn it off, you had to physically press a button, and since Sam didn't think to do that very often, the song just beat like a mallet on my already battered brain. "Cute" was the furthest thing from my mind.

"He's a punk," I said.

Jake sank down on his hands and knees in front of Sam, and kissed his brother on the forehead. "He's cute."

"Punk," I said.

Suddenly a coughing fit rocked Jake's body, and it crossed my mind that maybe he needed a breathing treatment. In time, though, he returned to his semi-normal wheezing, and I let the moment pass. The three of us sat on the floor playing with their mountain of toddler toys until Kathy came through the door for her lunch break.

Kathy was dressed casually in a pair of jeans and a Bruce Springsteen concert shirt. Still, she was a wonderful sight for my tired eyes. She scooped up Sam and covered him with kisses. She repeated the ritual with Jake, and the smile didn't slip from her face until she heard Jake speak.

"Dad said that Sam's a punk," Jake said.

"Wow, you don't sound so good. Did Dad give you a breathing treatment?"

"I didn't get to it," I said.

Kathy headed for the hall closet. She set up the breathing machine for Jake. I followed her into the kitchen where she poured Sam's cereal into a small, red bowl.

"My mother is going to stop by and give you a break," Kathy said. "She'll take the boys to her house for naptime."

I wasn't about to argue. I needed all the help I could get. "Your mother's a saint. She watches 'em all week, and now she's giving me a break. I don't know how she does it."

"Mom knows you're going to the game. She just thought you might need a few moments of peace. Besides, she's worried about Jake. She's like me. We don't want anyone else watching the boys when they're sick."

I didn't even consider disagreeing with her. To be honest about it, I felt better when they were in charge of Jake and Sam too.

"I can use the time to finish up some loose ends with the book," I said. I had just received a contract for my novel, *In Real Life*, and I wanted to rush the paperwork to my literary agent.

"Or you could rest. You have the whole month of October to sign the contract, right?"

I played with the boys for another two hours before Kathy's mother, Carolyn, stopped by at eleven-thirty. Carolyn took a couple of steps through the front door, and the boys' moods immediately changed. Jake ran to her, and Sam cried in a longing to be held.

"It looks as though they're happy to see you," I said. "I am too."

Carolyn hugged both boys, and I saw her studying Jake's face for signs of his cold. "They got you up early again, huh?" Carolyn said.

"It was brutal," I said.

"Well, now you can get a break."

I helped Carolyn put shoes and coats on the boys. I kissed Jake on the left cheek. "Take a good nap so you'll feel better," I said. I placed him in the car seat in the back of Carolyn's car, and I strapped him in as Carolyn secured Sam in the seat beside him.

"Have fun with Grandma," I said.

I had the house to myself for just over an hour. I scrambled to put the finishing touches on the manuscript of the book, and I listened to soft music as I worked. I was well beyond tired, but something drove me to complete the work.

I splashed a handful of cold water on my face and dug through the closet for a heavy coat. I had just finished dressing for the game when Kathy opened the front door.

"Should I take the cell phone?" I asked.

"Why?" Kathy asked. "We'll be sleeping through most of it."

"Maybe you'll get the urge to call and tell me how much you love me."

"You won't need the phone," Kathy said jokingly.

I kissed her and grabbed the phone anyway.

We live just over two miles away from Ralph Wilson Stadium. I wasn't even out of the driveway when the cell phone rang.

"Miss me already?" I asked, believing that Kathy was trying to reach me.

"What the hell are you talking about?" Jeff Renaldo, my longtime friend said.

"I thought you were Kathy," I said.

I backed out of the driveway and turned left on Lake Avenue.

"Which way are you coming into the stadium?" Jeff asked.

"I don't know. Should I take Abbott?"

"Yeah, we're in the huge lot behind the 7-Eleven. John and Al are here already, and we just cracked our first beers. Al's making sausage on the grill."

"I'll be there in two minutes," I said.

I clicked the phone off and smiled at the thought of seeing my buddies. I had grown up with John Cataldo, Jeff Renaldo, and Al DeCarlo and we've grown closer as our children have grown. Yet the fact of the matter is that we don't see each other as often as we might like. It had been at least five years since we met at the stadium for a game.

Jeff was waiting for me at the entrance to the lot, and he ushered me into a parking spot with the wave of his hand. The parking area was alive with Bills fans, and the sights and sounds of the tailgate party were like an attack on my senses. I heard the Bills pre-game show blaring from a 97-Rock radio remote van, and there were at least five footballs being tossed back and forth by young guys that dreamed of playing ball for a living.

Jeff handed me a bottle of beer and patted me on the back. "It's good to get away from the kids for a few hours, isn't it?"

"You have no idea," I said.

We soon met up with Al and John. I drank the beer quickly, and Al handed me another. "It's good to see you, man."

"You too," I said. "I'm glad we did this."

We stood around the grill. Al offered to make a sausage sandwich for me, but I was content to just drink the beer. Suddenly a loud commotion caught our attention. A group of guys were chanting, "USA! USA! USA!"

"What's that all about?" I asked.

"We just started bombing Afghanistan," John said.

"Man, it makes you wonder if playing football is so important," I said.

John fished in the barrel for a couple more beers. "Americans like to be amused."

The chant grew louder. Within minutes there was a teenage girl on the shoulders of a big guy. Each time that the crowd chanted USA, the girl lifted her shirt. John was at my shoulder as we watched the scene across the crowded parking lot.

"Geez, wouldn't you be proud to call her your girlfriend?" John asked.

Our tickets were a few rows from the field, and we stood in place as the Jets marched down and scored a quick touchdown on our beloved Bills. Just as the kicker banged the extra point through the goal post it started to snow.

"God, isn't this fun?" I asked. John laughed as he poured a little more beer in my cup.

"You know what I'd rather do?" I asked.

"What's that?" John asked.

"I'd rather go back to my place, make a batch of sauce, and watch the game on television."

By the time the Jets scored again and as the snow got heavier, we were all ready to go. Instead of going home, however, we worked our way into one of the stadium luxury boxes. We wound up eating and drinking enough to make it all worthwhile. My ringing cell phone put it all to an end.

"Didn't you get my messages?" Kathy frantically asked. "I'm at Children's Hospital with Jake. He wasn't breathing right. I took him to the Mercy Ambulatory Center and they took a chest X-ray. They found a mass." Kathy was on the verge of hysteria. She was crying through each word, but maybe it was the beer. Maybe it was the fact that I was with friends in an absolute carefree atmosphere, but whatever the reason I shrugged off the seriousness of the situation.

"I've got to go," I said to Jeff and John, "they're saying something about a bad X-ray. Looks like I'll be at Children's Hospital all night."

Now, anyone that has kids can understand what I was thinking. There are temperatures of 103. There are nights when you honestly think that they aren't going to make it to morning. And there is a great moment of clarity when you understand that a mother's shriek of alarm isn't all that it is meant to be. I was caught in that moment as I hurried toward my car in the packed parking lot. Maybe Kathy was just being dramatic. Perhaps it was just another moment in a long string of moments meant to keep me from relaxing.

But my hopes evaporated when I hit the voice mail option on my telephone. All three messages were from Kathy. The first was just a crying, rambling diatribe that brought tears to my eyes. "Something's wrong with Jake," she cried. "I'm serious. It's bad. Something's wrong." The second message was a bit more controlled but even more alarming. "They took a chest X-ray at the Mercy Ambulatory Center and found a mass that might be leukemia. We're taking him to Children's Hospital. Call me." The third message simply said, "Please! Please call now!"

The parking lot was packed, and even though I was leaving early, so were thousands of others. "Damn Bills can't even stay in a game long enough for me to leave early," I grumbled to myself. I slammed my fist on the steering wheel. The cell phone rang again.

"It's me," Kathy said. "We're at Children's Hospital. Can you stop by the house and grab Jake's blanket and a couple of sandwiches? We haven't eaten a thing since nap."

"What is it?" I asked.

"I don't know," Kathy cried. "I was making dinner. He started really gasping for air. I thought he was going to die in my arms."

"How is he now?" I asked, a little too loudly.

"He's breathing better now, but I'm so scared. God, bring me something if you can."

"Just hang in there," I said. "I'll be there as soon as I can."

I'm an impatient man. I don't enjoy sitting through meetings at work. I can't stand waiting in line or being delayed at the grocery store. Yet this was something different. I was trapped in traffic leading away from the stadium, and every shortcut I tried only led me into another line of cars filled with Bills fans that couldn't possibly have had anywhere important to go. It took me twenty minutes to cover the two miles from the stadium to my home.

I busted through the door and grabbed a couple of sandwiches and Jake's blanket. I held his blanket to my face and cried for the first of what would end up being a hundred times. Kathy rang me up on the phone a few minutes later as I was on the skyway heading toward Downtown. I couldn't remember the name of the street that I had to turn on.

"You have to turn on Hodge Street," Kathy said as though she were reading my mind. "We're at the emergency room, and they're going to take us upstairs for a CT-scan. It'll probably take a little while."

"What're they saying?" I asked.

"He has a mass. They don't know what it is, but they'll be able to tell in a little while."

"Could it be a virus infection or something?" I asked.

"I don't know," Kathy said. "God, I hope so."

There were tears in her voice, and I knew that I had to get to her soon. I'd seen enough of her as a mother to know that her heart was about to break, if it hadn't already. I said the first of what had to be a million prayers. "Come on, God, please don't let it be bad. Get us through this."

It was a simple, crude prayer that stuck in the back corner of my mind like a butterfly smashed against a windshield. It was also the way I'd be starting my prayers every night for a month.

* * *

Hands down, one of the worst places in the world is the waiting room at a children's hospital. The kids are wailing, the parents are anxious, and nurses and doctors are running around seemingly without direction like so many bewildered sheepdogs. Everyone has to wait their turn, and unfortunately, they all want to be first. There isn't a parent in the waiting room that doesn't feel their child's affliction is the number one problem. Kathy and I were not exceptions.

I pulled up outside of the emergency room doors. The street was empty, and it registered that I was real lucky to get the very best parking spot. I slammed the door of my SUV hard, but my seat buckle was caught. The door remained partly open but locked. I unlocked the door, removed the seat belt, and slammed it again. Out of the corner of my eye I saw a *No Parking* sign, but it was Sunday night. I would be all right.

I ran up the sidewalk, and the emergency room doors opened to let me through. The crowd of people in the waiting room stopped me in my tracks. There were kids all over the place. Some of them were wearing bandages, most were crying, and the faces of the anxious parents sent me headlong into a wave of anxiety. Somewhere in this mess of anonymous faces my wife and child were waiting for me. I clutched Jake's blanket and the brown paper bag with two roast beef sandwiches. I locked eyes with an obviously harried nurse behind the reception desk.

"My son has a mass in his chest — Fazzolari," I said. The woman didn't even look down at a chart. She didn't hesitate for even a split-second. Instead, her face took on a look of utter despair. My heart sank. "Your wife is with Jacob in room four."

I hurried through another room that bustled with activity. There were nurses all over the place. The sound of the crying children was even more deafening. I couldn't help but wonder if Jake was adding his voice. I had an overwhelming feeling of dismay regarding the condition of our healthcare system. It just seemed like the demand far outweighed the supply, and there were just too many kids depending on Children's Hospital.

I rushed into the room to see Jake seated on a table. He was wearing a small gown, but his pajama bottoms escaped from underneath the gown. He smiled sheepishly as though I had caught him doing something bad. Kathy's back was to me, and she was looking at the back wall. When she turned to face me, I saw evidence of tears in her blue eyes.

"I brought your blanket," I said to Jake. I also extended the bag of food to Kathy. I wanted to pull her into an embrace, but I held my ground. For some reason I figured that we needed to show Jake that it wasn't that big of a deal. I heard voices coming from behind the thin curtain that separated us with another set of parents and an obviously sick child.

"You have to get an enema," the mother said.

"I won't do it," a young girl cried. "You gave me one at home, and it hurt!"

Kathy edged close to me. "She's eight years old," Kathy whispered. "She hasn't had a bowel movement in three weeks."

I didn't have time to worry about someone else's child. "Hey, buddy," I said to Jake. "How do you feel?"

Jake stared at the tiled floor. "I want to go home."

"They'll do the enema better here," the mother begged from behind the curtain. A nurse talked sweetly to the child, and Jake stared at the curtain.

"I'm not doing it, and that's final," the child wailed.

"Alright then," the mother yelled, finally losing her patience. "The crap will fill you up and then it's going to come out of your mouth."

Even Jake laughed at that, but in the coming month, I would certainly understand the mother's frustration. Sometimes a sick kid doesn't see it from an adult point of view. Thankfully, the story had a happy ending. The staff was able to hold the kid steady long enough to finish their work, and inside of ten minutes, the child was speaking in level tones.

A nurse finally arrived on the scene to examine Jake. She talked in an even tone, and her smile soothed me. "Okay, Jake, we need to get your temperature."

Jake accepted the thermometer under his right arm. It beeped in a matter of a minute, and the nurse jotted a note on her clipboard and moved toward the door.

"We'll be back for him in a few minutes. The doctors ordered a CT-scan, and there's only one other patient ahead of you."

I knew better. It was less than a month to the day when we sat in the very same waiting room trying to get help for Sam. From day one, Sam hadn't been right. He would fill his diaper ten times one day and then not go again for three days. When we brought him to the emergency room in mid-September he was soiling his diaper every three minutes. During that visit we waited for nine hours, only to learn that he'd been constipated for a long time and was now overflowing.

There wasn't much to do as we waited for our turn to be called. Kathy ate one of the sandwiches, and Jake took two bites of the other one. I paced the floor, occasionally stepping into the nurse's station to see if our number was going to be called soon. Kathy sat on the table beside Jake, holding him tightly. When Jake leaned in and kissed her cheek, I feigned jealousy.

"Get your own wife," I said. "You can't be kissing my wife."

Of course this made him kiss her over and over, and he giggled wonderfully as he imagined stealing her from me.

The gathering of people at the nurse's station suddenly grew larger. I counted seven people gathered around an X-ray. "It's a huge mass," one of the nurses said. A second nurse dialed our family doctor on the telephone. I glanced over my shoulder at Kathy and Jake. Kathy caught my eye, and there were prominent worry lines creasing her forehead.

"My brother was here," she said. "He mentioned pneumonia. Would that show up as a mass?"

I shrugged. I was praying for some sort of respiratory ailment that could be cured with a pill, but the doctors and nurses that were gathered around whispering about my son didn't leave me feeling overly optimistic. It just had the feel of something bad. What I was really considering was cancer or leukemia, and it was impossible to comprehend.

"It'll be fine," I said. "It'll be just fine." I've had a lot of practice at reassuring people, and sometimes it seems as if this is a dad's main purpose. From squashing bugs to making sure there aren't monsters under the beds, it is a full-time job. I thought of my father and in that single moment in time, I understood something that he had told me a long time ago. Dad once said that when he got married, life became fifty percent about him and fifty percent about my mother. Figuring in the birth of six children, Dad divided himself time and time again. "I'm about three percent of the man I once was," he said, at age fifty. "And I've enjoyed every minute of it."

That's what a great father does, and standing in that waiting room, I realized that it was my turn to reach for greatness.

The doctors and nurses came into the room like a band of thieves, stealthy and grim-faced. They were looking to "steal" my child and take him upstairs for the CT-scan.

"They just want to take a picture," Kathy whispered.

"I'm not going," Jake announced through crying eyes. He shook his fist "Why can't everyone just leave me alone?"

The doctors held their ground. Finally, it seemed as though Jake resigned himself to the fact that he was trapped. He kissed Kathy on the cheek. I didn't miss the chance to make him laugh.

"Hey, you! Don't kiss my wife."

We rode up in a special elevator. I don't know why, but the fact that they took him the back way scared me even more. I caught fragments of conversations from all across the emergency room floor, and all of them seemed to be comments on the size of my son's mass.

The emergency room nurse led us into a darkened room. There was a huge table set up in front of the circular CT machine. I thought of an MRI I had endured one time, and I wondered about how we would get Jake to lie still. A husky young man greeted us. He seemed to be wearing a permanent scowl. "He's got to lay down real still. Hold him still! It won't work unless he's still."

Unfortunately, the best way to talk to Jake was one hundred eighty degrees different from the way this man was going about it. He might have made a good drill sergeant, but he didn't seem to have the demeanor to deal with a child.

"I'm not lying down!" Jake screamed.

"Jake, it won't hurt," Kathy said, trying to soothe him. "It's just a picture."

"Mom and Dad should leave," the man barked.

"I can't stay?" Kathy asked.

"It'll be easier if I try to settle him down," the man said.

I had little use for his tone, but I reminded myself that he worked with kids all day. I grabbed for Kathy's arm, but she gave me a look that said she had no intention of leaving.

"He's tired," I said to the guy. "Usually he's in bed by nine. This is the middle of the night."

The guy kind of rolled his eyes and huffed out of the room. He was back a minute later, but he hadn't done much to change his approach. "Jacob, you have to lie down. If you don't lie down, I'll have to give you a shot."

Jake didn't even blink. "Give me a shot then!" he cried in terror.

The man stepped back as though he'd been slapped.

"Hah! He called your bluff," Kathy said.

The man backed out of the room as if he were confronting an angry Chuck Norris instead of a scared four-year-old.

"I don't like that guy," Jake whispered.

I stifled a grin and headed for the door as Kathy tried to explain to Jake why he should be nice. Moments later, two nurses and the drill sergeant returned with a mild sedative. Finally, Kathy was able to coax Jake onto his back. The husky man took the scan with Jake's hand locked with Kathy's. The room where the computer gathered the images was off to the left, and I wandered in, actually believing that I might be able to make sense of what was happening. In an effort to make small talk, I turned to the nurse who was working a mouse in front of the computer. As far as I could tell, she was locking the images in.

"What's he looking at?" I asked.

"Oh, it's definitely a tumor," she said. "It's huge."

My legs turned to jelly, and I felt a huge burn work its way through my head. I'd never felt that way before, but it was a sensation I would get used to real quickly. I kind of half-stumbled to the wall and held my left hand out to steady myself.

"I don't know what kind of tumor, but there's a buzz downstairs. His X-ray was pure white."

"Maybe they screwed it up."

She rolled her eyes, and a second wave of heat hit me behind the eyes.

The procedure didn't take long. I returned to Kathy's side. We watched Jake's eyes droop as he tried, unsuccessfully, to lick a lollipop.

"I feel real tired, Mommy."

"It'll be all right," I said. I felt like a mechanical doll capable of making only one statement.

Kathy's eyes were full of tears, and I knew that she understood I wouldn't be able to reassure her about this particular set of circumstances.

"It's a tumor," she said.

"We don't know anything for sure yet," I answered. I draped my arm around her shoulder and pulled her close. I wonder if she knew that I was absolutely clueless. The same nurse that let the cat out of the bag met us in the elevator.

"Do you feel okay?" she asked. "You're awful pale, Dad."

"You think? Why would I be pale, I wonder?"

As we headed back to the emergency room waiting area, I thought of the little girl who couldn't poop. She'd received her treatment and was on her way. She'd go home, sleep in her own bed, and get up and go to school in the morning. She'd laugh and quarrel with her parents, and everything would be normal for her. But not for us. As I've said, I'm not a patient man. I wanted Jake to be well, and I wanted him well *now*. I wanted the doctors to give him some medication or tell us that it was all a big mistake. I would wake up at four in the morning every day for the rest of my life if I had to in order to make my wish come true. I just wanted to leave that hospital with my family intact.

Kathy helped Jake back up onto the table in the emergency room waiting room number four. She sat on his right side. "Da-aaad," Jake taunted me. He kissed Kathy over and over again. I scolded him for robbing my wife, and I couldn't help but let a couple of tears escape and run down my cheek.

"They're doing a blood test, and then they're going to admit him," Kathy said. Her voice shook as if she was on the absolute brink of a breakdown.

"Where'd you hear that?" I asked.

"They told me when they were doing the scan. You were looking at the computer. I'm staying."

"Me too," I said.

Kathy shook me off. I put my hand on her back. We were sparring a little bit to see where the boundaries would be set. Normally we slipped into the roles that were most comfortable, but this was new territory; nothing was comfortable.

"You have to take care of the dogs," Kathy said. "Mom has Sam, and Matt can stay with Jack and his parents."

A nurse popped her head into the room.

"We'll admit Jacob into ICU as soon as we have a bed ready." Jake's eyes fluttered as he fought sleep. Kathy's eyes were red with tears. "Go home. This is where a mother belongs."

Kathy lowered Jake onto the table. She nuzzled him and closed her eyes. "He'll be fine," I said.

"Yes, he has to be," Kathy answered. "There's no other option."

I wanted to agree with her, but I stopped short of making any guarantees. This sort of thing happened every day to lots of loving families and wonderful kids, but not to us.

"I love you," I said. At least I could guarantee that. I knelt down by the side of the bed, and she put her hands around my neck without rousing Jake. Kathy hugged me so tightly that it crossed my mind that she might be trying to hurt me. "Try to sleep," she said.

It was a little before two in the morning, and the sky was the color of lead. I sucked in the cold, October air and repeated my crude plea to God. I ran to the car and when I opened the driver's side door, a twenty-dollar parking ticket floated to my feet.

"Rhino-rrific," I said. "Son-of-a-bitch!" God must have been in an ironic mood that day.

Chapter Two

Monday — October 8, 2001

I slept a little over an hour. The thought occurred to me that I'd gladly spend the rest of my days as a dancing rhino if I could avoid going to the hospital to see if my child had cancer. I took an unbelievably fast shower and broke into tears before the steamed mirror.

"God, why are you doing this to us? We treat our children right. Why us?"

I knew that I wasn't going to get a quick answer, but my heart filled with dread as I considered that, perhaps, I had passed this affliction on to my son. Maybe I was paying for the sizeable quantities of beer that I drank in college. Did my habit of chewing tobacco have anything to do with his illness? Was it because Kathy smoked?

"Don't do this to yourself," I scolded my reflection. "It's nobody's fault, not yours and not even God's. We just have to deal with it."

The tiny voice in my head told me that I didn't want to have to deal with it.

"Tough crap," I said out loud. "Ninety percent of life is how you react."

I fed the dogs and let them out long enough to take care of their business. I made a couple of mugs of coffee and started the truck. The house was way too quiet. I headed into Jake's room for a change of clothes, and my heart jumped into my throat as I looked around at the toys scattered everywhere. I held the plastic King Kong to my chest, and I couldn't stop the tears from coming. I set King Kong down and picked up his Godzilla action figure. "My beautiful boy is in trouble." Yesterday, he was just a child with a cold, and today... I didn't even want to think about it.

Traffic heading into the city was light. It was just a few minutes past six, and the working world wasn't quite rolling yet. I used my cell phone to call Bob Overhoff, a co-worker at Scott Danahy Naylon Insurance. Bob's voice mail picked up. I toyed with the idea of leaving a message, but I couldn't form the words. There wasn't anything about work that interested me.

I pulled into the parking ramp on Hodge Street and ran across the street to the hospital. I was carrying a bag filled with clothes for Kathy and Jake. I took the elevator up to the second floor, and my stomach churned as I made my way down the short hall to the intensive care unit. Just inside the door to the ICU I spotted a chalkboard. The name Fazzolari was etched in the column under room four. The door was closed, but the lights inside the room were on.

I'm not sure what I expected, but I walked through the door into a normal everyday scene. Kathy was beside Jake's bed, and Jake was under the covers, watching cartoons. The huge bed dwarfed my little boy, but he looked all right. Instantly, I imagined that last night's news was just a dream or an error.

"The doctor will be in shortly. I guess they're still deciding what to do," Kathy said.

"Who's the doctor?" I asked. "Would Doctor Novelli come here to treat Jake?"

"It won't be Doctor Novelli. There's a whole team of cancer doctors," Kathy said. "I don't know any of their names." Her voice quivered when she said cancer.

I sipped the coffee. Jake was laughing at Bugs Bunny's antics, and he invited me to watch along. I wasn't sure I had the stomach to handle bad puns and falling pianos, but the amazing thing about kids is that they're so enthusiastic that they draw you in. The time passed fairly quickly, and by the time the doctor arrived, I was laughing too.

We met with Dr. Grossi in the center of ICU. He asked us to step into the conference room, but it was occupied. There was no shortage of patients.

"At least we have an idea of what we're dealing with," Dr. Grossi said. He was a short, impressive-looking man, and I was struck with the thought that he was now the number-one man in our lives. He was the first person to approach us about Jake's chances to get through this, and he seemed like our only hope for guidance.

"The tumor covers his entire chest area."

"I saw the X-ray," Kathy said.

"Frankly, we haven't seen many like that. Our educated guess is that it's a teratoma, and those are usually benign, but we can't be sure."

I breathed a sigh of relief, and Doctor Grossi caught it. "The problem is that it's on his airways. We can't risk putting him under to do a biopsy, so basically, we're going to try and treat it blindly. We're going to be aggressive, but it's the only chance we have. We'll give him chemo, and hope it shrinks. Then we can go in and treat it. This is if you agree with our plan, of course."

I stole a look at Kathy. She was crying, but I thought that she took the doctor's news fairly well. I didn't fully understand what Doctor Grossi meant, so he kindly broke the information down for me. "If we attempt a biopsy, the anesthesia will relax his airways, and because the tumor is resting on the center of his airways, they could collapse. We've decided not to put your son at risk if we don't have to. Although I just told you that we feel it is a benign growth, we are going at it as if it is a malignant germ cell tumor in an attempt to shrink it."

"So, what am I rooting for?" Kathy asked, her voice trembling. "Should I actually hope that it's cancerous so it'll shrink?"

Doctor Grossi fielded the question with ease and gave the safest answer in the world. "Some of it might be cancerous, and most of it might not be. We do have to hope for some shrinkage, I guess. We're flying blind here."

I immediately respected the man. How in the world could he be expected to break such news to loving parents? Somehow he had managed to give us the straight dope without alarming us. When I walked away from him, back down the hall to Jake's room, I couldn't believe that I'd just been asked to hope to expect cancer in my beautiful boy. Yet, that's where we were.

For millions of people all over the world, cancer is still highly regarded as a death sentence. Maybe that was the case twenty years ago, but in the back of my mind I understood that it didn't necessarily have to be so. If the tumor needed to shrink, than that was what we needed to pray for and work toward.

Jake's nurse for the day was Susan Mazurchuk, a pretty woman about the same age as Kathy and me. Susan was in the room when we returned from our visit with Doctor Grossi, and she offered a sympathetic smile. Her eyes reflected the sadness that we were feeling. "Jacob and I were just talking, weren't we?"

"Yes," Jake said. He rolled his eyes, but both Kathy and I were amazed that he had allowed Susan anywhere near the bed. Jake doesn't normally take kindly to complete strangers.

"I was telling Jake what a brave boy he is, right Jake? I showed him how we would take his temperature with this little blue thing."

"Under my arm," Jake said, smiling at Susan.

"What else?" Susan asked.

"They have to give my leg a hug," Jake said.

"That's to take your blood pressure, right?" Susan asked. Her voice was soothing, and I stole a quick glance at Kathy, who was also smiling.

"Dad, are we going to watch cartoons?" Jake asked.

"In one minute, buddy," I said.

Susan fluffed Jake's pillow and rearranged a stuffed animal near his head. "You're such a good boy," she said. Susan edged toward the door. I stood on her right side and Kathy moved into place on Susan's left.

"I can't believe he wasn't screaming bloody murder when you were alone with him in here," Kathy whispered.

Susan looked to be on the verge of tears. She smiled sympathetically once more. "He's such a doll. I have a boy just about the same age. He's just so beautiful." Her eyes took on a faraway look as though she were trying hard not to think about how she would feel if she were in our shoes. "Doctor Grossi scheduled the first treatment for later in the morning."

I looked blankly at Kathy. "The chemotherapy," she whispered, and the weight of the world came crashing down on my head. I swallowed hard and blinked back the tears.

"Dad, are you going to watch Bugs with me, or not?" Jake called out from the bed.

I felt like the world's biggest hypocrite. He wanted me to laugh at Bugs while medical professionals were in the back room preparing to give Jake his first dose of chemotherapy.

Jake and I watched one cartoon after another. I did my best to distract him whenever one of the doctors, nurses, or interns popped in to take a peek at him. Thank God Susan was usually in the room because she faced all of our worried looks with the cool professionalism of a seasoned veteran. She also continued to speak softly to Jake, and though it might not sound like much, the fact that she was his nurse on Day One eased quite a bit of pain for him and for us.

By noon, just as I was preparing Jake for a nap, my parents came through the door and seeing them sent daggers of pain through my heart. I had always looked to my parents to solve my problems for me, but it didn't look like they had an easy answer. Dad's head was down, and there were tears in his eyes. My mother looked to be on the absolute brink of hysteria, and Kathy and I took turns embracing them. My mother extended a huge plastic bag toward the bed.

"I got some presents," she said to Jake.

Jake struggled to sit upright, and Susan was right there to help him.

"Did you get me a Power Ranger?" Jake asked.

"You have to look and see," Mom said.

Jake peeked into the bag and a huge smile made its way across his face. "Dad, I got a red Power Ranger!"

I opened the package for him and listened to Kathy and my mother's conversation.

"Carrie's flying in from Baltimore," Mom said. Carrie is my youngest sister, and given the instability regarding air travel, this had to go down as a most amazing act of kindness. "Carrie took the week off from work so she could be here. She feels bad but Mike couldn't break free."

"That's okay," Kathy said. "We appreciate that she would do that for us."

The thought of Carrie being so giving sent me into a crying fit that resulted in a sob. I turned away from the bed so Jake wouldn't see me, but in doing so, I allowed my father to witness my pain. He bowed his head and stepped from the room. I saw his shoulders shake as he walked.

Jake, on the other hand, couldn't understand this extravagant show of attention. Why were they bringing him presents? Why were they looking at him as though he'd grown an extra head?

Mom and Dad stayed for a little over an hour. Jake's eyes continued to droop, and I was getting real anxious because I honestly felt that he needed a nap. I turned the television off and sat beside the bed until he drifted off. Then I slowly left the room. Kathy was waiting in the ICU waiting area, and

I hurried down the hall to be by her side.

"This is an absolute nightmare," she said as I hugged her to me.

"Do you want some lunch?" I asked.

"I can't eat," she said. "I've had too many cups of coffee to even think about eating."

Our long embrace came to a natural end, and I stepped back to examine her tired face. "Poor Jake," she said. "He was born on Friday, June thirteenth. He was five weeks early and crying from the start."

"Remember how he'd wail if you walked out of the room?" I asked. "God, you couldn't even go to the bathroom without him screaming. I always felt completely inadequate, and right now it's even worse." I could feel my eyes welling up with tears, and I battled hard to try and hold everything in. "I'm his father, for God's sake, and I don't know what to do."

It was the wrong thing to say because my sadness overwhelmed Kathy. "What about me?" she wailed. "I'm his mother. I was supposed to protect him. Deep down I kind of knew that it wasn't asthma, but I feel like I did everything I could."

I grabbed hold of Kathy again. She squeezed me close, and I moved her hair away from her face and kissed her. "We can't blame ourselves. We didn't do anything to deserve this."

We comforted one another for a few more minutes, and when my head cleared just a little, I let go of Kathy. "I'm going to get some fresh air," I whispered. "We do have to eat sometime. I'm not going to nag you, but we need to be strong and rested to get through this."

"I know," Kathy said. "I just don't feel like eating today."

I ran down the back staircase and exited the hospital through the emergency room doors. I hadn't wanted to let my guard down around Kathy. I wanted to be the strong, level-headed one. I couldn't help but feel that I had let her down in some way. I did know of one person that would truly understand my pain, and I punched my brother Jeff's telephone number into my cell phone. Hearing his voice set off a barrage of volatile emotions that left me saying that I wanted to switch places with Jake. "Why can't it be me?" I cried. "Why didn't God choose me?"

Jeff listened stoically. He didn't have an answer, but he tried to calm my fears and said enough of the right things to keep me still clutching my sanity.

My next telephone call was to my employer. Thankfully, the company offered support. I knew that Kathy had also contacted her supervisor at Bethlehem Steel, who was also very understanding. Neither of us could be absolutely certain that we'd be paid for our time off, but it was the least of our concerns. We'd live under a log somewhere and eat bugs if it meant that Jake would recover completely. We'd borrow as much money as we had to.

The most important thing was that Jake would know we'd be there for him through every minute of his illness.

One other consideration was our health insurance. We were covered through Kathy's policy at work, and for the first time it became readily apparent that not having health insurance would have put us in the streets. I couldn't possibly imagine not being able to treat my child, but for 14% of Americans, it's a hard fact they live with every day. If there's a worse predicament to be in, I don't know what it might be.

At four o'clock in the afternoon, Susan brought the chemotherapy medicine into the room. I didn't take a close look at the medicine itself, but another woman happened by with a huge binder filled with information about treating a child with cancer. That woman shall remain nameless because, as numb as I was at that time, I can't recall a thing about her.

"Here are some cut sheets about the medication," she said. "He'll be receiving three different meds — cisplatin, bleomycin, and etoposide. There are several side affects associated with each one, so you might want to familiarize yourself with what could happen."

But I didn't want to familiarize myself with any of this. Here was a situation for a character in one of my novels. This didn't happen to *my* child, for God's sake! Kathy took the sheets from my hand and read aloud.

"Nausea, vomiting, hearing loss, hair loss, kidney damage, mouth sores, and low blood counts."

"You've got to be kidding me." I shook my head in disbelief. Susan hooked up the bag of medicine to the IV line that Jake already had in place. Jake squirmed a little, but he had no way of knowing about the hell that we were about to put him through.

"I'm so sorry you have to go through this," Kathy said. She leaned into the bed and kissed his face three or four times. Jake looked a little shocked, and I figured that I had to do something to keep him from knowing that the next five days weren't going to be pleasant.

"Hey, get your own wife," I said, trying to smile.

"She's kissing me," Jake said, laughing.

Susan backed away from the bed. The bag of medicine was hanging from the unit staged to the left of the bed. "He's getting the first dose, and it should be done in about an hour."

I watched the yellow liquid drip into my poor boy, and I was completely overwhelmed by the thought that my son was being treated for cancer. Thank God our family members were near.

* * *

It galls me to watch television and listen to a thrice-divorced politician speaking about family values. I also cringe when a sports star brags about taking care of a child that lives with its mother three states away. Raising a child is far and away the toughest job in the world, and Kathy and I must have been brought up the right way because our priorities were in line. At the time of Jake's illness, we were in a comfortable rut that centered on the children. It wasn't like we were looking for an award for it, either. We were doing what we were taught to do, putting our children's needs first. I was the third child in a line of six. My parents were always there for us, and I've spent my entire adult life wondering about the amazing sacrifices that they made for us. The same can be said for Kathy and her parents.

In the early evening, Jake and I were watching a movie. Kathy sat across the room, working a crossword puzzle. Jake's first dose of chemotherapy treatment was done, and although he looked a little tired, he hadn't experienced too much discomfort. Margie, the ICU secretary, opened the door slowly. "You have a roomful of guests in the waiting room," she said. "They all have presents too. I think it's best if they visit two at a time.

"I'll go take a look," I said to Kathy. "I'll send them in. You can stay here, right?"

I honestly didn't expect what I saw in the waiting room. My sister Corinne and brother-in-law Chuck were waiting in the hall. I hugged both, and Corinne handed me a small rosary. "I figured that you might need this."

My brother John and sister-in-law Dana were next in line, and the tears in my brother's eyes sent my mind reeling. John is a year older than me, and for many years he spent every day beating the holy hell out of me. We were brothers, plain and simple, and we battled about everything. John wrapped me in a hug, and the tears streamed down his face. At that moment in time, I couldn't help but marvel at the sort of family that my parents had created. The chips were down, and they were right there for us. Our support system was nothing short of phenomenal.

Kathy stayed in the room as John and Dana and Corinne and Chuck handed Jake gifts and well-wishes. I sat in the waiting room, explaining the day of treatment to Kathy's brother John, her sister Carilee, and my brother Jeff and sister-in-law Lynn. As I talked about the care Jake had received so far, I began to feel better about Jake's prognosis. I'm not sure what it was, but explaining the procedure made me feel as if we were on the road to recovery. I had no way of being sure of such a thing, but faith and hope were suddenly in my vocabulary again. Lynn handed me a photocopied image of St. Jude, and Jake's smiling face was directly underneath St. Jude's watchful eye. "Don't forget your faith," Lynn whispered.

"I won't," I said. "Where would I be without it?"

I followed Kathy's brother John down the hall toward Jake's room. John was holding a stuffed dog that looked a lot like Shadow, our black Lab. I'm sure that it was a pretty expensive gift, and he presented it to Jake with a flourish.

Jake wasn't impressed. "It's kind of boring."

I couldn't believe my ears. I glanced nervously at John, and he tried to laugh it off. "Doesn't it look like Shadow?" he asked.

"I wanted a Power Ranger," Jake whined.

John didn't back down. He knew Jake well, and he carefully planned his response. "I thought you might like something different. Everyone got you a Power Ranger."

"Besides, you're supposed to say thank you when someone gives you a present," I said.

"Thank you," Jake mumbled.

John scanned the room and focused in on the tubes coming from under the covers. I saw the look of utter dismay in John's eyes, and it occurred to me I needed to comfort John somehow.

"What do you think about the Yankees' chances in the playoffs?" I asked.

"They're playing Oakland in the first round, right?"

"Yeah, it's going to be a tough series."

"You know I hate the Yankees," John said, "but I'm going to root for them this year. I want them to win it all for Jake."

I smiled, and John extended his hand. "You take it easy, bro. Jake, I hope you like the dog."

"Well, I don't," Jake said, but his smile told John that he was only teasing.

* * *

The hospital staff also included Maureen from Child Life. As far as I could tell, she was the Bob Hope of the facility, and Child Life was simply a group of people who moved through the hospital making sure that the children had toys if they wanted them, or enough cartoons or Disney movies to make it through the day. Maureen brought Jake a bank shaped like a fat robot that shouted out a warning of danger when you put a quarter into the slot. Jake's eyes lit up, and I wonder if Maureen realized what a difference she made.

"What's his name?" Jake asked me.

I had no idea, but since the robot was blue, I thought fast. "That's Mr. Blue, and from now on everyone that comes into the room has to give him money."

Jake thought this was a terrific idea. By the end of the night, doctors, nurses, and visitors had filled Mr. Blue with more than $15.

"Can we use it to go to the arcade when I get out of here?" Jake asked.

I answered, "Sure, we can stay at the arcade for a week."

It was nearly 9:30 before everyone left the hospital. Jake was on the verge of slumber and Kathy, Susan, and I were standing just outside the door.

"How's he doing?" I asked.

Susan nodded and smiled through her sympathetic gaze. "He's a good patient. I just wish we could get him to go to the bathroom in the bottle so we can measure his fluid intake."

"I'll try to talk him into it," I said.

Susan held a finger up. "Let me give it one more try."

A few minutes later, Kathy and I entered the room. The bottle was hanging on the end of the bed, and to our amazement it was partially filled. Kathy smiled at Susan and shrugged as to ask how she talked Jake into cooperating.

"I peed in the bottle," Jake said proudly.

We both looked at Susan, and she blushed. "I had to give him a kiss and a hug," Susan confessed.

I was proud of him. He was a smart boy, already working the pretty nurse.

Kathy always got the boys ready for bed, and on this Monday night, it wasn't any different for Jake. He more or less ignored my presence as Kathy went through the nightly ritual of discussing the worst and best parts of their day. Just before she pulled the covers up around his neck, she asked Jake to say his prayers. I had heard his prayer before, but for obvious reasons, it stuck in my head that night and resonated through every move I made for the next month.

God Bless Mommy and Daddy, Matt, Jake, and Sam, Max, Shadow, and Nobody (the hamster), Grandma and Grandpa Foutz, Grandma Spiffy and Poppa John, aunts, uncles and cousins. Make me be a good boy, God. Amen.

That night, as I drove out of the hospital parking lot, I couldn't shake the feeling that I was failing. I wasn't bringing my child home with me. What kind of father was I? The overwhelming urge to cry dominated my every thought. It was strange, but I felt as if I needed to hear something familiar. I turned on a Springsteen CD and listened to a song that Jake danced along with. "My Love Will Not Let You Down" was at full volume, and I sang right along with the Boss.

"God, please help us," I said over and over. "Please, make Jake a good boy and me too."

Of course, I couldn't sleep, so I got up and ran around the empty house at breakneck speed, putting in a couple of loads of laundry and gathering up movies, games, books, and anything else that might make Jake's stay a little easier. Before I turned in for the night, Kathy telephoned to say that Jake was fast asleep and that, hopefully, she'd catch a couple of hours herself. I wasn't sure that sleep would ever come, but I lay down between the two dogs and said the rosary until I drifted off into a dream of our old, simple existence, with Matthew, Jake, and Sam playing in a huge field with the dogs. I set the alarm for five, but didn't even make it that far. I started awake at 4:20.

—————Chapter Three—————

Tuesday — October 9, 2001

It was still extremely dark outside that morning, and even the dog, Max, seemed to know that the night wasn't over. I turned in the bed, and it suddenly occurred to me that I had clutched Corinne's rosary throughout the night. I turned the rosary over in my hand, and my mind went straight to prayer. I said the prayers quickly, as though the faster I said them the more power they would have. I also knew that going back to sleep was virtually impossible. I placed my feet on the floor and rubbed my hands across my tired eyes. "Thanks for the day, God," I whispered. "Please make it a good one."

I was in the shower when the telephone rang just twenty minutes later. I scrambled out of the bathroom, and Max ran down the hall as though I was chasing him. I grabbed the telephone on the third ring, just before the answering machine kicked on.

"Hey, you should see Jake," Kathy said.

My heart skipped a beat, but she didn't really sound alarmed. "Is everything okay?"

"His breathing's awesome. I don't know if the tumor shrunk, but he's breathing better."

I couldn't help but think about what might happen if it had shrunk. Was it possible? One day of treatments had shrunk the thing? Maybe it was completely gone! Should I even be hoping that it shrunk? "I'll be there in a half an hour," I said.

I was initially elated, but as I drove the twelve miles to the hospital, something began to gnaw at me. Why in the two years of being treated for asthma had Jake never had a chest X-ray? I didn't want to start second-guessing at this stage of the game, so I tried to push the thought from my mind. Still, it drove me crazy to think about it.

The morning radio station talk show was in full swing, discussing the Yankees upcoming playoff series with the Oakland Athletics. On any other day, my mind would have been dominated with thoughts of baseball. I've been a Yankee fan since birth, and I live and breathe every minute of their season. I used to joke with Kathy, saying that my first and last thoughts of the day belonged to the Yankees. But not anymore. I turned off the radio.

I arrived at the ICU by 6:20. The room was relatively quiet, with just a few of the nurses milling about, looking after their patients. I headed straight for room number four, but I stopped at the sink just outside the room in order to wash my hands. Yesterday, Susan had warned us about Jake being more susceptible to germs, so I wanted to make sure that my hands were clean. Jake spotted me through the window, and he stuck his tongue out and laughed uproariously. I pressed my face against the glass and the sound of his laughter sent a chill up and down my spine.

Jake was sitting up in bed, and his breathing was unbelievably better. He stuck his tongue out again and then turned his eyes back to the television. Bugs Bunny and Daffy Duck were arguing about something, and he didn't want to miss even a second of it.

"How do you feel?" I asked.

"I feel great." His hoarseness was gone, replaced with the usual sound of his strong voice.

Kathy was in a small, blue chair beside his bed. She offered a sleepy smile, and I couldn't help but pity her for having had to sleep in a chair all night. "How did it go?" I asked.

"I slept all right," she said. "Jake woke up for a couple of minutes when they checked his vitals, but we got right back to sleep."

"You could sleep on the freeway," I said.

Kathy smiled. We constantly discussed how easy it was for her to fall asleep, compared to me.

"You look tired," she said.

I shrugged. I tossed the *Buffalo News* and the *USA Today* on the chair beside the bed and sat on Jake's left side. He pointed to the television. Bugs Bunny was dressed-up like a girl bunny in an effort to entice Elmer Fudd. "This one is so funny," Jake said.

We watched in silence for a moment, and while he concentrated on the cartoon, I scanned the room. He was hooked to an IV-line, and the machine behind the bed flashed his vital statistics, as though he were a piece of equipment. It didn't matter how funny Bugs was, I couldn't feel entirely normal. Jake rolled onto his side and fluttered his eyes at me. "I need to ask you something."

"What's that?"

"There's a new Scooby Doo movie coming out on video. We saw the commercial. Can I get it? Mom told me to ask you if I could get it today instead of waiting for my birthday."

I glanced at Kathy, who smiled. She was going out of her way to let me be the hero. Jake was just hours away from the start of his second day of chemotherapy. If he had asked me to go to the moon, I probably would've given it a shot. "You'll have it by tomorrow morning."

The morning went by quickly. Jake was initially disappointed because Susan wasn't his nurse for the day. Ellen Eckhardt was assigned to him, and she quickly gained his trust by explaining each procedure before she actually approached the bed. She also made references to Superman and

Spiderman, and I couldn't help but be amazed by her patience in dealing with a young child.

A group of interns were making rounds, and they stopped in front of the open door and whispered to one another about Jake's progress. I didn't actually hear any of the words, but their mere presence made me a little uncomfortable. Jake's eyes never left the television screen.

"Hey, buddy, do you think it would be all right if I went downstairs and had coffee with Mom?"

"Can you bring me some potato chips?" Jake asked.

I didn't know how to answer him. I was a little surprised by the request, as I had imagined that his stomach would be upset because of the meds. "Can he eat anything he wants?" I asked Ellen.

"I'll check with his doctor," Ellen said. "I don't see why not."

"All right, buddy, I'll be back."

"I'll be here," Jake answered, and I couldn't help but laugh.

Kathy was walking in as I was walking out. She held two cups of coffee and a basket with about thirty Beanie Baby stuffed animals.

"Where did you get that?" I asked.

"They had it at the front desk. It's from Mike and Denise Palmer."

I shook my head as a smile made its way across my face. Mike and Denise have been friends for over twenty years. They live near Philadelphia, and we haven't visited with them since Jake was born. Somehow they heard about Jake's tumor, and they responded quickly and kindly.

"There's a balloon bouquet from Yvonne and Tony Conza too. I couldn't carry everything. The woman at the front desk said that everyone knows who Jake is. She's never seen a patient receive so many gifts." Kathy extended a cup of coffee to me.

I couldn't believe that Kathy was holding it all together. I started crying as I took a step back from her. I couldn't explain it, but at that precise moment, I felt absolutely overwhelmed. I felt grateful for having such wonderful friends, but unbelievably naive for not having understood anything about what it meant to be a husband or a father.

Kathy's eyes misted over at the sight of my tears. "Geez, I didn't know that I'd have to be the strong one."

"I can't help it. Seeing him in that bed is killing me."

"I know," Kathy said, "but we have to use today to get strong. We need to eat a little bit, and we need to get some more information."

A couple of nurses passed close by and smiled at us. Kathy returned the smile and motioned toward the waiting room down the hall. I followed close behind, wiping the tears away as I walked. I took a sip of coffee and sat beside Kathy on the couch.

"We need to figure some of this out," she said. "I know you looked at the informational sheets on the chemotherapy, but there's a whole booklet of information. Did you read it yet?"

I bowed my head. "I haven't had a chance. I was kind of busy."

Kathy took a cigarette out of her purse and held it in her hand. I knew she wanted to light it right then and there, but I also knew that she'd wait until she got outside. "I'm going to go home and shower soon, and hopefully, I'll eat a little bit more today. Maybe when Jake takes a nap, you can look at that book."

I sighed heavily. I grabbed Kathy's hand, and she let the unlit cigarette fall to the carpet. "I can't believe I didn't make the doctors do more," she said. "I always had a sneaking suspicion that it was worse than asthma, but I trusted the specialist."

"It isn't your fault," I said. "I don't see any medical degrees hanging on your wall. Someone missed something. That's why we're here."

I hugged her for a long time, but my thoughts inevitably shifted to Jake and how he was handling his time in the room alone. "Go home and take a shower," I whispered. "If you promise to stop blaming yourself, I'll promise to eat."

She smiled and nodded. "Okay. I think I'm getting close to being all cried out anyway."

"I definitely feel more determined," I said.

Kathy was nearly to the exit door when she turned back around. "Your buddy, Mike LiVecchi dropped off a couple of sandwiches. They're in the refrigerator in ICU. Eat one, right now."

By mid-morning, Jake settled in for his nap. I watched his peaceful sleep for a few moments before I started turning pages on the 200-page document from Roswell Park Cancer Institute and Children's Hospital of Buffalo. The topics were listed one after another: initial shock, helplessness, guilt, anger, and fear. The book touched on changes to the family structure, taking care of yourself, and a litany of support services that were available.

I found myself wondering about a breakdown on the type of tumor that they were treating. Doctor Grossi had mentioned that it was called a teratoma, but the parent/child handbook didn't specifically identify this type of tumor. I found a passage about malignant germ cell tumors, but that certainly sounded awful.

I decided to start with the basic information. A tumor was defined as any abnormal growth in a localized area. The definition explained that the tumor could be either malignant or benign. That sounded simple enough. Perhaps Jake just had an abnormal growth. Happens every day, right?

Yet, the more I read, the more confusing it became. Unfortunately, without a biopsy, there wasn't any way to elicit this sort of statement: "Your son Jake has a teratoma tumor that is benign, and the chance of curing it is one hundred percent."

I spent the entire morning, with Jake sleeping comfortably beside me, searching for that elusive sentence. I took a few bites of the sandwich as I read, and I washed it down with black coffee. I learned that solid tumors account for three-fourths of all childhood cancers. Leukemia accounts for the other quarter of all cancers, but I skipped over that portion of the handbook because I had not heard the doctors mention leukemia. Jake definitely had a solid tumor. It was there for the entire world to see on the CT-scan.

There were several types of tumors, none of which I wanted to know personally. I didn't know anything about an embryonal tumor known as a neuroblastoma. I didn't want information on a retinoblastoma or a hepoblastoma. A sarcoma was a soft tissue cancer I didn't want to become familiar with. The scenarios that flashed through my mind weren't pretty. The realization that cancer was the second most common cause of death (after accidents) didn't do much to improve my mood. This was the paragraph that I focused on, however, and I read it over and over.

Most childhood cancers are highly curable. Cure rates have increased with advances in basic research, leading to improvements in chemotherapy, radiation therapy, and surgery. Many children who years ago would have died after being diagnosed with cancer are now successfully treated and are preparing for college, career, marriage, and parenthood.

Those were the types of sentences that I needed to read. I didn't need to understand that Jake might not go through college. I didn't want to even imagine life without him. I buried my head in my hands and felt overcome with despair. It was a moment that I truly wasn't comfortable sharing with anyone, even Kathy, but thankfully the negative thoughts quickly faded from my mind.

Kathy returned approximately five minutes after Jake woke from his nap. He was sipping Pepsi when she walked through the door, and he smiled brightly at the sight of her. She had a plastic bag behind her back, and she spun around so that Jake could see it.

"Did you bring me anything?" he asked.

Kathy produced a box of fruit candy and a container of cheese crackers. Jake looked mildly disappointed. "I'll take some crackers, I guess."

"What about this?" Kathy asked, pulling out a Power Ranger coloring book. Jake's eyes came alive, and he tried to sit up.

"Can you take a look at that while I talk to Dad in the hall?"

Jake happily took the coloring book, and he motioned for Kathy to come toward the bed. She leaned in, and he kissed her on the cheek.

"Stop kissing my wife!" I yelled.

We stepped into the hallway, and spoke in hushed tones just outside the door.

"What's the most curable cancer to have?" Kathy asked.

"I don't know. Who the hell knows? All I know is that when I was growing up everyone told me God is great, and God is good. How do we reconcile this? What does merciful God mean?"

Kathy shrugged. I wasn't sure it was the conversation that she expected to be having, but I was battling through the shock and trying to make sense of this nightmare.

"I don't think we can reconcile God's mercy with cancer," she said.

I didn't want to try and figure out what life was going to be like a year from now if things didn't turn out the right way. I imagined myself drinking myself into oblivion each and every night as I considered what Jake's life would have been like.

"We are going to handle this, right?" Kathy asked.

I nodded. "Maybe there is someone in our life who needs to learn how to handle adversity. Maybe we have to show them what love is all about," I said. It was an awfully egocentric way of looking at things, I knew, but a comfortable place to hang my hat. "We'll make it," I said. "And no more crying in front of him."

Before we even made it back to the room a tall, lanky man approached us. He wore a tie covered with cartoon characters, and he never raised his voice much higher than a whisper. There is a definite talent in developing a good bedside manner, and this man appeared to be overflowing with the talent. He extended his hand, and I shook it quickly. I couldn't place the face, and I was sure he was new to Jake's case. I thought about why we couldn't have just one doctor to turn to.

"I'm Doctor Brecher," he said, "an oncologist. I split my time between Roswell Park Cancer Institute and Children's Hospital. I work with Doctor Grossi. You've met him, correct?"

"Yes, and where have you been all day?" I smiled to show that I appreciated his presence now.

"We've been monitoring Jacob's case. I would like to examine him now if that's all right."

Kathy stepped into the space between Doctor Brecher and the door. "Do you think the tumor shrunk already?" she asked.

Doctor Brecher immediately won me over with his soft, reassuring manner. "From what I was told, his breathing is better today."

"It's much better," I said.

"Did it shrink?" Kathy asked, once more.

"Normally, that doesn't happen for awhile," Doctor Brecher said. "The biggest testament, however, is how he feels. If he's acting better and breathing easier, we're happy, right?"

I needed to cut straight to the heart of the matter. The thought crossed my mind that I should just grab the doctor by his cartoon tie and hold him close until he gave us the answer we were looking for. But Doctor Brecher didn't deserve such behavior. "Will he be all right?" I asked in an even tone.

Doctor Brecher shrugged. "There may be cancer cells in there. If there are, the chemo will take care of them, and we can gauge the situation better after the biopsy. One day at a time, right? Has he been sick at all?" I opened the door, and we looked in on Jake. He was eating potato chips from a small bowl. His breathing and color were at least fifty percent better than two days ago. I held my hand out as if to allow my son to be inspected once more.

Jake caught us looking at him and rolled his eyes. "What's up, doc?" he asked.

All through the evening friends and family stopped by the room to wish Jake well and hand him presents. The most important aspect of the visits was that Kathy and I began to find a way to speak about Jake's illness. It wasn't that we wanted to accept our predicament, but we were becoming conditioned to handle what was ahead of us as far as getting Jake well.

It was nearly nine o'clock before I decided to leave the hospital for the night. Jake was propped up in bed, the stack of presents in his lap. Kathy was in the chair beside the bed, helping him sort through the gifts.

"Dad is going to get going," Kathy said.

"You'll be back in the morning for cartoons, right?" Jake flashed a look of worry.

"Of course," I said. I leaned across the bed and kissed Jake on the forehead. He turned to Kathy with a mischievous smile. "Your husband is kissing me."

Kathy laughed. "You can have him," she said.

Kathy walked with me to the emergency room exit. I held her close for a few moments under the bright lights of the emergency room vestibule. "We're going to be all right," I whispered.

"We have to be," she answered.

I walked down Bryant Street in the darkness. I glanced at the blinking message light on my cell phone. I didn't feel like calling many people back. My most urgent need was to make it to Toys-R-Us before closing time. I had promised Jake that I would buy him the new Scooby Doo movie, and one way or another, I would have it with me in the morning.

I turned into the parking lot of Toys-R-Us and ran to the front door like a lunatic. The sign posted on the door stated that closing time was 9:30. I had missed it by less than three minutes. A young girl smiled at me from inside, and I yelled to her. "Do you have the new Scooby Doo movie?"

She nodded and smiled. She turned to a co-worker, and they both burst into laughter.

"I need a copy!" I yelled.

"We're closed," she answered sweetly, and the two of them guffawed some more.

I was on the verge of utter despair when it hit me that there was a Media Play Store open until 10:00. I covered the three miles in a couple of minutes and stormed into the store like the 7th Cavalry. A teenage boy in a red smock spotted my hurried approach and eyed me suspiciously.

"Do you have the new Scooby Doo movie?" I was sweating and breathing hard, and I didn't care who knew it. I must have looked like a wild-eyed terrorist, because the kid backed away.

"Yeah, calm down," he said. "I hear it's really good."

On another day, I might have laughed along with the kid, but not that day. He handed me a copy of the movie, and I headed for the checkout counter. Now, I've been on sports teams that have won big games. I've graduated from college, published five books, and been present for the birth of my children. But I honestly never felt better than the moment when I headed to the car with the new Scooby Doo movie clutched in both hands.

Chapter Four

Wednesday — October 10, 2001

My sleep was fitful at best. I alternated between tossing and turning in bed to flashing in and out of a dream that was filled with cartoon characters. The afternoons of watching cartoons with Jake at the hospital was catching up with me. In my dream, I was picturing Frosty the Snowman in the classic Christmas cartoon. I was stuck in the scene where Frosty is trapped in the greenhouse and slowly melts. I was identifying the horror that I felt as a child with the circumstances that were dictated by Jake's illness.

I finally sat upright in bed. Max edged closer to me, and I patted his head as if to say that everything was all right. It was still just a few minutes before four in the morning, and I knew that I needed to sleep a little longer. I just couldn't get Frosty the Snowman out of my head.

It took another twenty minutes or so and when I slipped back to sleep, my dream had changed. I dreamed that I was running across a field of green. There was something chasing me, and although I had no idea what it was, I ran quickly and just kept running. Just before I was caught from behind, I started to fly, and I soared high among the clouds.

Not knowing what any of the dreams meant, and feeling as though there were cobwebs in my mind, I stepped off the elevator at the 2nd floor. It was six-thirty, and the cup of coffee that I finished off on the way to the hospital hadn't done anything to clear the cobwebs. Kathy and I were surviving on pure adrenalin, but I was finding out that there wasn't an endless supply.

A young man in a light blue uniform was in the hallway, pushing a broom, but there wasn't a lot of effort involved. The broom handle was rigged to the front of his belt, and he was walking along very slowly. I said good-morning, but he didn't respond. I turned into Jacob's corridor with a twinge of anger surging through my veins. Why couldn't that man do his job the right way? Someone was paying him, but he was just going through the motions. I realize that everyone has a bad day, but for one reason or another, this guy's lackadaisical attitude really got under my skin. I've always believed that you should earn every cent. Hopefully, that man was just taking a short break, but I doubt it. Just seeing this man brought to mind something that my father had told me just after my graduation from high school. Dad said; "Do more than what is expected of you and never compete with anyone but yourself."

Jake was sitting up, but I could immediately tell that this ordeal was getting to him too. He complained to Kathy about the angle of the television set, and she rolled her eyes as she moved it until he nodded in approval. I distracted him with the new Scooby Doo movie, and we immediately put it into the VCR.

"Did you get the coffee and the papers?" Kathy asked with a note of desperation in her voice.

I extended them to her, and she broke for the door. Kathy is a happier person after coffee and a glance at the morning crossword. I fell into my chair beside Jake's bed, and it occurred to me that we had settled into a mind-numbing routine. The initial shock had almost completely worn off, and now it seemed as if we were dealing with the residue. For the first time that day, it hit me that we were preparing for day three of chemotherapy. My heart ached for the innocence of last week and the hassle of finding time to help stuff the Italian sausage. How I prayed that someday I would once again worry about something so unimportant in the grand scheme of things.

"Look what I got," Jake said.

He sat up a little bit and smoothed out a brand new T-shirt that he was wearing. The shirt had both of his favorite cartoon characters on it: Spiderman and the Red Ranger.

"That's cool. Did Mommy get you that?" I asked.

"No, the doctor," Jake said.

I was a little confused, but moments later the puzzle was solved. Susan came back on duty and admitted that she had brought the shirt for Jake. "I have a little boy the same age," she said. "He picked it out for Jake."

I immediately forgot about the man pushing the broom with his belt buckle. Susan was doing her job to the best of her abilities and beyond. *Do more than what is expected of you.*

"Thank you," I whispered as I clasped her hand.

"I thought about him all day when I was off-duty yesterday," Susan said.

Susan finished taking Jake's temperature and checking the various apparatus attached to my boy. She stepped out of the room, and I saw her chatting with Kathy, who was returning from her short break.

Kathy and I caught up a little bit while Jake watched the movie. We talked about how well we were being treated by our employers and the friends who had stopped to see Jake since Sunday. We discussed Sam and Matt for a few minutes, but they were doing well.

"Don't forget Matt's party on Saturday," Kathy said.

I gave her a bit of a blank look, but the situation came back to me quickly. Matt had asked if he could have his birthday party early. Considering it was October and his birthday wasn't until May, we had agreed that he didn't need a reason to have friends over. "We can't cancel it."

"The thought had crossed my mind," I said.

"He'll blame Jake forever. He's only eight. He doesn't know what's going on."

She was right, of course, but that didn't do me much good. The yard wasn't ready for ten little boys playing baseball. The dogs had filled the backyard with their daily business, and I hadn't mowed the grass in a couple of weeks. I was a little unsure of what the garage looked like, too.

"I'm going to have to find some time to straighten up things," I said.

"Jack is Matt's father. He'll help out. I'll ask him to stay for the party."

I knew Kathy's ex wouldn't mind. He played ball with Matt every day. Hopefully he felt comfortable enough to do it at our home.

"What else?" Kathy asked.

Before I could mutter anything to such an unanswerable question, she finished her thought. "Did you see Max's paw? There's something stuck in it. He keeps biting at it."

"Wonderful. I'll check him out tonight."

"Oh, I also forgot to tell you that Father Judge dropped by yesterday to bless Jake."

My eyes filled with tears, and Kathy laughed. "Still a little emotional?"

"It's the people," I said. "We must be doing all right if so many people are willing to do these great things for us."

"You reap what you sow," Kathy said.

"I didn't sow this," I said as I pointed at the chart hanging from Jake's bed. Yet we both understood what she was speaking about. If any of our friends needed help, we'd be there. "Some people are doing a lot more than expected," I whispered.

"Like your brother, John," Kathy said. "He's here every fifteen minutes, and the tears in his eyes just kill me."

"I never doubted anyone in our family," I said, my voice quivering like a leaf.

"Maybe it's a good time to get another coffee," Kathy said, patting my shoulder.

Later that morning Jake and I watched a cartoon about a robot, a little boy named Billy, and a skeletal character named Grim. All three were walking along the sidewalk of a strip mall when they noticed costumes in a storefront window. The skeleton turned to the other two and said, "That's what I want to be for Halloween." The little boy turned to the robot and said, "Grim wants to be a window."

I couldn't believe that Jake understood the joke, but it sort of became our mantra. Anytime that Jake faced a major crisis, such as having a piece of tape removed, I reminded him of the joke, and we shared a laugh. My mind shifted to the dream of Frosty melting away. I was terrified and amused at the same time, and I reached into the bed and tickled Jake's belly quickly.

"Grim is funny, isn't he, Dad?"

"It's my favorite cartoon ever," I said.

Jake didn't touch anything on his lunch tray, and it was just shortly after noon when he confessed that he was sick of cartoons. "When can I get out of here?" he asked. His lip quivered, and I knew he was just barely hanging on to his sanity.

"You need to get a little more medicine," I said. "You're getting better, though." I had no way of knowing if what I was telling him were true. I was focused on the fact that Susan would be starting the chemotherapy around four o'clock.

"I'm almost ready for a nap," I said.

"Me too," Jake said.

"Let me talk to Susan for a second. I'll see if we can get her to stop people from bothering us."

Susan was sitting at the nurse's station. She smiled as I approached. "Does he need anything?"

"He needs a little sleep," I said. "Is it possible to keep everyone away for a little while?"

"Sure," Susan said. "Just close your door, and I'll stay clear."

Jake's eyes were already closed. I shut off the television, and we settled in. The large balloon dinosaur that my mother had bought earlier lurked in the far corner of the room.

"Okay, we're sleeping now," I said.

Jake closed his eyes and smiled. As soon as I closed mine, he made a loud, burping sound.

"What was that?" I asked, as if in shock.

Jake pointed to the dinosaur. "He did it!"

For the better part of fifteen minutes, I pretended to close my eyes, and Jake and the burping dinosaur woke me up. We laughed all the way through it, and just for good measure, every few moments, Jake said, "Daddy wants to be a window."

A few moments later the doorknob turned. I couldn't believe that someone was trying to get in, particularly since I told Susan that Jake desperately needed a nap. The door swung open and my good friend, Chris Heinold, held out a bag with about twenty presents. Jake smiled and sat up quickly. "You brought me something?"

I couldn't quite put my finger on it, but Chris seemed real nervous. He held the bag open, and Jake picked out a pack of matchbox cars.

"That's boring," Jake said.

I took the cars from Jake's hand. "That's not very nice. Chris brought you all of these presents, and you're being mean."

I smiled at Chris. "He's grown a little immune to all of the presents,"

I said. "He'll play with every single one. Thank you."

Chris shrugged as Jake reached in for another gift and fished out a huge candy bar. "Can I have a piece?"

I broke off a piece of chocolate. "As soon as you finish that we have to nap."

I turned the television back on so Jake would have some company, and then I touched Chris on the arm and motioned for the door. "You hang in there, little buddy," Chris said to Jake.

"Thanks for the presents," Jake said.

Chris and I stepped into the hallway. I noticed tears in Chris's eyes.

"Man, I'm sorry," Chris said. "I can't imagine what you're going through. If anything like this happened to either of my daughters, I'd be out of my mind."

"I am out of my mind. I never dreamed I'd ever have to face something like this."

Chris and I were best buddies for a lot of years. We spent more than our fair share of time in bars, and we grew up together as men and as fathers.

"It's tough enough to be a father. No one should have to go through this," Chris said.

"A lot of people do. Try not to look around. There's a lot of pain here."

Jake emitted a tremendously loud burp, and Chris turned to the door with alarm in his eyes.

"That's the burping dinosaur," I said. "We're trying to nap and he keeps us up."

"I'll let you go," Chris said. "Call if you need anything."

I shook hands with my good friend, and watched him walk out of the ICU. His shoulders were slumped and he didn't look anywhere but at his feet. I knew Chris was hurting for me and for all of the fathers that ever had to go through such an ordeal.

But Jake and I had one more bit of business to take care of before we settled in for the much-needed rest.

"Why are you being so mean to people bringing you gifts?"

Jake considered this for a moment. He darted his eyes away.

"These people are coming a long way to see you. They're spending a lot of money to make you happy, and you're being mean to them. Why?"

He fingered one of the packages. In his eyes I saw a glimmer of true sadness. "I hate everyone. I want to go home. I miss my brothers."

I had no idea what I could say to make him feel better. I rubbed his hand and smoothed out the covers. "You know what?" I asked.

"What?" he answered through tear-stained eyes.

"Jake wants to be a window," I said. Jake started laughing, and I tickled him for a moment.

Thank God for cartoons. Jake fell asleep watching Batman. He slept for two hours. I sat beside the bed, replaying his complaints over and over in my mind, and saying the rosary.

* * *

It wasn't often that I got an afternoon break, but Jake had received the same GameBoy Advanced game from two people, and it was my job to return one of them for a new game. I quickly drove to Toys-R-Us. It was a beautiful, sunny day that betrayed every thought in my head. Pulling into the parking lot, I saw a familiar car in the spot near the door. Kathy's mother had taken Kathy's car home from the hospital on the first night, and three days later she was still driving it. I peered into the back window, hoping that I would see car seats. I saw Jake's blue car seat behind the passenger seat and Sam's gray car seat behind the driver's seat. I ran into the store, realizing that I might actually see Sam there.

The clerks at the store had to be shaking their heads again. Just hours after I had pressed my face to the glass door, looking for the new Scooby Doo movie, I was running through the store as though my hair were on fire. I'm surprised that they didn't call the police.

Carolyn and Sam were in the center of the store, looking at plastic action figures. Sam didn't even glance my way, and Carolyn held her eyes away. She couldn't look at me without crying. Their cart was filled with toys for Jake, and my heart was again on overload.

"He's doing great," I said. "He took a nice, long nap and Kathy's watching cartoons with him. He's going to be fine."

"I know," Carolyn said, her voice cracking. "I just want to hug him so bad."

I tried to change the direction of the conversation by playing with Sam, but he was far too interested in the balloons at the front of the store to pay any attention to me. I'm certain that he didn't even recall who I was until we got out into the parking lot. I think it was my vehicle that triggered his memory, but as we made our way to our separate cars, Sam started crying for me. I pulled up beside him and opened the side window. "Daaaa..." he yelled.

I kissed his face over and over, and he just kept reciting his abbreviated version of Dad. Carolyn cried all the way through our long good-bye.

* * *

I hesitate to say anything disparaging about The Children's Hospital of Buffalo, but I will anyway; the cafeteria food was just a notch above edible. As a family we don't eat much fast food. We cook breakfast, lunch, and dinner at home, and our meals are usually pretty decently balanced. I couldn't bring myself to try anything served downstairs, other than coffee. I considered buying a couple of meatloaf dinners, but I could tell just by looking at them that the mashed potatoes were instant, and there was a bright red sauce on the meatloaf that I couldn't identify. I knew I should be eating right, but I wasn't about to roll the dice on such fare.

It was late afternoon, and my trip to the cafeteria resulted in just a couple of cans of diet soda. I returned to the room and took up the question with Kathy. "What are we doing for dinner?"

"Oh, I forgot to tell you, your mother called," Kathy said. "She made roast beef, mashed potatoes, and corn. Corinne is dropping it off."

"Thank God!" I said.

"And your brother Jeff made sausage and potatoes and left it in the fridge at home. Did you have any?"

I hadn't seen the sausage and potatoes, but Jeff is a professional chef, and I knew what Kathy's next sentence was going to be. "It was awesome. I had three pieces of sausage and two huge potatoes."

"That's nice," I said. "I'm downstairs trying to figure out if I can chance eating the hospital food while you've been eating like you're on vacation."

Kathy laughed. "We can bring our own food in," she said. "Maybe tonight you can make a steak or something for Jake. He'll probably eat better if the food is home-cooked."

We settled into our usual spots around Jacob's bed and waited for Corinne to show up with our dinner. Doctor Brecher knocked softly on the door, and he entered with a huge smile on his face. "Hello, Jacob, how are you today?"

"I'm good," Jake said. He hadn't even turned his eyes away from the television.

"Do you mind if I take a listen?" Doctor Brecher asked. He waved his tie at Jake who was immediately interested in the cartoon characters on the tie. Doctor Brecher nodded in approval and smiled. He placed the stethoscope on Jake's chest and listened for a moment. "All right, buddy, you're doing well." He patted Jake on the head, and Kathy and I followed him to the door.

"Did the tumor shrink?" Kathy whispered. We all looked toward the bed. Jake didn't seem to be following the conversation.

"It is difficult to know at this point," Doctor Brecher said. "He sounds a lot better, though."

"So that has to mean that something is happening, right?" I asked.

Doctor Brecher nodded, but his eyes told me that he wasn't about to declare anything. Kathy must have picked up on it too. "How does the X-ray from today compare with the first few that he took? Does the tumor look smaller?" she asked.

"We will know more in a few days," Doctor Brecher said. "Rest assured, though, that we intend on curing Jacob. We are working toward removing the tumor and sending him home to you. At this point, we can't be sure that the tumor is shrinking, but that may be because there are no cancerous cells. We need to take it a moment at a time, okay?"

I shook Doctor Brecher's hand, and he stepped out into the hall. I hugged Kathy for a moment, and together we turned back to the bed that held our beautiful child.

"I like that guy," Jake said. "He talks real soft."

"I like him too," I said.

It suddenly occurred to me that when things look bad there's usually someone around the scene that reminds you that God exists. I was beginning to understand that the doctors and nurses of The Children's Hospital of Buffalo were our salvation in all of this.

Jake slipped off to sleep at a few minutes after nine o'clock. Once again, a steady stream of visitors had been by to say hello, and Jake seemed worn out by the whole ordeal.

"I'll walk you downstairs," Kathy said a few moments after Jake's eyes closed.

We took the elevator down and headed for the emergency room doors. The ward was jammed with parents and children, and I thought back to the horrifying scene of a few days ago. Was that all the time that had passed? It seemed like we had been in the hospital for a year.

"The Yankees are on," Kathy said.

"You know, I don't even care," I said.

I wrapped my arms around Kathy's waist. I felt as though I was nearing the end of a sadly demented date. "How did you feel dealing with it today?" I asked.

"I'm doing what I have to do," Kathy said. "What choice do I have?"

Kathy's question was ringing in my ears as I headed for my car. I listened to six messages that had been left on my cell phone voice mail. There was a telephone call from my childhood buddy, Al DeCarlo, and as I drove over the skyway leaving the city, I punched in Al's telephone number. All throughout our lives, Al's timing has been impeccable. It's almost as if he has a beeper that tells him when I'm lonely. He had lost his mother to cancer when we were adolescents. His father raised the family to adulthood and then, tragically, succumbed to a heart attack. If anyone had cause to be down about life, it was Al and his brother Aaron and sister Tracy, but they weren't. They have been an inspiration to me all through my life. I only wish that everyone had the chance to meet any of the three.

When Al answered the phone I talked a blue streak. I told him of the treatments, and I talked about the fear controlling my heart.

"You're doing it the right way," Al said. "Be strong for Jake. There isn't a lot you can do about his illness, but you can teach him love. You're supposed to be teaching everybody, pal."

I pulled into the driveway at home just as our phone conversation ended. I turned the key in the front door, and the dogs jumped all over me. I let them outside to do their business, and most of the conversations that I had throughout the day worked their way through my mind. Doctor Brecher and Al DeCarlo were right. We did need to take it a moment at a time, and Kathy and I had to teach everyone that we came into contact with that love would carry us through this.

I broiled a steak and cut it into pieces to take to Jake, hoping that he'd eat something more substantial than crackers.

I let the dogs back in from outside, and again they jumped all around me, begging for attention. I located the remote and turned on the Yankee game. It was game one of the American League playoffs, and I knew that if Jake wasn't sick, the game would have been the most important thing in my life. I would be on the edge of my seat for each and every pitch. Now, it was simply a distraction.

Jason Giambi hit a long home run for the Athletics, and I shook my head in disappointment as he rounded the bases. I lay back on the couch, and the dogs took their turns jumping on me, looking for love and affection. Al DeCarlo was surely on the mark; everyone needed to feel love, even the dogs.

The game ended just before midnight, and despite having their chances, the Yankees lost. I headed up to bed with the dogs at my heels. As my head met the pillow, I began reciting prayers over and over. I can't even remember drifting off to sleep, but the dream of Frosty the Snowman melting before my eyes returned. I woke up scared and sweating, knowing that there hadn't been anything I could do to save Frosty.

Chapter Five

Thursday — October 11, 2001

I had no way of knowing what day it was. It's strange, but life is set up so that each day gives you a certain feeling. We all know the bad rap that Monday gets, but even a Thursday has its own unique feel. Having a child in the hospital strips you of any feeling of familiarity. The alarm rang at 5:15, and I jumped from the bed with the dogs trailing close behind. I remembered what Kathy had said about Max's paw, so I held it in my hand, searching for a sign of a thorn or wound. Since I didn't see anything that looked as if it were causing him discomfort, I patted him on the head and sent him on his way.

There's a lot of misery in the world. Normal, everyday life often pulled me away from thoughts of other people's suffering, but there was no escaping it in the hallways at The Children's Hospital of Buffalo. The worried looks on the faces of the other parents frightened me into realizing that life can change at any moment. I tried to look away from the children in the other rooms in the intensive care unit. I respected the nurse's wishes to vacate the hallway when a discussion of another patient was taking place. I even hesitated to make personal contact with the other parents lurking in the corridors. My heart was filled with emotion and despair, and I didn't think that I could take the story of another sick child. Still, I couldn't avoid the misery and the general atmosphere that settled over the ward like a heavy mist.

I entered Jake's room at a few minutes before seven. I leaned into the bed and kissed Jake on the forehead. Bugs Bunny was chasing someone around on the screen, and Jake giggled. I turned to Kathy, and she offered a smile that flashed a tired impatience. Kathy's philosophy of life had always been to ignore pain. On more than one occasion she referred to this defense mechanism as, "living in my bubble." She felt that we had a perfect little life that didn't allow for thoughts of despair. But suddenly, our life had been invaded by despair, and her bubble had broken.

"The poor guy down the hall has been here for three months," Kathy said. "His daughter has intestinal problems, and it's pretty bad. The doctors told him there isn't much hope. The girl has been doing better the last few days, but the poor dad got laid off from work. To top it off, the kid's mother has been battling the father for custody."

I held up my hand to make her stop. While promoting my fourth book, *Desperation*, I had visited the Buffalo City Mission. The visit to the mission had changed my perspective on life. I tried to donate time and money in an effort to make myself feel better, but deep down I knew that my token gestures to the function of the City Mission wouldn't change the world.

"There's nothing we can do. There are so many people hurting. Right now, we can only help Jake."

"I know, but I feel so bad," Kathy said. "Did you see the girl in the next room?"

I nodded, but I was afraid to hear the story.

"I saw her mother in the elevator, and I told her that Jake would be here at least another week. The lady said, 'My daughter is never going home.'"

"That's too bad," I said.

"My heart is so full of hurt," Kathy said. "I just feel so bad."

I tried to pretend that my hands were tied. Stories of heartbreak and pain are around us every day. Just this past year, a couple of close friends had lost their father to a sudden illness. Children, mothers, and pets pass on, despite the protest of those who love them. Jake was lying in a hospital bed with chemicals rushing through his veins. Misery was enveloping us now, and we just wanted to avoid the grasp of eternal despair.

It was a Thursday that was taking on a feel of its own, and I didn't much care for it.

* * *

Later in the morning Jake worked on coloring a couple of pictures in his Red Ranger coloring book. I was cleaning up the empty soda cans that had accumulated around the room, and Kathy was working a crossword puzzle that seemed to be getting the best of her. In fact, frustration seemed to be the order of the day. Kathy tossed the paper down, and I saw the question forming behind her blue eyes. "Who's in charge of Jake's care?"

I abruptly stopped cleaning things up, and I knelt on the floor beside Kathy's chair. "What are you talking about?"

"So far there have been about eleven doctors in here looking at him this morning," Kathy said.

"Eleven?" I asked. "I've told you a million times not to exaggerate."

She smiled at my little joke, but her face was immediately contorted by a look of frustration. "One of the men from surgery was here asking about the biopsy. Two of the residents stood outside the door and whispered like high school girls. I never saw the residents before in my life. I just want to know who's in charge."

I glanced nervously at Jake. Kathy had every right to be upset. God knows she wasn't getting proper rest. But we didn't need to fight with the staff that was responsible for helping us through this nightmare.

"I think Doctor Brecher is the guy we need to talk to."

"Where is he?" Kathy asked.

"We talked to him yesterday," I said. "I know we didn't get a lot of information, but this is going to take some time."

Kathy shrugged. I caught a glimpse of Jake, who had turned in the bed to listen to our conversation. There were dark circles under Jake's eyes, and I wondered about the chemicals in his body and what they might be doing to him. Kathy chugged so much of the coffee so fast that I wondered if she could hold it down. "They're in here all night long. Every hour I see a new face, and I don't know what any of them is doing."

I sat in the chair across the room. We had been married long enough for me to understand that this was a time for her to vent a little bit, and that my job was to simply try to understand her point of view. Besides, she was right. I agreed that we deserved to know the intentions of everyone poking and prodding at our son. Yet I was more interested in the bottom line, and the more people making the effort to get Jake back on his feet, the better off we were.

"I'm going to ask the nurse who's in charge," Kathy said.

"We are," I said. "More specifically, you are."

Kathy didn't want to hear any more of my patronizing bunk. She grabbed the new coffee I offered her and picked up the crossword puzzle again. "I am going to ask someone."

"If you want, we can just pull him out of here and treat him at home," I said. I was trying to make her laugh and at least I got a smile. I settled in beside Jake, and we concentrated on Bugs and Daffy. Jake's first sentence of the day, after Kathy was out of earshot, was an instant classic; "Mommy wants to be a window," he said.

Just before lunch Kathy's sister Lori stopped by Jake's room for a visit. Kathy had headed for home for a shower and a change of clothes. Lori's husband Mike was carrying a bag of presents and one of the gifts opened up the greatest debate since Lincoln versus Douglas. Jake's eyes flashed pure excitement as he removed a red Power Ranger costume. The costume was complete with a red and white mask, belt, and gloves.

"It's awesome! Halloween is pretty soon, isn't it, Dad?"

"Just a couple of weeks," I said.

Jake wanted to put the mask on his face, and I helped him pull the strap over his head. I gave a passing thought to whether or not it might affect his breathing, but it was just for a few moments.

Halloween is a truly exciting holiday for children, and Jake was no exception. He had been talking about what costume he was going to wear since mid-July when Matthew handed Jake his *Scream* mask from last year.

"Which one should I wear this year, *Scream* or the Red Ranger?" Jake asked me. He looked at me through the eye holes in the mask, but I could almost tell that he was smiling.

"You look pretty tough in the Red Ranger mask," I said. "Maybe tomorrow I can bring the *Scream* mask from home, and we can see which one is scarier."

Jake lifted the Ranger mask up and left it resting on his head. Lori and Mike wore ear-to-ear grins, happy that their present had brought their nephew a moment of happiness. Fear moved across my mind like a wave to the shore: What if he didn't have the chance to don either costume this Halloween?

Lori and Mike didn't stick around too long. They knew that Jake was just about ready for his nap. I walked out into the hallway and hugged Lori. "Thanks for stopping by," I said.

"Do you and Kathy need anything?" Lori sighed heavily and looked me straight in the eye.

"Just be around for us, huh?" I asked. I hugged her again and then I shook Mike's hand.

Before returning to the room, I unwrapped the cut-up steak and heated it in the microwave in the nurse's station.

"I bet you can't eat it all," I said as I handed the bowl to Jake.

"I'll bet you a dollar," he said. He dug his hand into the bowl and pulled out three or four small pieces. He popped them into his mouth as if the steak was candy. I pretended to be amazed, and he smiled through his chewing. "I'm going to do it," he said. Before Kathy made it back from her trip home, Jake had cleaned out the entire bowl.

Jake was asleep when Kathy returned. She was holding a stack of cards and letters and a few pages of material printed off the internet.

"Let's go to the waiting room and sift through some of this," Kathy said.

I followed her down the hall into the ICU waiting room. There were three other people in the room who were sitting in chairs around the television set. The inane banter of the Jerry Springer show filled the room.

"I can't keep up with thanking all of the people who've sent cards and letters," Kathy said.

"We'll have plenty of time to thank everyone when this is all over," I said.

Kathy spread the letters out on a small table, and we sat side-by-side reading through them.

"Chuck and Karen Renaldo sent a gift certificate for Blockbuster. How long has it been since we even saw them?" Kathy asked.

"It's been about a year since they visited from Baltimore, but they're friends for life," I said.

"Look at this one from Chris Colantino," Kathy said. There was a photo of a church in the distance, and the card read. *A faithful friend is the medicine of life — Bible, Ecclesiastes 6:16.* Chris had also included the statement, *Now faith is being sure of what we hope for and certain of what we do not see — Bible, Hebrews 11:1.*

"It's unreal," Kathy said. "Jake's touched so many lives. God has to have a plan for him."

"He'll do big things," I said. "He's never known anything but love."

As parents of an ill child, we were totally overwhelmed by Jake's illness, but our friends went out of their way to help us through.

"Your father called. He said that his telephone hasn't stopped ringing. People are calling him night and day to see how Jake's feeling. Your aunts, uncles and cousins are praying for him. Your cousin Carol had a mass said for him in New York City."

"The only thing about this that makes me want to cry right now is thinking about how wonderful everyone has been," I said, taking a deep breath.

"Daddy wants to be a window," Kathy whispered.

Jake slept for a little over an hour. By that time, Kathy and I had returned to our all-too-familiar chairs. I was on the left side of the bed up near Jake's head and Kathy was on the left side down near his feet. Jake was askew in the huge bed, his head turned toward the television.

"What do you need to get ready for Matthew's party on Saturday?" Kathy asked.

I had thought about what needed to be done, but that was as far as I had proceeded. "I need to mow the lawn and clean the dog crap out of the backyard."

"Well, it's raining pretty hard today, so cutting the lawn will have to wait."

I didn't think Jake was listening to the conversation, but apparently he was. "Dad, I've been meaning to ask you," he said. "Did the grass we planted grow?"

I nearly fell out of the chair. I couldn't fathom that a child going through so much could possibly recall that we planted grass seed the day before his hospitalization.

"Yes," I said. "We have a lot of grass now."

"God made it grow?" he asked.

I nodded, and he turned toward Kathy.

"Mom's proud, right?"

I was pretty sure that Kathy was proud, but it was hard to tell on account of the tears glistening in her eyes. We shared our first real smile of the day.

* * *

Shortly before nine o'clock, Jake fell asleep watching cartoons. Kathy and I slipped out of the room to discuss his tumor with the resident doctor.

"Did the tumor shrink?" Kathy asked. "He's breathing so much better, so it had to, right?"

The young doctor was extremely hesitant. He looked to be just out of medical school, and I'm not entirely sure that he was comfortable with our double-barrel assault. "I don't think we can tell for sure if it shrank. Normally, chemotherapy doesn't work that fast, but who knows? Everyone handles it differently."

"They've been taking X-rays every day," Kathy said. "Are they discussing the results?"

The doctor offered a half-frown that seemed to indicate that he thought the question was a little naïve. "Sure," he said. "We've all seen the X-rays, but it is so hard to tell. Once they do the biopsy we'll know exactly what it is."

I was having a difficult time formulating my questions. Half of me still wanted to believe that Jake didn't even have a touch of cancer. The other side of my brain was hoping that the tumor had shrunk so that they could perform the necessary operations. The young doctor looked at me, expecting me to say something, but I just stared blankly.

"Can we see this morning's X-ray?" Kathy asked. "I mean, we saw the initial X-ray. Maybe we can tell if it looks different."

If the doctor was put off by our request, he did a great job of hiding it. He made an excuse and slipped off into another room. Kathy looked at me hopefully. "We should be able to tell, right?"

"I don't know," I said. "Remember all the sonograms they did when the kids were developing?"

"Sure," Kathy said. "I can still picture Jake's in my mind."

"I never saw a thing," I said.

The doctor returned and led us to a large white poster board in the far corner of the nurse's station. As he hung the latest X-ray, I wasn't sure what to expect, but I gasped for air again. The reality of it all came crashing down on my head once more.

"It looks better, doesn't it?" Kathy asked.

The X-ray was pure white. I'm sure that I was too.

"See, over there on the right side? It looks clearer, doesn't it?" Kathy said.

I didn't see much of a difference. "What does he think?" I asked.

The doctor wasn't about to bail me out. He bobbed his head from side to side and squinted as though he were truly studying the X-ray. I'm sure that he knew exactly what he was looking at, but he was in a tough position. He didn't want to offer us false hope, and he didn't want to crush us, either. "It may have shrunk," he said at last.

"But we'll know more when we have the biopsy," I said.

"Exactly."

It was evident that Kathy felt better. Just having a little bit of information seemed to fortify her, and I did an excellent job of pretending that we were, indeed, making progress.

We thanked the doctor for his time and headed back toward Jake's room. I poked my head in and confirmed that he was still asleep and sighed heavily.

"Why don't you head out now?" Kathy asked. "Maybe you can get a little more sleep."

I kissed her and headed out the door. I was waiting for the elevator when I realized that I had forgotten the car keys. I returned to the room and Kathy stepped back outside with me.

"By the way," she said, "I was on the Internet today, and I sent an e-mail to a lady in New Mexico. Her son had a teratoma tumor removed from his chest, and he's doing fine now."

"We don't know if that's what Jake has," I said.

"I know, but I asked her for more information. It can't hurt, right?"

I kissed her again and headed back toward the car. The rain was falling hard and cold. I didn't even feel like walking fast enough to get away from it. Something in my mind clicked, and I began saying The Lord's Prayer over and over. I felt as if I were trapped in an absolute nightmare. I thought of the family in New Mexico and all the pain they had been through. There was just so much misery in the world.

It was a little after ten when I turned onto the skyway in an effort to leave Buffalo. I couldn't help but think about how odd it was that Jake's entire ordeal was playing out mere minutes from our wonderful home. The thought of our relatives visiting all day again put a lump in my throat. We couldn't have had better siblings or parents. I turned on the radio and Springsteen's voice filled the car. My heart did a flip when I realized that Kathy had also been playing his music for inspiration. "Reason to Believe" was her song of choice, and I listened to it twice. I needed to find a reason to believe, and I begged God to help me catch a break. I thought about the Yankees and their playoff series. Couldn't God let the Yankees win just for me? Lord knows that I was searching for any sort of distraction.

Friday — October 12, 2001

Kathy's passing reference to the other teratoma victim piqued my interest, and my first order of business upon waking up in the morning was to check the e-mail. I read the story of a thirty-year-old man named Eric, and it immediately sounded eerily similar to Jacob's story.

For years, Eric had endured bouts of rough breathing. His problems had been routinely attributed to allergies, and he had never had a chest X-ray either. When Eric's tumor had been discovered, his parents and girlfriend had battled through the pain and helped him get ready for surgery. The tumor had been removed, and Eric has been healthy ever since. His surgery had taken place three years ago, and his mother reports that Eric suffered no ill effects. Now, this is where it gets interesting; Eric's tumor weighed approximately ten pounds!

I had to read Eric's story a few times before the importance of it sank in. It was like something out of "Ripley's Believe it or Not". I stared wild-eyed at the computer screen as I sorted through the details of a story that had played out thousands of miles away.

I scrambled around the house to make sure that I had everything we needed for day five of our hospital stay. The steak worked out so well that I thawed another and broiled it as the dogs went about their morning routine. I also tossed in a load of laundry, believing that we would be able to handle that chore on a tag-team basis. Kathy would transfer the wet clothes to the dryer on her afternoon break and start the next load, and I would finish it up at night.

Max's paw was bright pink and grotesquely swollen. Again, I looked for a stone or a thorn, but he didn't sit still long enough for me to study it very thoroughly. "You're going to have to suck it up," I told him. "You can't get sick now."

It was strange, but the dogs seemed to sense that the family dynamic was a bit off kilter. They grudgingly entered the front room where they would be locked in until Kathy came home. Max and Shadow were used to a lot of attention, and they seemed a little sad now that they were being all but ignored. I patted each dog on the head and made sure they had enough water. I opened the front door, and Max and Shadow followed me to the threshold. "Sorry, guys, I have to go."

The morning sky was gray. If it rained again all day I wouldn't have a chance at mowing the lawn before Matthew's party. I slipped in behind the wheel and checked the dashboard clock. It was twelve minutes after six, and if traffic cooperated I'd be at the hospital before the nurses made their shift change at seven. An idea flashed across my mind, and I jumped from the truck and headed back into the house.

The sadness was almost overwhelming as I sifted through Jake's toy box, handling his abandoned toys, but a sense of elation flooded over me when I found his *Scream* mask behind a couple of stuffed animals. I just wanted to make him smile a couple of times.

Kathy was wide awake and already working on a huge cup of coffee. Jake eyed me with a look of confusion and sadness, and I imagined that the white-coated man at the foot of the bed was causing his discomfort. I barely noticed the man as I tossed my coat on the chair in the back corner of the room. The man was studying Jake's file, and his stone face told me that he was extremely concerned. "We haven't seen a lot of these types of tumors," the man said. "Yet it is very important that we work with Jake to get him coughing up some of the phlegm in his chest."

Who was this guy? Was he a new doctor assigned to the case? Maybe they needed a specialist. I glanced at Kathy, and she rolled her eyes. I'm pretty sure the man didn't see it, but I quickly understood what she meant.

"Who are you?" I asked.

The man adjusted his glasses and smiled. "Ken Smith. I'll be Jacob's nurse for the day."

"Are they changing his treatment in some way?" I asked.

"No, but I can't emphasize how important it is for you to make him cough."

"Why?" I asked. "And how am I going to make him cough? Should I tickle him?"

Ken flashed me an impatient look, and Kathy grabbed me by the arm.

"Jake, we have to go outside for a few minutes. We'll be right back." Before I stepped out, I reached into the bag and tossed the mask onto his bed. He smiled and held it up to his face.

We barely made it into the corridor leading away from ICU. "What's up with Marcus Welby?" I asked, jerking my head toward Jake's room.

"He's very thorough," Kathy said. "He's trying to familiarize himself with Jake's case."

"I'm beat," I said. "I'm not sure I can handle someone so diligent."

Then Kathy uttered the phrase that I was tired of hearing. "Let's get another coffee."

* * *

In July of 1996, I tore my Achilles tendon. I suffered the injury when rounding second base in a slow-pitch softball game. I remember the incident so clearly because when it happened I was as busy as I had ever been. My third book was due out before the end of the year, and my full-time job was extending me as much as it possibly could. Kathy and I saw each other every day, but we were still shadow boxing with thoughts of the future. I was fairly convinced that I didn't need much of anything. That ill-fated trip around the bases changed everything.

I underwent surgery the next morning. My leg was put into a cast, and the couch was my new place of business. I can remember thinking that God wanted me to take a timeout to assess my life up to that point. A few real important things came out of my months in front of daytime television. First and foremost was the thought that life can change on a dime. Secondly, I understood that I did need someone in my life, because without Kathy I wouldn't have even been able to open the windows during the hottest Buffalo summer ever. Finally, I understood I just couldn't handle pain. As I sipped the coffee, I worked to recall the story of my torn tendon. I asked Kathy if I had complained. She smiled and said, "You're a man. All men complain."

Jake's illness was having a similar effect on me, in that it made me think. Life was surely filled with things that would knock you down before you could see them coming. Also, I understood that he was in that bed, holding my heart in his hands. I couldn't have possibly needed anything more than his full recovery. In five short years, I had gone from the man who was convinced he could do fine on his own to the man who couldn't even fathom the thought of having a part of a new, wonderful life ripped away. The only thing missing was the complaining.

Jake had been in the hospital for nearly a week. During that time, he must have been poked with twenty needles. He had had lines stuck in both arms and fresh air blown into his face. The alarms beeped and blinked around him all day long, and he was shaken awake from his nightly sleep for just about a week. To top it off, he had lived with a cantaloupe-sized tumor in the center of his chest for two years. His right lung had collapsed sometime in the past year, and every breath had been a struggle. Despite all of this, he never complained.

I returned to the room while Kathy slipped outside to smoke a cigarette. Ken wasn't around, and Jake smiled brightly as he fingered his *Scream* mask.

"How are you feeling?" I asked.

"Good," he said. "Mom said there's a tumor in my chest, but there's nothing in there."

"Mom told you about the tumor?" I asked.

"Yeah, but I don't have one."

I could imagine Kathy discussing it with him. I was sure she had made it sound like a day at the beach, but I was a little surprised that he was so well informed.

"Did you ever have a tumor?" Jake asked.

I started to say no, but then I remembered that I had had outpatient surgery during college to remove a benign tumor in my neck. (I had complained through that, too). "Yeah, yeah, I did," I said excitedly, "but the doctors did their magic and took it away. Now, it's all gone."

Jake turned his attention back to the cartoon channel. A good ten minutes went by before he resumed the conversation. "I'll let the doctors do their magic on me if they want," he said. "My tumor can be all gone too. They can throw it in the garbage. I'll be just like you."

Up to that point, this was as close as he came to complaining. I kind of understood that my days of moaning because of my simple torn tendon were behind me for a little while.

* * *

The best part of the care received at The Children's Hospital of Buffalo was that every doctor and nurse we ran into treated us as human beings. We weren't just another case, and Jake wasn't just another sick child. Ken reassessed our situation and changed his method of operation. He went from being slightly overbearing to the picture of patience.

In the late morning, the rumors started to surface that Jake might be moved out of intensive care. Doctor Brecher approached us at the end of his rounds. As usual, his demeanor calmed us.

"He's breathing real well," he said. "We have arrived at the conclusion that he really isn't in a lot of danger at this point, and we're talking about moving him to the eighth floor. He'll receive his last dose of chemo today, and we'll keep an eye on his blood counts for a couple of days, but in all likelihood, we'll give him a break before we do the biopsy."

"A break?" I asked. "As in going home?" It felt wonderful to finally hear that Doctor Brecher didn't think Jake was in a lot of danger.

Brecher smiled. "Exactly like that."

We could hardly contain our excitement, but we didn't want to jump the gun and tell Jake that he was on his way home. There was still a long way to go, but a single day without doing the hospital shuffle was enticing to all of us. Kathy immediately left to shower and let the dogs out, hoping that she'd be back in time for Jake's transfer to the upper floors. There was just one stumbling block: Jake.

I slipped into the blue chair and leaned into his bed. "We're going to move upstairs," I said.

"I don't want to move." He turned his back. The excitement of just moments ago evaporated.

"It'll be a lot better on the 8th floor. The nurses won't bother you. We'll have a bigger room."

"I want to go home," Jake said turning back to face me. "If I can move, why can't I go home? I miss Sammy and Matthew."

It was hard to argue with his logic, but I changed the subject quickly in order to give him the time to mull over the change. "Do you know what these balloons say?" I asked, grabbing the strings of several brightly colored balloons that hovered at the foot of the bed.

Jake rolled his eyes, apparently a little annoyed with my attempt to distract him.

"Get well soon," I said. "And this one, 'I hope you're feeling better.'" He turned away again. "This one says, 'Daddy is a dork'."

Jake laughed. "Read them again."

I repeated my performance, and he laughed every bit as hard. It was a beautiful sound. "You don't really care if we move out of here, right?" I asked.

"No," he said. "Not really."

"Do you want to try a nap?" I asked.

"That dinosaur is going to burp."

I slapped at the head of the big dinosaur balloon, and it bounced off the ceiling.

"Keep your mouth shut!" I yelled.

Jake laughed as the dinosaur bobbed back to its resting place. "You're so funny, Dad."

"Are you ready for nap?" I asked. I kissed his forehead, and he squirmed away from me.

"I'm ready," he said.

He was asleep in a matter of minutes. Of course, that's when the door swung open. My brother John appeared for what had to be the tenth time. He dropped a candy bar on the desk and sat down in a gray chair at the foot of the bed. We spoke in hushed tones for a couple of minutes, and then I started packing up toys and clothes for our move upstairs. John asked questions about Jake's progress, and I recognized the look of desperate love in his eyes. Like me, he wished he could trade places with Jake.

Ken appeared just a moment later, and I feared that Jake's nap would be too brief.

"The bed is ready for him on eight," Ken said.

"We don't have to move now, do we?" I asked.

Ken didn't answer right away. He stepped into the hallway and reappeared with the head nurse. "Unfortunately, we need this bed for another child," Ken said.

My heart sank as I thought about the misery of another child taking his turn in the intensive care unit. The anonymous child would take Jake's place and bring with him another set of worried parents and concerned aunts and uncles.

"I understand," I said.

I really wished that Kathy were there for the move. Going out that door was a huge step toward recovery, and I almost felt guilty enjoying it alone.

John and I piled the gifts on the edge of the bed as Ken circled us, unhooking all the machines that Jake would be taking with him upstairs. There was still one dose of chemotherapy to come, and that realization curtailed my excitement. Although Jake's breathing had improved, he was a long way from being cured.

John helped steer the bed out of the intensive care unit. I could see in his eyes that helping steer the bed meant a lot to him and gave him a sense of being able to control *something*. Room 819 was much bigger than the ICU room. We actually had enough space to store all the presents and move around with comfort. We had our own bathroom and telephone. There was even a recliner that would serve as a much more comfortable bed for Kathy during her long-night vigils. John stayed until we settled in, but left before Jake woke up. He had no idea how lucky he was.

I was right beside the bed when Jake opened his eyes. He rolled over onto his side and immediately cried, "I want to go back downstairs. I hate this room."

When it comes to organizing my life, I'm a tad inflexible. I actually asked Kathy to print out a schedule detailing our activities, and it is posted on the refrigerator as a maddening reminder that I'm wound a bit tight. To further illustrate the point, I have kept a journal of my life, chronicling each day, and it dates back to the 3rd grade. I mention this for one reason; Jake's the same way.

That was why I was frightened by the mammoth change to the new room. Jake won't brush his teeth with anything other than his regular toothbrush. His Pre-K teacher explained that before the start of every day she has to go over her planned activities, and that Jake gives her a difficult time if she deviates from the plan. We've noticed the same things at home, and of course, I take the blame for his crazed attention to detail.

Thankfully, Kathy returned about ten minutes after Jake woke up. "This is great," she said. "I love the new room, don't you, Jake?"

"I hate it," Jake said.

"I brought your video games from home," Kathy tried.

"I don't care! I don't want to play!"

Kathy glanced at me. I shrugged, and she smiled. I was worried that Jake wouldn't cooperate with the nurse that would be setting up his chemotherapy treatment. Kathy tried to reason with him. "There's a boy downstairs that needs that room more than you do," she said.

"He can have this room," Jake said. "I don't care! I want to go home! I hate it here!"

Kathy sat on the bed right beside his right shoulder. Jake moved away from her, but she put a hand on his knee. "We are going to go home," she said. "The doctors told me that I have to stay in this room a little longer, and then you and I are both out of here. Will you stay with me?"

Tears began to fall from his eyes. This was too much for me to handle, so I started to pace around the room. All of the excitement of being moved up was being stripped away by the tantrum I knew was coming.

"Can we go home forever?" Jake asked.

It was a question that doomed Kathy's chances of persuading him to relax. She tried to hug him, but he thrashed around so much that I feared he'd rip the tubes from his arms.

"I want to get out of here!" he screamed. He slammed his fists onto the bed. My heart was in my throat as I tried to figure out if he was causing himself harm. There were a couple of robots at the foot of the bed, and Jake kicked them onto the floor. Naturally, the door swung open, and our niece, Jennie, made a couple of steps into the room, then pretended to back out.

"Jake's having a fit," Kathy said, stating the obvious.

Jennie and her sister Katie are Jake's secondary babysitters. Since his birth, they had seen Jake in all of his glory. Jennie sat in the chair beside the bed and watched as Jake threw punches into the air and screamed, "I hate everyone!"

"He's just being Jake," Jennie said. "Everyone knows he doesn't like change."

Maybe there were lessons to be learned here. As I watched Jake struggling to adapt to his new hospital room, it occurred to me that it wouldn't kill me to be a little more flexible, too.

"I wonder where he gets it from," Kathy said. She smiled in my direction, and I smiled back.

"I promise that you won't even recognize me when this is all over," I said. "You're going to be calling me 'Mister Happy Go Lucky.'"

The sound of her laughter took the edge off Jake's fit. Within ten minutes, he was under control and playing video games like a real trooper.

Kathy and I had dinner, and Jake played one video game after another. After I finished eating, I played a dragon-themed video game with Jake, and he kissed me on the cheek just as the game ended. "I like the new room," he whispered.

"You're a tough guy," I said.

Jake's eyes were looking quite heavy. I wondered about the effects of the chemotherapy, and both Kathy and I understood that we should get him to rest as much as he could.

"Are you ready to say your prayers?" Kathy asked.

Jake lay on the pillow and smiled. The words were automatic. *God Bless Mommy and Daddy, Matt, Jake and Sam, Max, Shadow and Nobody, Grandma and Grandpa Foutz, Grandma Spiffy and Poppa John, aunts, uncles, and cousins. Make me be a good boy, God. Amen.*

It just plain killed me that he was asking God for help in being a good boy. On some level, it struck me as ironic that we were praying for God's help when Jake actually seemed to have been born with a defect that was of God's own making. I'm not the only one that's struggled with maintaining faith through thick clouds of doubt, but Jake's simple, nightly proclamation brought it all full circle. Here was a child that didn't truly understand what he was asking, but night after night, he asked, believing that God would make him a good boy. In his limited knowledge, I'm absolutely certain that he believed that God would carry him through.

As I drove home, Jake's prayer gnawed at my brain. Who was I to think that I knew more about God than Jake did? I considered Jake's understanding to be limited, but when I thought about it carefully, what more did I know?

"God, help make Jake a good boy," I cried. "And me a good father."

I hated walking into the empty home, but as I turned my key into the front door lock, Shadow jumped up to meet me. Max was still lying on the floor, and I immediately noticed his sore paw. It was blood red and swollen to three times its normal size. He had chewed away all the fur on the foot and, although he was thrilled to see me, he couldn't do much more than limp to the door. Guilt and shame swept through me as I dropped to the floor to comfort him and examine his paw. His undying loyalty was evident as he wagged his tail and jumped to greet me. Max, by all rights, should have been furious with me. If he were a more reasonable being, he would have bitten me when I walked through the door. For a week, he suffered with a sore, swollen foot, and I had ignored him. Now, at the pinnacle of his pain, he was rejoicing in my mere presence. Maybe I'm giving Max too much credit, but he sure seemed like a testament to faith and loyalty.

There wasn't a lot I could do for Max at that hour on a Friday night. I wandered through the empty house with the dogs trailing close behind, and I tried to plan what needed to be done before Matthew's party. I flicked on the television and mindlessly watched the second game. The Yanks were losing again, and I was pretty sure they weren't going to provide me with a lot of comfort.

"Just perfect," I whispered to the television screen as the final out was recorded and the Yankees had lost. "When I need the distraction of baseball the most, the Yankees are going to get knocked out in the first round."

Max and Shadow followed me to the bedroom. I allowed both of them to get into bed beside me, and surprisingly, I was the one that couldn't settle down enough for sleep to come. I tossed and turned in the bed so many times that I finally just got up. It was after two o'clock, and I desperately needed rest. My plan was to mow the lawn, take Max to the vet's, and clean up the garage a little so that Matthew's party would go off without a hitch. There was only one problem; I couldn't do any of it if I didn't get some rest.

"Son-of-a-bitch!" I yelled, as I threw the covers off onto the floor.

Both dogs jumped up and slunk away. I sat on the side of the bed, squeezing my head in my hands in an effort to quiet the voice that was planning my day. I grabbed my shirt and pants and headed down the stairs and into the back yard. The dogs followed right behind me.

It was a cool night, and the moon was shining brightly. Clouds darted across the moon's face as though they were being pulled on a string. Every so often a star appeared from behind one of the clouds, and that stupid, "Star light, star bright" saying popped into my head. "God, can we cut a deal here?"

I recalled a scene from a movie called *The End* in which Burt Reynolds, convinced that he was dying, made a pact with God to donate sixty-percent of his income to the church. Reynolds's character was struggling to swim to shore, but he kept his dialogue with God running. Every fifty yards or so, the amount of the donation dropped until Reynolds stepped out onto the beach, guaranteeing God that the three-percent was on its way.

"I'm not asking you to heal Jake. I'm not asking for a miracle. I just want to go to sleep."

The dogs waited at my feet. I was glad that their understanding was somewhat limited; otherwise, one of them might have called a psych center. After all, I was standing in the backyard, screaming at the moon to let me go to sleep. Come to think of it, maybe they could relate to such behavior.

I had a fleeting thought to mow the lawn right then, by the light of the moon, but I imagine that, if I had actually done that, my neighbors would have been making the call to the looney bin.

"What do you say?" I asked God again. "I'll try to be a little more patient if you'll let me go to sleep."

I headed back to bed. It would be a perfect ending if I said I was asleep by the time my head hit the pillow. That didn't happen. It was, in fact, about a full minute later that I finally drifted off.

Chapter Six

Saturday — October 13, 2001

It took me half an hour to clean the dog crap out of the backyard. My mind was still frenzied from that experience as I hit the remote control to raise the garage door. Instead of rising, the door slipped off one of its tracks, crashed downward and hung by a thread over a pile of furniture and boxes that weren't ours. After a few moments, I vaguely remembered telling our friends Mike and Carla they could store some items in the garage until their deal closed on their new home.

"What did you do to the door?" I asked as though Mike were right beside me. The dogs ran away again, and I imagined they now knew I was completely insane. Then it hit me. How could I possibly expect ten eight-year-old boys to attend Matthew's party and not touch the garage door?

"Why, God, why?" I screamed.

The dogs ran to the furthest corner of the fenced-in yard, and I followed with the lawn mower. It was still only six-thirty. I was running the risk of truly irritating the neighbors, but what choice did I have? Now, on top of mowing the lawn and taking Max to the vet, I had the garage door to worry about. Besides, I wanted to get to the hospital early enough to give Kathy a break. She had planned to chaperone the party. She needed an hour or two of solitude to prepare herself mentally.

I yanked the cord on the mower, and thankfully, it started right up. I spent the next forty minutes introducing a new sport to my neighborhood. I call it aerobic lawn-mowing. I ran behind the mower, cutting the grass as frantically as the wheels in my mind were turning. I could almost sense the communication between Max and Shadow: "He's gone off the deep end."

I hustled back into the house with sweat pouring down my face and fresh-cut grass blades clinging to my arms. I made a fresh pot of coffee and stood at the kitchen sink with the telephone in my hand. Who could I call at such an hour to fix the garage door? Also, was there a way to get Max to the vet and still make it to the hospital on time to spell Kathy?

I tried my brother John, and his wife Dana answered the phone on the first ring. I was happy they had kids and were up at the normal children's hour. Dana was alarmed when she heard my voice, but I assured her that Jake was fine. I explained the problem with the garage door, and she promised to pass the message along to John.

Next, I tried the vet, but while the lady on the other end of the line appreciated my problem, she didn't exactly bend over backwards to help. "We have an opening at ten." she said.

"Nothing earlier? I have to get to the hospital to see my boy. Can you bump someone?"

"What about Monday?" she asked cheerfully.

"By Monday the dog will gnaw his foot off," I said.

She acted as if she were going to do something to help, but her cheerful voice sent me over the edge with her next aggravating sentence. "Ten o'clock is the best I can do."

"Forget it, I'll find another vet," I said.

I slammed the telephone down and fired my empty plastic coffee mug off the wall in the kitchen. It shattered into hundreds of pieces, and a little voice in my head mocked me for my impatience. The phone rang before I could calm myself.

"Hey," Kathy said. "What's going on?"

"Aw, you know, nothing much," I said, hoping my ragged breath would not give myself away. "Just reading the paper and hanging out."

"I just wanted to let you know that there's no hurry to come up here. Jake's playing video games and watching movies. He knows that you have to get things ready for the party."

I felt better instantly. I crawled around the floor, picking up the little plastic pieces that used to form my coffee cup and made a couple of half-hearted efforts to see if my sister Corinne or my brother Jeff could take Max to the vet. They were both busy, so I called the clinic back and, feeling like a total jerk, asked if they could hold that ten o'clock appointment for me.

"Sure," the cheerful woman said. "I explained your situation to the doctor. We might be able to sneak you in a few minutes early."

I had to lift Max to get him into the back of the truck, and he spent the first three minutes of the ride licking his sore paw. The radio sports show was talking about the Yankees' loss from the night before, and I clicked the radio to silence. I was badly in need of a lucky break and I couldn't be sure that one was coming.

I used a leash to drag Max to the front door of the clinic. Sensing that he was about to be examined, he tried to pull me back toward the car. After a few minutes of pulling, Max seemed resigned to his fate, and he followed me into the clinic.

For the first time since Jake went into the hospital, I found myself in a setting that had absolutely nothing to do with his condition or the human members of my family. Max sat beside me on the bench in the crowded vet's office. His paw was just a raw nerve, and I did my best to keep his mouth away from it. One by one people entered and exited the shop. They were looking for flea powder and discussing annual check-ups, and I wanted to stand up in the middle of them all and scream at the top of my lungs that I should be going first. My kid was sick. Didn't anyone understand that? Who cared if Fluffy had fleas? I had a child with a tumor! Thankfully, the coffee mug was the only real casualty of the morning.

"Oh, that looks painful," the veterinarian said. She examined Max's injured paw and sighed. "It can be one of two things. He probably got something stuck and then infected it with his saliva. Or, he may have a tumor in the paw. It's been known to happen."

"You've got to be kidding," I said.

She looked at me kind of sideways. "No, like I've said, I've seen it before. What we'll do is clean it out and give him some medication. If it isn't any better by Tuesday, we'll have to think about what else we can do."

I felt like someone had a voodoo doll with my name on it. Max's sore paw was just another needle into the side of the doll. We left the office with a wallet that was a hundred dollars lighter and a bag filled with medication that had to work.

* * *

I didn't feel comfortable that morning until I sat in the chair beside Jake's bed. Over the course of five days, feeling inadequate in almost every way, I realized that I needed to be beside his bed. I was sure that playing video games and watching movies was my main contribution to humanity. Kathy headed home for the party. It had been days since I laid eyes on Matthew, and I had only seen Sam for those few minutes at the toy store. The party was a good idea, and Kathy's presence would afford Matthew a wee bit of much-needed normalcy.

I hadn't realized it at first, but the move to the eighth floor was horrifying in several different ways. First off, the other children on the floor were free to roam the halls, and many of them stopped by the room to get a look at Jake's gifts. A six-year-old boy stationed directly across the hall was the first to actually knock on the door. "What's your son's name?" he asked.

The kid stood about four feet tall. His colorful Pokemon pajamas and his toothless smile brought an ache to my heart. He was dragging a couple of monitors behind him, and an oxygen tube was hooked up to his tiny nose.

"That's Jacob," I said.

The kid smiled at Jake as his eyes darted across the room at the pile of gifts. "I'm Christopher," he said. "Do you want to play?"

Jake squirmed in the bed. He cast a glance Christopher's way, but I could almost read his mind. He didn't want to play with Christopher. He didn't even want Christopher in his room.

"Maybe we can play in a little while," I said. "Jake needs a nap now. We're thinking of going down to the game room later."

Christopher smiled, but I sensed his disappointment. There aren't too many things as evident as a disappointed child. A light went out in his eyes, and his shoulders hunched forward slightly.

"See you later," Jake said, although I'm sure he wanted to say, "Get the hell out of my room!"

Christopher sighed and began to leave, dragging his equipment behind him. A nurse held the door for him and patted him on the head as he passed.

"I have to check Jake," she said. "Christopher, you can play on the computer if you want."

The nurse took Jake's temperature and blood pressure. She noticed me watching Christopher. "Chris pretty much runs the place. He's been here most of his life. It's a blood disorder."

My heart sank. Of all the heartbreaking stories I had heard in the past week, Christopher's affected me the most. It was the first time that I actually talked with one of the living, breathing victims of a demented lottery that doled out illness, suffering, and disability to children. "Is he getting better?"

The nurse shrugged. "Hard to say." The thermometer beeped, and she ruffled Jake's hair. "Everything is good here though."

"How do you do this?" I asked. "How can you possibly separate yourself from the pain?"

"A good nurse doesn't separate herself," she said. "Every day I hurt a little bit. I have kids at home, and I just thank God that they're healthy. Doing this work makes it impossible for me to take anything for granted."

So, there it was. I had come into the hospital telling everyone that would listen that we didn't need a lesson. We didn't need to change. We had established a wonderful family. We loved our children above everything else. Why were we picked to go through this? The answer was quickly becoming apparent; in a relatively short span of time I was learning life lessons that would stay with me forever. Before Jake became ill, I had never felt I was taking things for granted, but as I stared into the face of suffering, I realized that I had.

Jake and I played video games for most of the afternoon. I detailed the injury to Max's paw, and Jake asked if I would give Max a kiss for him when I got home.

"Tell him I said to get better," Jake said.

"I will. Max told me to tell you that he hopes you get better."

Jake smiled. "Uh, Dad, dogs can't talk."

"He barked it," I said. "Didn't I tell you that I can speak dog-language?"

Jake laughed, but all at once a worried look creased his brow. "Do you think I could sit in the chair with you?"

"Sure," I said, silently wondering if he was okay. I pulled the chair closer to the bed. He struggled to sit up, and I lifted him into the chair onto my lap, making sure that his monitors stayed hooked up. He felt so good in my arms, but I could also tell that he had probably lost a few pounds. I wasn't sure that what I was doing was right, or smart, but after the longest week of my life, I just needed to hold him. He slipped his right hand around my neck, and we settled in together, his face just an inch away from mine. He was looking up at the television, and it's a good thing, too, because my eyes instantly filled with tears. I didn't want him to see me cry. It would probably have hurt him terribly to see me upset.

"I was sick of that bed," Jake said. I sensed him looking at me. Then he turned his head, and I looked at the window to hide my tears. He kissed my right cheek. "Thanks for sitting with me."

"Yeah, this is fun," I said.

Jake and I spent the next hour or so watching cartoons. A couple of nurses visited to check his temperature and blood pressure, but we were both waiting for Kathy. She arrived at dinnertime. Jake had just started playing a video game, and I was reading an old copy of *Reader's Digest.*

"Hey, guys, what's going on?" Kathy asked.

I could tell there was something different about her. She looked more relaxed. But wait! She had spent the afternoon with a bunch of manic eight-year-olds. How could that be relaxing?

"I have a confession," she said. "I had three beers. The party went great, and I was sitting outside watching the boys play ball when it occurred to me that we had beer in the refrigerator."

I don't know if I was jealous because I hadn't thought of it, or irritated because I couldn't understand how she could even think of a beer with Jake in that hospital bed.

"Jack was great too. He played with the boys and even had a beer with me."

Well, that was good news. I was at the hospital trying to lift Jake into the chair to watch a few minutes of television, and she was sitting on the porch drinking beer with her ex-husband.

"Did Matthew have fun?" I asked.

"They had a blast. They were running around with the dogs and playing ball. I'm sure that he felt like a normal kid for a little while."

"That's all that's important," I said, but I'm not sure I meant it.

We needed dinner, which was fortunate because it gave me an excuse to get out and clear my head. I left the hospital and walked down Elmwood Avenue until I came to a pizza joint. I ordered a couple of subs and had to wait ten minutes until they were ready. In that short time, I realized that Kathy had needed the afternoon at the party as much as Matthew did. She was the one sleeping in a chair every night. No matter how many games Jake and I played, she was still his mother. Kathy and Jake were always together, and if she needed to blow off some steam that was fine with me. The thought that she had a beer with Jack was also of little concern. Hell, Jack and I had a six pack riding on the Oakland-New York playoff series. We had set up our lives so that jealousy and pettiness weren't a part of our relationship. By the time I returned to the room, I was actually happy that Kathy had got away from the stress for a little while. Lord only knew how much longer we would have to go on this way.

As much as it didn't matter, my life returned to normal a little later that night. Although the Yankees were down by two games to the Athletics, I still believed that they would prevail. Max and Shadow found comfortable spots on the floor at my feet, and the announcers irritated me to no end by exclaiming that the Yankees reign as baseball's champion was coming to an end.

"It ain't over until it's over," I said, quoting legendary Yankee Yogi Berra. I couldn't help but think of Jake's illness and the growing sense of determination that was filling my heart. "All the Yankees have to do is take it a day at a time."

Shadow jumped into my lap, and I rubbed her ears. Mike Mussina was pitching the game for the Yankees, and right from the start, I could tell that he was operating at a slightly higher level than the Oakland batters. The Yankees took a one-run lead in the middle innings on a long homerun by their catcher, Jorge Posada.

"That's all we need," I said happily.

Between innings, I gathered items to take to the hospital the next morning. I was never more than ten seconds away from thoughts of my family, but slowly, the Yankees efforts captured my imagination. *They're down, but they're not out,* I thought. *They're going to handle this situation an inning at a time, and they will prevail.*

The game slipped into the late innings. In the bottom of the seventh inning Oakland had the tying run on base. The Yankees baseball life hung in the balance. Oakland's Terrence Long lined a base hit into right field, and my heart sunk. Jeremy Giambi raced around third and headed for home plate. Yankee right-fielder, Shane Spencer, threw the ball toward home plate. I screamed out as I saw that the ball was nowhere near the plate. "Son-of-a-bitch!" I yelled.

Suddenly, from out of nowhere, Yankee shortstop Derek Jeter sprinted toward the errant ball. All in one motion, he scooped up the ball and tossed it backhanded to the plate. The catcher tagged the base-runner out and the Yankees hung onto their lead. Immediately, the telephone rang. Kathy was on the line, and she was whispering. "Did you see that play?"

"Unbelievable," I said. "How's Jake?"

"He's been sleeping since you left. I just had to call you though. I think the Yankees are going to pull it out. They're going to do it for us."

I laughed. "Baseball and life aren't one and the same," I said.

"I just think we should adopt the Yankees' attitude," Kathy said. "They never give up."

"I'm not giving up," I answered. It was amazing to me that Kathy was watching the game and drawing some of the same parallels. We were both using the Yankee game as an inspiration.

"I love you," I said.

"I love you too, but I'm telling you, think about it. Believe that they can win, and they will."

For the first time in over a week, I was truly smiling. I clicked the telephone off and watched the end of the game. As the Yankee players ran out of the dugout to celebrate the victory, I felt an emotional stirring in my heart. *They aren't going to just give up their championship,* I thought, *and I'm not going to just give up my family.*

Sunday — October 14, 2001

I woke up dreaming about blood cell counts. I don't know how many times during the entire ordeal that I woke from a sound sleep as though I were being electrically shocked, but this was definitely one of those times. What did I know about blood counts? The short answer was absolutely nothing, but the nurses and doctors all seemed to be concerned with it. When Jake's blood counts returned to normal, they said, "You'll all be able to go home."

The shower was particularly soothing, and I stayed under it until the water started to cool off. I thought of the Sunday mornings of my youth and the scent of garlic and onion simmering in olive oil. There were so many mornings when that was the scent that shook me from sleep. My father was always in the same seat at the kitchen table, and his first question was usually the same. "What time are you going to church?"

That's what Sundays were all about. We would attend mass, eat pasta, watch the Yankees or the Bills, and take a nice, long nap. Sundays were a day surrounded by family and friends, and we used to joke that it didn't matter how many people showed up at dinnertime. There was always enough to go around. Even after marriage, Sunday dinner was still a big deal at my parents' home, and we tried to attend as often as possible.

It doesn't look like I'll make church or pasta today, I thought.

Even though it was just a little before seven in the morning, my father contacted me on my cell phone. "I made a huge batch of sauce, and Carrie made meatballs," he said. "What time do you want to eat? I have to get it to you somehow."

My father's sauce was still the best, and Carrie would definitely garner top honors in a Fazzolari meatball-making contest. "It doesn't matter what time. I'll eat a dish now."

Dad laughed. We talked about Jake for a few minutes, and I understood that the whole ordeal was eating a hole right through my parents' hearts.

"I'll get it to you somehow," he said.

At least we had that going for us.

I parked the car in the ramp on Hodge Street across from the hospital. I was still trying to control everything about my life as I pulled into the exact same parking spot that I had used on the previous two days. I ran across the street and up the steps so that I would be in Jake's room before the Bugs Bunny cartoons started.

Jake was sitting up in bed. He smiled brightly when he saw me washing my hands in the sink outside his room, and I pressed my face against the glass to make him laugh. I entered the room quickly and moved straight to the bed.

"The Yankees won," Jake said. He appeared to be symptom free. In fact, he looked better than he ever did at anytime in his life. His breathing problems had nearly subsided, and I couldn't help but think that the tumor must have shrunk. What else would explain his improved appearance?

"He's ready to start eating," Kathy said.

"Did you bring me a steak?" Jake asked.

He was eating everything in sight. Jake had always been a poor eater (I wonder why), but the chemotherapy treatments had changed that. I removed a bowl from the shopping bag I had set on the table. I handed Jake the bowl, and he grabbed a handful of steak and filled his mouth.

"You've been eating like a monster," I said. "Yesterday you ate steak, potato chips, cookies, chicken nuggets, ice cream, and three candy bars!"

"I'm hungry," he said.

I removed a cup of coffee from the bag and handed it to Kathy. She smiled, but I couldn't help but notice how tired she looked. She puckered her lips, and I kissed her quickly. "That was a good game last night," she whispered. "You have to believe, right?"

"I believe," I said.

Jake was no longer hooked up to an IV or the machine used to check his pulse. The chemo was done for now, and the picc line, which was a thin plastic tube used to pump the medicine into his body, dangled from his arm. A nurse knocked softly on the outside door, and it occurred to me that we had found a rhythm in the midst of the maddening routine. Jake moved forward in the bed. "I'm eating steak, and I drank a little water," he said.

He knew that the nurse would be asking him what he had ate and drank, and he beat her to the punch. Jake lifted his arm so that the nurse could place the thermometer properly, and he exposed his left leg for the blood pressure hug. As the nurse finished up, Jake looked at me. "Can we play air hockey today?" he asked.

I glanced at Kathy, and she smiled as bright as day.

"Mom talked to the nurse. The doctor said I could get up and walk around."

"Oh, yeah," I said. "We're going to play, and I'm going to beat your butt."

We argued about who the best air hockey player was, and we agreed to decide it after the afternoon nap.

"They said he could walk around?" I asked.

"Not all afternoon," Kathy said. She reached for the newspaper, and I knew that she would be working the crossword puzzle in a matter of seconds. "They're also talking about letting us go h-o-m-e if they don't do the biopsy early next week."

I wasn't sure what I thought about that. Although the hospital stay was difficult on all of us, it would be torture if they sent us home without actually figuring out how to treat Jake's ailment. Kathy did a good job of reading my discomfort. "I want it to be gone too," she said. "But I think we could all use a break."

She hugged me tightly and gave me a long kiss.

"Get your own wife," Jake called out. We all laughed.

Kathy picked up her purse, the newspaper, and her coffee cup. She paused at the door, and a troubled look creased her brow. "You know, I used to be able to do most of the crossword puzzle without much of a problem. Since we've been here, though, I haven't been able to come even close to finishing." She just let the sentence hang in the air as she disappeared into the hallway. I shrugged my shoulders, and Jake laughed again.

We watched cartoons all through the morning. Jake slipped off to sleep for half an hour. I sat beside the bed, watching him sleep. I couldn't help but think about the carefree Sundays of my youth and how I wished that I was still a child in my parents' home. I had always felt loved, protected, and secure. I wondered if I was offering Jake the same sense of security and love.

During Jake's short nap, there was a constant stream of nurses, residents, and nurse's aides banging in and out of the room. Perhaps, in hindsight, it was because they were considering sending Jake home, but it seemed as if they formed a line and were taking turns driving me crazy.

Jake woke up when my sister Corinne and brother-in law Chuck arrived for a visit. Kathy had headed home for a shower, and the Yankee game was just starting. Corinne proudly handed me a container with pasta and meatballs. "Our mommy and daddy are still watching out for you," Corinne said.

I thought about the love and security that Mom and Dad had always provided. It seemed that the job of being a parent was neverending.

Corinne and Chuck didn't stay long. They kissed and hugged Jake good-bye, and Corinne struggled to hide tears as I followed her and Chuck out into the hallway. "Thanks for bringing dinner," I said. "The worst part of living in the hospital is trying to live a normal life."

"I don't know if that's the worst part," Corinne said, "but we're proud of you. Jake is as comfortable as he can be."

I thought of the huge container of pasta. "That's what parents do, right?" I asked. I hugged Corinne and shook hands with Chuck. They both worked hard to fix smiles upon their faces. "You know I hate the Yankees," Chuck said, "but I'm rooting for them now."

"That means the world to me," I said.

A nurse followed me into the room. Jake lifted his arm so that she could take his temperature, but his face was a picture of annoyance. He suddenly looked extremely tired, and I knew that he needed another nap. The nurse was in and out quickly. The Yankee game was just starting, and the scent of the pasta was driving me crazy. I just wanted to watch the game and eat without the constant interruption of the nurses.

"Are we going to watch the game?" I asked Jake.

"We want the Yankees to win, right, Dad?"

"That's right, buddy."

Thankfully, we had two televisions. I hit the mute button on the overhead television and tuned in the game. I popped a video into the portable television/VCR, and Jake alternated looks between the game and a Scooby-Doo video.

By the third inning, with a belly full of pasta, the exits and entrances of the nurses were wearing on me.

"Hi," a nurse's aide said as she banged open the door. "I have to take his temperature."

"The main nurse was just in here," I said, in a not especially pleasant voice.

"I have my orders," she whispered. She attempted to make small talk with Jake, but he didn't even look up. She went about her business quickly and closed the door slowly. "I don't think anyone is going to bother you for awhile now."

Oh, how wrong she was! The Yankees took an early lead, and Jake slipped back to sleep. His naps were more frequent, and I hoped that this would be a restful one. Everything seemed peaceful and relaxed. For about two minutes. Then a young nurse I hadn't seen before slammed the door open and crashed it against the back wall. She was dragging the thermometer behind her.

"Time for his temperature," she announced as if she were speaking through a bullhorn.

"Someone was just here, and he's asleep," I said. "The poor kid has been trying to take a nap all afternoon. He can't get more than half an hour."

She giggled and pretended to tiptoe into the room. In doing so, she kicked my soda can across the floor, and it banged off the wall. "I'm sorry," she said, aloud.

"Can you try and keep it down?" I asked.

By now, I suppose she was equally annoyed with me. She stood at the foot of the bed for a full minute, seemingly lost in thought.

"What's wrong?" I whispered.

"Did you see my clipboard?" she roared. She still hadn't figured out the concept of talking quietly, and it really sent me over the edge.

"It's in your other freaking hand," I said.

She looked down at her left hand, and her face flushed with embarrassment.

"You know, I can probably do this later," she whispered. She closed the door quietly.

Jake woke up a short time later, and by then the Yankees were on cruise control. I kept making the comparison between how well they were playing and how good my ailing son looked now. Jake continued to alternate looks at the Yankee game and the Scooby Doo movie.

"Mom said that Derek Jeter saved the game last night," Jake said. "Which one is Jeter?"

I pointed out the Yankee shortstop, and it struck me how powerful the circle of life truly is. My father used to watch the games with his father. I used to watch the games with my father. Now, I was watching them with Jake. Some of the most powerful memories of my childhood involved Billy Martin, Reggie Jackson, Thurman Munson, and Ron Guidry. Despite the success of the Yankee teams of my youth, the best part of it all was that my father was every bit as excited as my brothers and I. It is a connection that I still share with Dad, and God willing, Jake and I will share the same passion for the next fifty years or so.

When the final out was recorded and the Yankees had evened up the series, Jake pumped his fist in the air. "Are you glad the Yankees won, Dad?"

"Of course," I said. "They're the best."

"Can we play air hockey now?" he asked. So that was the reason he was so pumped!

I wasn't comfortable with the thought of taking him out of that bed and down the hall. He hadn't been on his feet in just about a week.

"You promised," he said.

I swallowed hard and smiled through the nervousness. "I'm going to beat your butt."

Gingerly, I lowered him from the bed to the floor. I slipped a pair of sweat pants on his skinny legs and a T-shirt over his head. He looked every bit as nervous as me.

"We're going to have a good time, right, Dad?"

I can't even remember if I answered him. We stepped into the hallway. My left hand was coupled with his right, and we were walking real slowly. I can't exactly put my finger on it, but it was almost as if I was afraid that he was going to break into tiny pieces.

"How do you feel?" I asked.

He squinted and smiled to let me know that my question was absolutely ridiculous.

"I'm going to crush you," he said.

The air hockey table was unoccupied, and I found a step Jake could stand on to keep the game at eye level. I handed him the paddle and the puck and turned on the game. The small plastic puck was pushed around by the air being pumped through holes on the tabletop. Jake slammed his first shot into my goal before I made my way around the table. "I'm winning," he yelled.

"That's cheating. I wasn't ready."

His smile didn't dim all the way through the game. He beat me five to one, and he reminded me of the score every three minutes or so for the next two days. (For the record, I let him win.)

About three minutes after the game ended, his skin was chalk-white. I asked him if he was tired, but he shook me off and made his way around the recreation room. The selection of toys was top-notch, and again I was reminded that The Children's Hospital of Buffalo was a first-class operation. We played with army figures, and I noticed that his breathing was a bit labored.

"I'm ready to go back to bed," he said. "We can come back, right?"

I was relieved that his little journey out of the bed was over. "Absolutely. We'll come back later, and I'll beat you next time."

"I always beat you," Jake said. "You stink at everything."

I tousled his hair, and he smiled brightly.

"Can I sit on your lap while we watch cartoons?" he asked.

I couldn't think of any better way to end the afternoon. Kathy came in about halfway through one of our favorite shows. "You two look cozy."

"We're buddies, right?" I asked.

Jake seemed to be thinking about it. He reached out for Kathy, and she kissed his face three or four times. "I spanked Dad in air hockey," Jake said. "And now I'm kissing his wife."

I tickled him, and Kathy's face came alive with a satisfying smile. I couldn't help but feel that we were starting to turn a corner. Kathy, Jake, and I had battled through the initial shock and sadness of discovering the tumor, and we were starting to believe that our lives would be normal again some-day soon. The thought of normalcy in a completely abnormal setting stayed with me throughout the rest of the evening. Yet, as I left the hospital and headed back toward the Hodge Street parking ramp, the overwhelming fear of what was ahead of us came rushing back at me.

I settled into my red Mercury Mountaineer and turned the radio off. I picked up the cellular telephone and checked the voicemails left behind by friends and family. My co-workers had left messages, and their kind words sent my mind into a whirlwind of thought about parents who weren't blessed with such understanding employers or helpful families. I knew that we were in an enviable position, since we had the love and support to fight through this terrible battle. We truly understood the meaning of the word *faith*.

Suddenly, I felt bad for snapping at the nurse's aide. She was just trying to help. My heart ached for all of the other children facing a night in the hospital without a parent by their side. Why was there so much pain in the world? It was a question I wasn't prepared to handle.

I drove in silence and tried to frame the heartache of what was happening into the context of a typical Sunday during the days of my youth. The city lights beckoned to me as I passed over the Skyway and along the steel plant that was all but shut down. A long train on the tracks near my home delayed me. "I'm still scared as hell," I said aloud. "God, please make me a strong father. You entrusted me with a wonderful family. Help me make them feel secure and protected."

Chapter Seven

Monday — October 15, 2001

I woke up feeling almost numb. In the back of my mind I knew that the doctors might send Jake home without doing the biopsy, but part of me wanted him to stay in the hospital until the tumor was completely removed. It was just a few minutes after six o'clock in the morning when I stumbled toward the shower. My cell phone was on the dresser in the bedroom, and I picked it up and checked the message box. There were six messages and I took a few minutes to listen to each one. My best friend for about twenty years, Jeff Renaldo, had left a message, and he had sounded as if he were beside himself with worry about Jake's illness. Jeff and I grew up together, playing sports, double-dating, and just being there for one another. Our friendship had grown more solid with each passing year. It suddenly occurred to me that it was also Jeff's birthday, and I sat on the edge of the bed and punched in Jeff's cell phone number. His voice mail came on and I clicked the telephone off and covered my head with my hands.

Jeff was born on October 15, 1963, and I came into being almost exactly a year later. Every year, we shared the same ritual. I would present him with a gift on the fifteenth, and he would return the gift to me on the eighteenth. I looked at the cell phone as if it had betrayed me. I needed to talk to my buddy right now, and although it was impossible to imagine that he might be awake at such an ungodly hour, I talked with him anyway. "I didn't get you anything this year, buddy," I said as though Jeff were sitting beside me. "But I'm thinking of you, and that's all I want back this year. I feel like I'm losing my mind, pal, but have a happy birthday anyway."

I took a couple of deep breaths before heading to the shower, but out of the corner of my eye, I saw Max limping toward me. I patted his head and bent down to examine his swollen paw. It didn't look as if the medicine had helped him one bit, and a few tears escaped as I battled the helplessness that was threatening to overwhelm me.

I was able to battle through the early morning routine of gathering everything we would need for day eight of Jake's hospital stay, but I couldn't shake the desperation in my heart. I kept the radio off as I drove through the quiet streets, and I slowly began to formulate a game plan for the day. Jake would have to have a CT-scan, and although it is just a glorified X-ray and there isn't any pain involved, Jake considered a CT-scan akin to torture. He didn't want to lie still on the table. Being slowly lowered into the whirling image machine scared the hell out of him.

I entered the room slowly and Jake smiled as I walked through the door.

"Hey, Dad, did you bring food?" Jake asked.

I searched through the plastic grocery bag that I had brought with me, and slowly, I pulled out three large, chocolate chip cookies. His eyes widened at the sight of the cookie, and a stray thought crossed my mind. Was he supposed to eat before the CT-scan?

"Can I have one?" he asked.

Also, it wasn't even seven o'clock, and Kathy wasn't real big on feeding him junk food for breakfast. "How about if I get you a bowl of cereal first?" I asked.

Kathy was deep in thought. "What's wrong?" I asked.

"I'm not sure if he's supposed to eat before the CT-scan," Kathy said. "They mentioned something about using dye, and if they do, he can't eat for something like six hours."

"Let's ask the nurse. The kid is hungry."

Kathy went out to the main desk while I distracted Jake with cartoons and an update about Max's paw. Kathy returned a couple of moments later. "She said he could eat. They aren't sure when they're going to take him up, but she didn't think it mattered."

I poured a bowl of cereal and handed Jake one of the big cookies. He ate a couple of spoonfuls of cereal and had only about two bites of cookie left when the nurse came through the door. "I was wrong," she said. "They want to take him up for the CT-scan at nine. He can't eat."

I looked to Kathy for help. As I've said before, I am not the world's most patient man, and since they wouldn't be making a decision about the biopsy until the CT-scan was done, I quickly figured that we had lost about six hours. We would be left waiting because of a few bites of cookie and half a bowl of Fruit Loops.

"He's already eaten a little bit," Kathy said. "Will that delay it?"

"I'm afraid so," the nurse said. "We'll schedule it for one o'clock."

I made a conscious effort to just go along with the situation. Okay, so they made an honest mistake. At least he ate a little something. He'd be all right until one o'clock.

Jake watched cartoons, and Kathy worked on the puzzle. I read about the baseball game.

"I'm glad the Yanks are still alive," I said. "It'll help distract us a little bit if they can get to the World Series this year."

"It would be good for New York too. Those poor people really need a distraction," Kathy said.

I tossed the sports page to the floor and scooped up the front page. I read a couple of articles pertaining to the ongoing war against terrorism, and I thought about the morning of September 11th and the pain that I felt in my heart on that horrific morning. Like millions of other Americans, I will always remember the moment of impact. When the second plane hit the World Trade Center, my heart sank. I didn't consider myself overly naïve, but I never truly considered that Americans would be attacked in such a brutal manner. I also wasn't alone when the overwhelming sadness shook me to the very core. It was natural to be horrified by the actions of the men responsible. It shattered every one of my sensibilities, and the attack was the most atrocious thing that ever happened to me as an American.

What galled me even more was the reaction of some people as the planes hit their marks. If I heard one person scream for blood, I heard a thousand. The idea that anyone could hate a group of complete strangers scared me almost as much as the act itself. My initial thought, when I realized we were being attacked, was that I wanted to be with my family. I wanted to hug the people that I loved before I internalized the hatred I felt for whomever was responsible.

I looked across at Kathy. Her head was bowed as she contemplated the crossword puzzle. I glanced back over my shoulder at the bed; Jake must have felt my stare because he turned and smiled. I scanned the front page, and September 11th took control of my mind once more.

The main office closed early on the afternoon of September 11th, and I drove home quickly. I sat in front of my computer and typed out a letter to the editor. I just wanted anyone who read the letter to be patient and to take stock in their own lives. I condemned our need for revenge and our thirst for blood. Maybe I was a little too bleeding-heart for my own good, but I sent the letter to everyone on my mailing list. A half hour later my telephone rang and the editor for *USA Today* asked if they could use my letter in the next day's edition. The *Atlanta Constitution* and the *Buffalo News* also called, and inside of three days, anonymous people were calling my house to let me know that my peaceful, loving attitude was part of the reason why America was being attacked. Kathy fielded a call that began with the pronouncement, "Your husband is an asshole."

In my mind, their reactions cemented my point. Perhaps I was a bit idealistic in my view of the situation, but right or wrong, I felt that we all were afforded an opportunity to look inside. A lot of media people proclaimed the attacks as a wake-up call for the American people, but what were we waking up to take a look at? There are sixteen thousand murders a year in this country. Millions of Americans are starving and without health care, and the educational system is seriously flawed. The fundamental difficulty, I have always believed, is a lack of respect for human life. Why, during the height of the crisis, was everyone from President Bush to Geraldo Rivera telling us to pray when the fact was that kids weren't allowed to pray in schools?

I didn't think we should let the opportunity to change ourselves pass us by. I suppose that history will judge our reaction, but on the morning of October 15th, with my son battling a huge tumor in the center of his chest, I focused on the pages of the city section of *USA Today*. The attack was still the biggest story. Another item detailed a domestic battle between a husband and his wife. Another chronicled a drug ring investigation that led to dozens of arrests. Eleven murders were being investigated, and a gym teacher was caught spying on high school cheerleaders through a hole in his office wall.

I couldn't help but think that maybe I was an asshole for spouting off about being thankful for what was right in our lives. It might just always be the same old story. Even though it seemed that every single American was horrified by the devastation and violence involved in the attacks, just over a month later the newspaper was filled with stories of miserable behavior.

Kathy glanced over at me. "What are you thinking about?"

"The Yankee game," I answered. We had too much on our minds to revisit September 11th.

"Are you worried?" she asked.

"It doesn't seem all that important," I said.

"Yeah, I know what you mean."

* * *

A few minutes before ten o'clock, a nurse's aide came into the room carrying a tray of homemade, oatmeal raisin cookies. I had already battled Jake's request for food on three separate occasions, but this was going to be a rough confrontation.

"Hi, I thought you might like a cookie," the woman said.

I stood up quickly and blocked Jake's view of the cookies with my body.

"He can't eat," I whispered.

"Oh, he can have one," she said.

"No, he's having a test. He isn't supposed to eat."

"I want one," Jake said.

The woman took a good look at my scowling face and began backpedaling out the door. She didn't mean any harm, but she should have known better.

"In a little while," I told Jake. "After the test you can eat anything you want."

As usual, Jake took the bad news with a degree of dignity. He eased onto the pillow and turned to the television. What Jake didn't know was that a little while would be more like four hours.

I lectured myself on the importance of staying patient. The nurses and doctors went out of their way to explain that Jake would be taking his cue from our mood and behavior, yet we were all pretty much at the end of our ropes. Jake was tired of cartoons, movies, and video games. The fact that he had been out of bed yesterday weighed on his mind, and he asked a lot more questions about going home. "I miss Sammy and Matthew," he said.

"I know. If you're good when they take your picture, maybe we can go home soon," I said.

"Forever?" he asked. "Will I be able to go home forever?"

I paused, not knowing just what to say. His heart was breaking right in front of me, and he seemed to be begging me with those big, brown eyes of his, not for anything special. Just for a normal life.

"We'll have to come back soon," I said at last. "Maybe we'll stay a little while longer now, so that we don't have to come back for such a long time next time."

"I don't want to come back," he cried. "I don't have a tumor anymore."

Oh, how I wished it were true. I tried to change the subject, but he was onto that trick too. He lifted up his shirt and pointed to the center of his chest. "See? There's nothing there."

How could I explain that it was inside, under his skin? How was I supposed to tell him that they had to open up his little body to get rid of it? Before I could even formulate an answer, the door banged open, and the lunch lady carried a tray to the side of his bed.

"We have peanut butter and jelly," she smiled. "Do you like peanut butter?"

I jumped from the chair as though I were shot from a cannon. It was all I could do not to grab the lady and shove her back out the door.

"He can't eat!" I yelled.

"I love peanut butter," Jake said.

The woman had the presence of mind to step into the hallway with the tray still in her hand.

"Can you hang a sign on the door or something?" I asked. "The kid can't eat until after his CT-scan, and you people are torturing him."

The woman was on the verge of tears, but I just couldn't help it. Jake was tossing unanswerable questions at me. I was beyond tired, and the staff didn't seem to have an idea of what was happening with one of their patients. Unfortunately, a respiratory nurse chose that moment to enter the room. "So, how's he doing today?"

"He's good," I said.

"And how's his asthma?"

I felt red-hot anger rise up inside. My entire head felt hot, and I gave her the full shot. "He doesn't have asthma," I said. "He has a tumor in his chest. They misdiagnosed it as asthma. Didn't you read the chart?"

The woman actually began to stammer. She backed up as I kept moving forward.

"He can't eat for six hours, and you people are bringing him cookies and peanut butter sandwiches. We are upset that he went two years as an asthma patient, and you come in here asking how his asthma is doing. Please, read the charts."

The woman apologized three or four times in less than a two-minute span. She posted a sign on the door that restricted the delivery of food to the room.

"I'm terribly sorry," she said again. "I guess I didn't have all the right information."

"Okay," I said. "Maybe we need a nap."

"I'll put a Do Not Disturb sign on the door. Again, I'm sorry."

She left the room, and Jake started laughing.

"What?" I asked. "What's so funny?"

"I thought you were going to stuff her in my pee bottle," he said between giggles.

* * *

We were able to nap for exactly ten minutes. Kathy returned from her trip to the shower, and almost immediately we heard a couple of nurses chatting outside the door.

"The doctor wants to check him," I heard one nurse say.

"They're taking a nap," the nurse whispered. "The father isn't in a good mood."

I pulled the door open, and the nurses reacted just as Jake and Matt did when they were talking in their beds a half hour after they were supposed to be asleep. One of the nurses looked down at her shoes, and the other one's face turned bright red.

"The doctor wants to see him?" I asked.

"He's making his rounds," the nurse said.

"I don't mind if he stops in."

"We'll try to get him upstairs for the CT-scan in about an hour," the nurse said. "We didn't realize he hadn't eaten."

Doctor Brecher knocked softly on the door a few moments later, and his demeanor was contrary to everything that had happened up to that point. I shook his hand. We were finally going to get a straight answer on the plan for the day. "After Jacob has the scan, we'll evaluate our treatment plan," Doctor Brecher said. "I don't know if surgery wants to do the biopsy tomorrow, but if not, maybe we can get you home for a little while."

The words were like a sweet tonic for my soul. I apologized for my erratic behavior, but Doctor Brecher just smiled.

"You two have done a good job." Doctor Brecher smiled at Kathy.

* * *

I'm not very good with directions. There are times when I'll drive right by my destination and curse myself as I double back, wondering how I could be so stupid. If it weren't for the horrible day we were having, I might have been able to forgive the nurse who came to walk us down to the 2nd floor for the CT-scan. She walked us right past the room, and we probably would've kept walking straight into the wall if Kathy hadn't been paying attention.

"Didn't we just pass the room?" Kathy asked.

The nurse blushed and smiled. "Yeah, I guess we did. Sorry."

It was just about the final straw. "They better let us out of here today," I said to Kathy. "I don't know how much more of this stupidity I can take."

As soon as Jake saw the huge circular CT unit he began to cry. He didn't want to lie on his back. It was going to take a tremendous effort to get him to cooperate. He cried and screamed loudly. The attendant was so unbelievably patient and understanding that I was almost ready to forgive the nurses for their gaffes.

"It's only going to take a few minutes," the man told Jake. "We just need to take a couple of pictures. I promise we won't hurt you."

I went into the hallway to get away from Jake's terror, but I couldn't keep myself from listening. Kathy's words of comfort soothed Jake for a moment, and I was convinced that everything would be all right after all.

"Okay, pal, just lie still," the attendant said softly.

There was silence, then Jake screamed again, and all at once I heard a muffled cry coming from the room to my left. I edged around the corner and saw a middle-aged black woman peering back at me through eyes filled with tears.

"Are you okay?" I asked.

"I'm crying for that poor little boy," she said. "He's so afraid."

It's strange, but through all of the emotional days and despite all of the gut-wrenching moments, that woman's compassionate reaction to my son's cries brought tears to my eyes. This woman would never see us again. She was obviously waiting to undergo tests to see what was wrong with her own child, and here she was, crying for my boy. I thought back to my earlier cynical thoughts about the fate of humanity. On September 11th it would have taken a lot to convince me that there was still compassion in the hearts of mankind, but the tears in that woman's eyes reminded me that God was alive and well, and just around the corner.

Jake battled through the CT-scan. I think it was the promise of another toy and a small, red lollipop that did it, but Kathy's gentle words of encouragement carried plenty of weight, too. I don't know what I was thinking, but I looked over the attendant's shoulder as he downloaded the images. I was still hoping for a miracle. A little voice in my head whispered that the attendant was going to turn around and tell me that they'd all been wrong.

"Geez," he muttered under his breath, "I've never seen one so big."

"Can you tell if it shrunk?" I asked.

"I don't see much of a change, but the doctors will have a better eye for that."

"Thanks," I said.

I had just about made it to the door when he cleared his throat and spoke again. "Don't worry, Dad. The doctors will fix him up."

"Thanks again," I said. I wonder if he honestly knew how much I needed to hear that.

* * *

When we returned to the room, the news came fast and furious. Kathy reminded me that my sister Corinne had dropped off a container of hamburgers and a package of fresh rolls.

"I need one now," Kathy said as though she were addicted to them.

"Can I have a peanut butter sandwich?" Jake asked.

I slipped off to the kitchenette, which was just a few feet from Jake's room, to prepare the food, but the microwave was about halfway through the cycle when I heard Doctor Brecher's voice. "We really don't think there's been a change," Doctor Brecher told Kathy. "We haven't heard from surgery yet, but I doubt if they'll want to do the biopsy right away."

I joined Kathy and Doctor Brecher in front of Jake's room. Doctor Brecher glanced at me and nodded. "I expect we'll send you home for a week or so, and then talk about the next step."

Doctor Brecher's smile couldn't have been more reassuring, but despite the fact that Jake would sleep in his own bed tonight, I knew we weren't much better off than eight days ago.

* * *

If I live to be a hundred years old, I will never see anything as beautiful as the smile that covered Jake's face when he laid eyes on his brothers. His mouth was agape, his eyes were gleaming, and I swear that I could see his heart jumping for joy. Instantly, tears filled my eyes, and I turned to see if Kathy had witnessed the look. She was a second late, and I wasn't clever enough to describe it. She didn't have to wait long to get a taste of what I was feeling though. Kathy's mom and dad came in right behind the boys and we were all waiting for the hug that Carolyn was about to lay on Jake. She pulled him so close and kissed him so many times that I began fearing for Jake's health.

No matter what — we had survived part one. Jake fell asleep fairly quickly, and although Kathy was looking forward to the ball game as much as I was, I watched the Yankees eliminate Oakland as she slept on the couch beside me. As Mariano Rivera recorded the last out, he pumped his fist into the air, and I clenched mine too. The Yankees came back. Jake would too.

I slipped into bed feeling a small degree of satisfaction. Jake was asleep in his own bed, and the Yankees had advanced past round one of the play-offs. Twenty minutes later, I was startled awake, realizing that I had once again dreamed about Frosty the Snowman trapped inside the greenhouse. In the darkness, I could clearly see the puddle of water sitting at a crying child's feet. It sent a cold shiver up and down my spine. It was a long time before I could sleep again.

Tuesday — October 16, 2001

I began the day by thinking about my life as a practicing Roman Catholic. I never felt quite right slipping off to sleep without first saying my prayers. I hated the way I felt when I missed Sunday mass, and for the most part, I consulted God, through prayer, on every significant event in my life. I even asked God to let the Bills win a Super Bowl. He didn't hear that one. As I prayed for Jake's recovery that morning, my mind slipped into a trance as I recalled a day long ago.

I was just nine years old. I'm not sure of the date, but my first day as an altar boy took place in the year 1973. My brother John was a member in my group, as was a life-long friend, Joe Mathis. The captain of our group was Michael Gullo. We were set to make our debut as a team in front of a Sunday congregation that filled every pew.

The regular priest, Father Bernard Weiss, was on a leave of absence, and I didn't know the name of his replacement; but he was definitely a scary old man. My father had actually referred to the substitute priest as "Father Barnfly" because of his filthy habit of reaching into his mouth and adjusting his dentures.

"I'm not taking communion from Father Barnfly," was exactly how my father put it.

Our group of altar boys met in the back of the church. We were handed a black gown, with a white pullover top that made us look like Sally Field in The Flying Nun. *I pulled the white top over my head and asked Joe Mathis to fix the back for me.*

"I'm nervous," I whispered.

Joe, John, and Mike had already served mass at least one other time.

"It's easy," Joe said. "I'll help you."

We met up with Father Barnfly in the priest's quarters. He was putting on his own version of our silly outfit, and right off, I knew he was in a bad mood. He eyed Mike suspiciously.

"Who is supposed to be lighting the candles?" Father asked.

Mike hesitated. He looked as though the question had tripped him up somehow. "The candle thing is broke," he said.

The priest whirled around and stared straight at me "You! Go light them by hand."

I grabbed a pack of matches and headed toward the door. If I hadn't left so quickly, perhaps John or Joe might have stopped me to explain that there was a smaller wick that I could've used instead of the matches.

I slipped out the door and gasped as I became suddenly aware of the packed house. Mom and Dad were out there somewhere, as was every single kid in my third-grade class. I struck the match and lit the first candle just fine. The second candle went even easier, and my breathing was a little more controlled as I realized that I could probably handle the assignment. Of course, the third candle was a bit more troublesome. As the match burned down, the flame contacted the index finger of my right hand. I jumped and screamed, as any other person might do, and the congregation erupted in laughter. I dropped the matchbook and headed for the door. John and Joe were in a state of absolute glee, but Father Barnfly's approach halted the laughter.

"Are you an idiot?" the priest bellowed.

At that moment, I wasn't in much of a position to answer his question. I didn't cry, but I didn't feel very good about the church, the priesthood, or any of the people that laughed at me.

* * *

"I wonder what happened to Father Barnfly," I said to myself as I sat up in bed that morning. I was still at a point well beyond tired, and I'm sure Kathy was too. I was highly functional throughout the day and tired enough as the day ended, but horrible thoughts invaded my mind as soon as my head hit the pillow. Unfortunately, those thoughts weren't silenced with Jake's return home.

Kathy and I needed to contact our employers. We were planning a return to work on Thursday, as we felt that the entire family needed a little time to readjust. I was scrambling out of bed at a little after seven when I heard Matt and Jake's voices. Matthew was getting ready for school, and Jake wanted to get started on playing with the toys that he so dearly missed. Kathy was already moving around the kitchen, and thankfully, the coffee was ready.

"Did you sleep much?" she asked.

I just sort of looked at her.

"Me neither," she said. "It just isn't fair."

We embraced in the center of the kitchen, with Kathy caught somewhere between teary-eyed sniffling and full-fledged weeping. Jake slipped in unnoticed and threw his hands up high in frustration. "What're you crying for?" he asked. "I ain't dying."

It was a proclamation that sent a chill up and down my spine, but I broke free from Kathy and playfully chased him down the hall. He ran away, and Kathy scolded me for making him run.

"He's not going to keel over," I whispered. "He's been living with this for nearly two years."

"Which brings me to my next point," Kathy said, clearly trying to control the anger in her voice. "What is the matter with those doctors? Couldn't they tell that it wasn't asthma? Even if they thought it might be asthma, didn't they think there was a slight chance that it might not be?"

"They half-assed it," I said. "There are too many patients, and they give you about three minutes to state your complaint. Insurance companies are scaring them off, and they aren't doing their jobs right. It's all about getting paid. They figure it's easier not to do the X-ray than fight with an insurance claims department that denies every claim."

"It's all crap," Kathy said. "I took him in more than a dozen times. He went to a specialist. What kind of specialist is that? The guy didn't even do an X-ray."

I knew that the doctors in question would love to have the chance to re-examine Jake, but it was too late. The chance to simply take care of his problem was long past.

"There aren't a lot of people that do their jobs right anymore," I said. "You can't even get an ice cream cone without getting aggravated at some-one behind the counter that doesn't feel like being there. Think about it — it takes you triple the time to get through a checkout line at the store and the bank that it used to years ago. The garbage man dumps the garbage on your lawn and he won't bend over to pick it up. It isn't just those two doctors. People everywhere are more lax."

I thought of the man pushing the broom with his belt buckle. My anger was taking over, but I also thought of the doctors and nurses that were bend-ing over backwards to help us.

"It just aggravates me," Kathy said.

* * *

Then there was poor Max. Twice a day I had to apply a cleansing solu-tion to Max's paw, and he was also ingesting a pill the size of a half-dollar, wrapped in bologna. I couldn't really tell if the paw was getting any better, but it wasn't getting any worse, either. The ironic part about it was that the veterinarian called twice to check on his condition. Max was getting better health care than Jake got for two years!

We also played nurse with Jake. He left the hospital with the picc line in his left arm and the tape and bandages still on his chest. He didn't want to remove anything because he figured they controlled the magic that would make the tumor disappear. Every couple of hours we took his temperature and discussed his blood count.

We restored normalcy as much as we could. We didn't talk too much, in front of the kids, about what we had left to face. During the afternoon,

I made a huge dinner of roast beef and mashed potatoes, and we all sat down at the table together.

"Can I say Grace?" Matthew asked.

"Of course," Kathy said.

Matthew rushed through the standard prayer, but at the end, he glanced at Jake. "Please help Jake get rid of his tumor."

We wanted normalcy, but Matthew's words were too much to ignore. Kathy's eyes filled with tears, and I looked away. Jake offered his one, sincere reaction. "I'm fine!" he yelled. "Matt, I don't have a tumor! I'm fine! I'm fine! I'm fine!"

Jake ran toward his bedroom. Matthew shrugged his shoulders and looked at me with big, blue eyes that were full of fear as he tried to guess my reaction. He actually thought he might be in trouble for sending Jake into a tirade.

"Thanks for saying Grace," I said. "You did a great job."

The evening hours passed quickly as Kathy bathed Sam and I played a video game with Jake and Matt. When I wasn't playing with the boys, I was pacing through the house, in complete fear with the thoughts that were running through my mind. I wasn't real sure how Kathy was handling the normal minute-by-minute routine, and I've always heard the expression that you're born into the world alone and that you'll leave it alone. I don't know why, but I understood that saying a little better in the time of Jake's illness.

Kathy is a tremendous companion in my life. We discuss every aspect of our lives, and for the most part, we think along the same lines. When we disagree, we get it out in the open and keep our pain from festering. Usually, our arguments begin and end in a short window of time. The thing is, it didn't matter how much we discussed the tumor, the doctors, or our fears. At the end of the day, we went to bed alone with our thoughts. I knew how much she was hurting and that she felt my pain, but there wasn't much we could do about it. We needed to handle it together, but we also needed to handle the pain alone.

I took to talking with God when I let the dogs out at the end of the day. There aren't many things more spectacular to me than the sky. I love to watch the sky fill with stars on a summer's night. I am almost mesmerized by the clouds gliding across the moon so bright, and when the sky is bright blue, I feel as content as I can feel.

It was a cloudy, cool night. There were a few stars poking out from behind the clouds, and I tried to concentrate on a single one, but my gaze drifted across the entire sky. Since the first day of first grade, I had come to understand that heaven was up and hell was down. I stared to where I imagined heaven to be. I thought of my grandparents and dearly departed family friends Albert and Susan DeCarlo. I thought of Nado Cataldo, Michelle McGrath, Robbie Kurek, Dan Alff, and Davine Horton — friends that left way too early. I thought of John Tezyk and Jason Bly — best friends and seniors in high school who lost their lives in a car accident. I pictured my father's father in my mind's eye. The dogs were running around the backyard, and I was talking to my grandpa and the sweet souls of the departed.

"Hey, everyone up there! This is Cliff. I need your help. My beautiful boy is sick. I can't handle life without him. I don't know how it works up there, but if you have any pull with the Man...."

The sound of my voice sent Shadow running toward me, and I cried as I patted her head. I seriously doubt that the dogs had ever heard the sounds coming from me just then. "God, why can't I build a wall around my children? Why can't I protect them the way I should?"

Shadow flicked her tongue out in an effort to lick my face. My respect for life was never sharper. I kissed her on the head, and Max limped toward us, his aching paw sending a wave of sympathy through my body. In the backdrop of that cloud-filled sky, I danced with the dogs in the moonlight. I hoped that Kathy wasn't looking down from the kitchen window above our head, but I had faith that I wasn't actually dancing out there with just the dogs. Old friends, grandparents, and children that left too early were out there with me too. I just knew they were.

Chapter Eight

Wednesday — October 17, 2001

We all slept a little later than normal on our second day back at home after the lengthy hospital stay. Jake and Sam quickly settled in front of the television for an hour of cartoons as they ate cereal from small, yellow bowls. Kathy and I sat across from one another at the kitchen table with steaming hot mugs of coffee in front of us.

"How are you feeling this morning?" I asked. "Are you a little more rested at least?"

Kathy shrugged. "I believe he'll be fine, but I'll probably never feel normal again."

I smiled at the thought of what Kathy considered normal. "It hasn't been normal since the day Jake was born," I said. I couldn't help but consider the days leading up to Jake's birth, and from the faraway look in her eyes, I knew that Kathy was also reminiscing. It's strange to look back on it, but our concern for Jake's well-being started on that very first day.

It was Thursday evening, June 12th in 1997. Kathy was still three weeks away from her due date, but she had spent the better part of two days at the doctor's offices. I wasn't offering a lot of sympathy because I figured that the reason she felt lousy was that she was carrying a baby around. As far as I was concerned, she was bloated, tired, and on edge as a result of the pregnancy, and nothing more. Kathy wasn't exactly sure what was wrong beyond the normal symptoms of pregnancy, but she knew that she didn't feel the same as when she had been pregnant with Matthew. The pediatrician and midwife agreed with me, so I steeled myself against the complaints and tried to be supportive. I massaged her back and talked real softly. I kept Matthew under wraps and tried to make a decent dinner. But Kathy knew her body better than all of us, and the nausea and dizziness led her to believe that something was horribly wrong.

I didn't have any vacation time scheduled for the middle of June, and things were hectic at work. I had spent an extremely stress-filled day at the office and decided on that Thursday night that we should all turn in early to be ready for the days ahead. Kathy felt very nauseated, so it didn't take much to convince her that a couple of extra hours of sleep were a good idea.

She woke me at a little after two on the morning of the thirteenth. She sat on the right edge of the bed and whispered, "We need to go to the hospital."

Max jumped to the left of me, and I shook my head in an effort to figure out where I was.

"Okay," I said. "I'm ready."

Kathy explained her symptoms, and I nodded. "I mean we have to go right now."

I tried to move. Max, who tipped the scales at ninety pounds, had pinned my left arm down, and Kathy, with an extra fifty or so pounds, was sitting on my right arm.

"I'd love to jump right up," I said. "But you and Max got me pinned here."

Kathy and I laughed, but I'm not sure that we were anything other than worried. Was it all right for a baby to make an appearance three weeks before he was due?

Matthew wasn't worried; he was indignant. He didn't want any part of the early morning trip to the hospital. "Can we do it tomorrow?" he whined as I tried to pry him out of his bed.

"Grandma will meet us at the hospital," I said. "You can go back to sleep at Grandma's house. Pretty soon you might have a brother."

Matt nodded. He wiped the sleep from his eyes and smiled. "I'd like to have a brother today."

I drove slowly to Mercy Hospital in South Buffalo. I had no idea how much pain Kathy was in, and she put on a real brave face. Kathy's mother and father met us at the hospital and Matthew gladly broke for their car. I was pretty convinced that the doctors and nurses would make Kathy comfortable and that we would be sent home for the remaining couple of weeks of the pregnancy.

They ran tests through the early morning hours. Kathy's platelet count was too low and her blood pressure was sky-high. At a little before five in the morning, the attending doctor made an announcement. "We'll induce her at six." He ducked out of the room like a scared rabbit.

"What's that mean?" I asked, completely dumbfounded.

"It means that Jacob will be here this afternoon," Kathy said.

I spent the time waiting in the lobby of Mercy Hospital. Was I ready to be a father? My relationship with Matthew was solid, but Jack was also around to help with the usual father duties. Could I handle all of the parental responsibility for a child? It was late to be considering if I was worthy, but my time in the waiting room was filled with self-doubt and reflection.

The doctor started the drip at six, and Kathy battled through labor without the aid of painkillers. Her health was my paramount concern, but I couldn't help worrying about the health of our child too.

I returned to the room in the early morning hours, and Kathy opened her eyes. She was crying, but smiled through the tears. "He has to be okay. He's coming out so early. I hope he's ready."

"He'll be fine," I said. "I hope we're ready for him."

At 2:56 in the afternoon, Jacob took his first breath. Since that time, I've told anyone who cared to listen that the miracle of childbirth is an absolute testament to the presence of God. The idea that a baby could be delivered into the world with a completely intact, functional body is almost preposterous. I remember focusing on his tiny feet and how absolutely perfect they looked to me. I was helpless against a sudden onslaught of tears, and I kept whispering over and over to myself that he was a miracle. All of the nurses agreed with me.

I called my friends as I left the hospital, sure that they would hear in my voice that I found living proof of God's existence. The whole world seemed different somehow, and I was certain that everyone who knew me would be able to figure out the difference. One such buddy, Tom Rybak, encapsulated my transformation perfectly for me.

"I know, right now, you feel like you're dancing on a cloud," said Tom, the father of two young boys. "But there will come a night within the next couple of months when you'll stand in your kitchen in the middle of the night, wondering what the hell you did."

It didn't take that long. Jake was miserable from the start. He screamed when I walked into the room, and as far as I could tell, the only thing he liked about his new world was Kathy. He was somewhere on her body nearly every minute of the day. His cooing was reserved specifically for her, and if I happened to pass by, he screamed. It didn't get much better as he grew older.

If I understood the miracle at all in those first few months, it was only when I observed the bond between mother and son. Kathy recovered quickly from the difficult pregnancy. Shortly after Jake's birth her blood pressure and platelet counts returned to normal. I saw a brand new light in Kathy's eyes, and I realized that the birth of Jake had certainly transformed her too. The connection between Jake and Kathy was almost too beautiful to take. The sight of a child in a mother's arms is more beautiful than all of the sunsets rolled into one. I have always had a wonderful relationship with my mother. After seeing Kathy and Jake, I understood that my great relationship with my mother was mostly her doing. Kathy's eyes definitely looked brighter to me in those first few months, and as Sam came along, and as Jake's illness progressed, those eyes didn't lose even a glint of their luster. The best way to describe a mother's love is to imagine lavender and roses, laughter and brilliant sunshine all combined.

I watched Kathy as she sipped her coffee and worked on the crossword puzzle. She still seemed to be having a hard time getting a puzzle done, and she pushed the pen away from her and leaned back in the chair.

"I've been having a dream about Frosty the Snowman," I said.

She looked at me quizzically, and a smile creased her lips. "Is it an erotic dream?" she teased.

"No, Frosty's locked in the greenhouse, and I watch him melt. I feel helpless. It's pretty scary."

"Santa saved Frosty, didn't he?" Kathy asked. "Didn't he put the hat back on Frosty's head and bring him to life?"

"I don't know. It's just weird how the mind works."

"Tell me about it," Kathy said. "I can't even finish a crossword puzzle anymore."

We talked about what we had to face for the day. There was never any doubt about who was going to be at Jake's side when Terri, the visiting nurse, came to our home that morning to change the dressing around the picc line. Jake screamed for Kathy as soon as the nurse rang the doorbell, and my first instinct was to hide in another part of the house. Kathy recognized my fear, and her maternal instincts kicked into overdrive.

"You can go outside if you want. He's going to be screaming."

I opened the door for Terri, and she smiled as she passed. I pointed to Jake's bedroom and she offered a nod of reassurance.

"He really hates taking tape off his skin," I said.

"We'll handle it," Terri said.

Jake begged Kathy to keep Terri away from him. He pulled out all the stops on every temper tantrum he'd ever thrown in his life. Kathy held him, wiped away his tears, and made him battle through it. She did it with a mixture of love, discipline, and bribery, as only a mother can do. I hid in the kitchen, pretending that I wasn't feeling his pain.

After twenty exhausting minutes, Kathy and Terri emerged from the back bedroom.

"We did it," Kathy said. "His dressing is changed, and the line is flushed."

"I wish I could have helped," I said.

"Oh, you did," Kathy said. "I promised him you'd take him to the arcade."

"It's a done deal," I said.

"He's a beautiful boy," Terri said in a voice that sounded like it was coming from a million miles away. Jake looked a bit haggard, but he settled down as Kathy kissed his right cheek and softly caressed the side of his face.

"We know," I whispered.

* * *

The trip to the arcade was significant for a couple of reasons. First and foremost was the fact that Jake and I were actually out of the house among the living. Secondly, I couldn't help but appreciate the fact that I was granted the opportunity to play with him for at least a little while longer. As I drove, Jake talked about his tumor and the magic that the doctors would do for him.

"I have to go to the hospital one more time," he said. "The doctors will get rid of the tumor, and I'll get to stay home forever, right?"

"That's right," I said. Telling him that he would have to return to the hospital was hard, but I figured that making it seem like no big deal was the way to go.

He was quiet for a few moments. We were waiting for a red light, and I stared straight into the lamp. I thought of all the moments spent waiting for the light to change, and I silently prayed for a lifetime with my son asking me questions.

"Why do they have to take the tumor out?" Jake asked. "Is it a bad guy?"

I couldn't believe that I hadn't thought of it before. Jake's entire life was centered on the idea of good guys beating down bad guys.

"Yes," I said. "The tumor is a bad guy, and the doctors are good guys. The doctors are going to crush that big, bad tumor, and then you'll feel better."

Jake seemed to buy the explanation. He pointed to the mall and talked excitedly of an arcade game the entire premise of which was based on good stomping out evil. I parked the car, helped him out of the backseat, gathered him into my arms, and carried him a couple of steps.

"I can walk," he said.

Of course he could. I reminded myself that he wasn't fine china and that he wouldn't break into pieces before my eyes.

"Dad, why is that bad tumor inside me?" he asked. "Did God put it there?"

It was a question I wasn't sure I could answer, but the right words popped into my head, and I found myself truly believing them. "Yes, God gave it to you because you can beat it up."

Jake smiled as bright as day. "That's because I'm tough, right, Dad?"

"You are the *toughest*," I said.

We spent about two hours in the arcade. I had about eighty dollars in my wallet when I entered the place, and I walked out with less than fifty. I would've spent every dime if Jake wanted me to.

After dinner, I played inside with Kathy, Matt, Jake, and Sam. We spent most of the night in front of the PlayStation video game, but we also took a few minutes to read a book with Sam. Jake was at my shoulder as Kathy changed Sam's diaper and got him ready for bed. I helped Jake change into his pajamas, and he kissed me as I bent down to remove his socks.

"Are you going to bed now?" he asked.

"In a little while," I said. "I want to watch the Yankees win."

Jake studied my face for a minute, and I could see a question forming in his mind. "Are the Yankees the good guys?"

"Yes," I said "And they're playing the Mariners, who are the bad guys."

"I always root for the good guys," Jake said.

I tucked Jake into bed, and Kathy visited with him for a long while before he actually drifted off to sleep. I couldn't shake the thoughts of good guys versus bad guys, and inexplicably Frosty the Snowman's image was stuck in my brain.

I settled in to watch game one of the series between the Yankees and the Seattle Mariners — a team that had won 116 games. Kathy sat beside me on the couch, and although we didn't say too much to one another, we were both beginning to really equate the Yankees on-field success to how well Jake's recovery would proceed. The telephone rang in the middle innings, and my father's voice carried over the line.

"Are the Yanks going to be all right?" he asked.

"They're good guys," I said. "The good guys always win."

I'm sure that Dad thought I lost my mind, but he had spent a lifetime making sure that we battled through all sorts of adversity, so on some level, he probably understood. The Yankees got an early lead and hung on to win the game, which ended a little after midnight. I went through the usual mind-dance in an effort to slip off to sleep, but I was still saying the rosary when Jake screamed out at 2:30. I ran down the stairs dressed only in my under-wear. Jake was crying hard, and I struggled to hear his words of complaint. Kathy tapped me on the shoulder, and I looked into her sleep-filled eyes. Jake ran to her and they held each other as the moon threw light on them. They hugged for a full minute, and I wasn't even sure if they knew I was in the room. The love they shared was more than I could fathom. All at once, Jake looked up. "Hey, Dad, you're in your diaper," he said as he pointed at my underwear.

Jake and Kathy shared a hearty laugh at my expense, and I slipped back into bed. The rosary was waiting for me on my pillow, and I picked up right where I left off. The significance of praying to Mother Mary wasn't lost on me.

Thursday — October 18, 2001

I remember the conversation as though it were yesterday instead of ten years ago. On my twenty-seventh birthday I stopped by my parents' home in North Collins. My father was cleaning out the garage to prepare for the coming winter, and I sat at the picnic table and had a beer with him. Dad was in a fairly philosophical mood on that day, and he said, "When you're thirty-seven, you'll look back and wonder what the hell you were think-ing when you were twenty-seven."

I'm not sure why Dad picked that day to make such a statement to me, but October 18th, 2001 was my thirty-seventh birthday. I realized that I had not known squat about life at twenty-seven.

When I opened my eyes on my thirty-seventh birthday, I honestly thought that I couldn't possibly face a tougher test. I had no way of knowing where I'd be at forty-seven, but I had a feeling that the day in front of me would have a bearing on the person that I would become.

Kathy returned to work. She was on the early shift, and I was on call with Jake, Matthew, and Sam. I don't know why, but my mind drifted to my thirteenth birthday. The Yankees won their first World Series championship in many years. My favorite player, Reggie Jackson, had homered three times in the final game, and I thought he did it in honor of my birthday. I sat on the bed and recalled cheering Reggie's final home run. I had split a salami sandwich with Dad as we basked in the win. I always believed that life would be as wonderful as it felt at that moment.

As I got dressed for the day I considered what it truly takes to be a father. It seemed to me that the most important thing I could do for my children was just to be around for them to rejoice when they were happy and commiserate when they were sad. I rubbed sleep out of my eyes and was in midthought about the coming day when I heard Jake's voice. "Dad? Is it time to get up?" he called from the bottom of the stairs. "Happy birthday!"

My life was still pretty wonderful. "Make him good again, God," I whispered.

I ran down the stairs and grabbed Jake in a hug that made him laugh.

Jake, Sam, and I spent the morning together. I couldn't help but consider how different spending time with them felt for me. In a span of just a couple of weeks, I had gone from completely dreading the moments when I watched the children while Kathy was at work to thoroughly enjoying every aspect of being with my sons. Jake and I read an animal book to Sam, growling like the tiger and whinnying like the horse. We even played the annoying rhino tape and Jake and I sang the theme song for Sam.

Just before eleven o'clock, Kathy's mother, Carolyn, stopped by for a visit.

"I thought I could give you a break," Carolyn said as she looked at Jake and Sam across the room.

"You just want to see the boys," I teased.

"You need a little time for yourself," she said with a smile.

"I don't know if I can leave Jake," I whispered. "I haven't spent more than a few minutes away from him in the last couple of weeks."

"I know," Carolyn said. "That's why it's important for you to take a break now."

I hesitated for a moment on my way out, but the boys didn't even notice that I was leaving.

"Just go have some lunch or something. They'll be fine."

I couldn't shake the anxiety. I backed out of the driveway, feeling absolutely ridiculous about not wanting to leave. I went around the corner to the local Greek restaurant and ordered a huge breakfast, telling myself that it was okay to feel semi-normal.

As I ate, I read the e-mail I had printed out from friends across the country. Old college chums who hadn't been part of my everyday life for a long time sent encouraging messages. Eric, the only other teratoma patient I'd ever heard of, also sent a message that detailed his surgery and recovery. I read his letter twice, and it became apparent that if Jake's tumor was similar, there was a great chance for complete recovery. But if the tumor was different....I didn't want to think about it. Yet I did. I couldn't keep the unsettling idea out of my head. Imagining life six months down the road was something I couldn't handle if things didn't work out as I had planned.

I scanned the sports page. The Yankees were playing again at night, and I occupied my mind with the pitching match-up for the game. I wasn't being normal. I was simply pretending to be normal. I left half the breakfast on the plate, paid the bill without even glancing at the waitress, and headed back toward home. My heart was aching as I thought of Jake and Sam playing with Carolyn. I couldn't stand being away from the boys for even a minute. I wanted to spend the rest of my life just playing with them and watching the rhino tape.

My mother and my sister Corinne were at the house when I returned. They had birthday gifts for me, and I opened them without much thought. They also came armed with cookies and presents for Jake, and although it was a celebration of sorts, it felt undeniably awkward to me. The only present I wanted was for Jake to be well, but I accepted the gifts with as much excitement as I could muster. I unwrapped a framed photo from Corinne that showed a baseball player making contact with a fastball. The caption read, *Drive: Every strike brings me closer to the next home run. Babe Ruth.*

"I picked it up six months ago," Corinne said. "It seems to fit right now, doesn't it?"

"God, I hope so," I said.

"You'll get that next home run," she said.

I don't know where she found that picture. I'm not sure if she'll ever realize how much I needed to see the caption, but that photo quickly found its way to my bedroom wall. Jake stood beside me as I hung the photo. "That's a really cool picture, Dad," he said.

I tousled his hair and smiled. "It sure is," I whispered.

* * *

The defining moment of my thirty-seventh birthday came as Jake struggled with the idea that he'd have to return to the hospital. He spent most of the day playing and spending time with his brothers. Visits from both grandparents and Aunt Carrie and Uncle Mike were out of the ordinary, and he was enjoying every minute of them. I was on the couch watching the pre-game for the Yankees-Mariners battle when he jumped up into my lap and kissed me on the left cheek.

"Dad, can I ask you something?"

"Sure," I said as I snuggled him in the crook of my right arm.

"Dad, why do I have to go back to the hospital?"

He didn't seem sad, but I knew he was. He wanted me to get him out of the situation somehow. "That tumor has to come out," I said. "It's a bad guy."

"I really want to keep it," he said. He looked down at his chest. "It's mine."

"It is yours," I said, "but it's bad. The tumor is like a bunch of aliens invading your body and making you sick. Me, you, and the doctors are going to crush the aliens so that you feel better then ever. You don't like being sick, right?"

He followed the action on the screen. They replayed highlights from the Yankee victory the night before. I pointed to Yankee centerfielder Bernie Williams making a catch.

"They're going to do magic on my tumor, right?" Jake asked. "The doctors and God, right?"

"Exactly. They'll do magic while you're asleep, and they'll get the bad-guy tumor out."

"Can I have it?" he asked.

"No, we're going to throw it in the garbage. That's where all of the bad guys belong"

I tickled him, and as he laughed and squirmed, I thought of my father and my thirteenth birthday. I had been so happy as Reggie Jackson's last blast settled into the centerfield bleachers.

"Are you and Mom going to be there when I wake up?" he asked.

"Of course," I said.

A full-screen shot of Yankee shortstop Derek Jeter flashed across the screen.

"There's Jeter," he said. "Dad, why do you guys stay at the hospital with me?"

"Because that's what moms and dads do," I said. "We'll always take care of you."

He smiled and nestled in even closer. I had grown up feeling secure in the love that my parents provided. I owed my children at least that much. I just never knew how intense the love could be. Maybe my father's excitement in 1977 wasn't all due to the Yankees' World Series win. Maybe it had to do with how it made me feel on my thirteenth birthday.

Kathy cruised around the living room, picking up flotsam left behind by the boys. Sam was already in his crib, and Jake must have known that his turn was coming.

"Give Dad a kiss and tell him happy birthday," Kathy said.

Jake kissed my right cheek and said "Happy Birthday" in his best gravelly, monster voice. I tickled his stomach again, and he swung his little fists wildly, screaming with delight.

"Good night, dude," I said.

"Go Yankees," he yelled as he followed Kathy out of the room.

That night, as I watched the 2001 Yankees play, I couldn't help of thinking about the 1977 Yankees and sitting beside my father as that team won. I hadn't really come all that far in twenty-four years; I had simply switched roles. I don't know how I knew this, but I was confident about Jake's chances of a full recovery and the Yankees game that night. The Yankees won effortlessly, making my birthday complete.

Chapter Nine

Friday — October 19, 2001

I felt a real need to establish a game plan. I didn't have any control whatsoever and it was really starting to gnaw at me. We hadn't so much as heard a word from The Children's Hospital of Buffalo since we walked out the door, and now it was time for some answers.

At five-thirty in the morning, I was sitting at the kitchen table with the lights off. Kathy had left for work an hour earlier. I stared, hypnotized, into a cup of coffee as Sam cried for attention. I took one more gulp of coffee and headed for his room. I lifted him from the crib and he smiled.

"Are we ready for Barney?" I asked.

Sam smiled again, and I hugged him close to me as I headed down the hallway. I slipped the tape into the VCR, and as Sam pointed at the fat dino dancing across the screen, I called Kathy. She answered on the first ring. She sounded vibrant, considering the time of day.

"Hey, I was thinking we should call the surgeon today," I said.

"I already have it on my list," she said.

I started laughing. I'm organized, but Kathy is exactly the opposite. "You made a list?"

"Yes, smart-ass," she said. "I take it I'm supposed to be talking to Doctor Marc Levitt. I don't remember meeting him, do you?"

"No, but he's the guy," I said.

"I'm really sad today," Kathy said. "Maybe it's being back at work, but I'm really struggling."

"He'll be okay," I said.

Her end of the line was silent. I knew her answer to that declaration, and she didn't disappoint me. "I told you," she said, "he has to be. There is no alternative."

Unfortunately, I couldn't guarantee her anything. Maybe Doctor Levitt would be able to help.

* * *

Later in the day, I prepared dinner with all of my attention attuned to the telephone that wasn't ringing. Kathy had called Doctor Levitt an hour earlier, and although he wasn't in his office, his secretary explained that he would get right back to us. The boys ran through the house like wild colts, and the dogs were whimpering for their supper. Kathy entered the kitchen, and we discussed questions that we had for the surgeon. I had compartmentalized everything, and I felt as though I had a decent understanding of the treatment plan. Jake was scheduled for another CT-scan on Monday and the biopsy, regardless of the results, was scheduled for Wednesday. After receiving the results of the biopsy, they would schedule the surgery.

"The waiting is the hardest part," I said. I paced the kitchen floor and Kathy stepped in front of me to stop my mad march across the linoleum. She opened her arms and I stepped toward her.

"I know," Kathy said. "I feel like we're being tortured."

"I wish I knew more about what they had to do," I said. "I just imagine them opening up his body. It keeps me from closing my eyes at night."

Kathy buried her face in my chest. She was probably visualizing an operation on a four-year old too, and it wasn't pretty.

"How do these doctors do this for a living?" she asked.

"They must be special people," I said. "Could you imagine that being your life's work?"

"Amazing," Kathy said. "It would kill me if I couldn't fix just one of them."

The telephone rang. Jake let out a blood curling scream from his room. As Kathy grabbed the portable phone, I ran in Jake's direction.

Jake's big crisis? Sam had switched the television channel. I separated the two boys and changed the channel back, then headed to the bedroom where Kathy had retreated with the telephone. I had only missed the first few minutes of Kathy's conversation with Doctor Levitt, but she was crying by the time I arrived. I felt as if someone had let the air out of me. It was hard to get much out of her end of the conversation. She kept saying nothing but "okay" over and over.

She summarized in a few seconds what Doctor Levitt had said in a couple of minutes. "Jake will have a CT-scan on Monday and a biopsy on Wednesday. You'll schedule the surgery for the following week as long as there are no surprises."

I nodded along with her. It was exactly what we had expected.

"I understand," she said. "You're worried about his breathing, right?"

Kathy paused for a moment, and her eyes filled with tears.

She clicked the phone off and sat on the edge of the bed. She was crying and rubbing her eyes, and I was standing beside her, waiting, my mouth hanging open.

"He's real worried about knocking him out," Kathy said. "The next CT-scan will tell them if the tumor shrunk. But if it didn't, if they have to knock him out and if his lungs collapse...."

She couldn't finish the sentence. I needed to turn the conversation around a little bit. "He feels comfortable about the operation though, right?"

"I don't know. We don't even know him and he's going to have Jake's life in his hands."

"He can do it," I said. "Children's is one of the best hospitals in the country. He's probably a real talented guy."

"Has he ever removed one this big?" Kathy said. "He seems real nervous about its position."

"They have to give you all the scenarios. They don't want you to be surprised if it doesn't work out just right."

But no matter what I said, Kathy was inconsolable. My arm around her just wasn't helping very much. I kissed her left cheek and wiped a couple of tears away. The kids were calling for us, and Max was barking at something outside.

"He could die," she said. "I knew we were still in a lot of trouble, but I can't get that thought out of my head. I was expecting the doctor to tell me that it was going to be fine."

I was in just as bad a shape as her, but we didn't have more than a moment to grieve; Jake was calling to me from the bottom of the stairs. "We can't let him see us crying," I sniffed, wiping my nose on a paper napkin.

"You don't know what it felt like to hear what Doctor Levitt said."

"Yeah, I do," I murmured, "but those doctors are going to fight for him as hard as we would."

"I hope you're right."

* * *

Even in a life-threatening situation, it is hard to stomach Barney and Scooby-Doo all day long. I spent the entire day preaching patience to myself, but the endless song and dance and silliness coming from the television was driving me crazy. I got dinner together, and we all sat down in the same seats that we've always sat in. We went around the table taking turns talking about our day. The boys finished their dinners quickly and retreated to the living room, leaving Kathy and me alone for a few precious moments. I put my fork down and pushed my plate to the center of the table. In all of the years I've known Kathy, she'd never seen me not completely finish a meal.

"It's wearing on you, isn't it?" she asked, reaching across the table to pat my hand.

I nodded. "You know what the most depressing thing about this is?"

Kathy offered a half-chuckle as though it were the most ridiculous question she'd ever heard.

"It's that we don't have control over anything that matters. I always thought I had all the bases covered, and, as it turns out, I'm not even in the game."

"Maybe that's the lesson we needed to learn," Kathy said.

"All right, I learned it. Now let him get better."

As I helped gather the dishes, I heard Jake and Sam in the living room starting the Barney tape over again for the hundredth time. Matthew was with his Dad for the night, and Kathy and I were pretending that our life as a family wasn't being threatened at all.

"I think you need a beer," Kathy said.

We rarely drank beer at home. If we were out with friends, we could drink with the best of them, but we didn't have a lot of time for entertainment. The thought of a cold beer was undeniably tempting. "I'm drinking Heineken," I said. "Life's too short to drink cheap beer."

I did have a beer as I watched cartoons with Jake. It was just before nine o'clock when Kathy broke up our cartoon festival to lead Jake to bed. I followed Kathy and Jake to the bedroom to say goodnight. This evening, I decided to listen in on his nightly prayers. Jake kneeled on top of his covers and held his hands together, pointing his fingers toward the ceiling with his eyes closed. *God Bless Mommy and Daddy, Matt, Jake, and Sam, Max, Shadow and Nobody, Grandma and Grandpa Foutz, Grandma Spiffy and Poppa John, aunts, uncles, and cousins. Make me be a good boy, God, and help the doctors get rid of my tumor. Amen.*

I kissed Jake goodnight and stopped by the refrigerator for a second beer. Kathy headed toward the shower, and I sat alone in the living room, surfing thru television channels over and over. I wasn't interested in much that was going on, but I stopped flipping to hear some of the war news. The big threat to America seemed to be the anthrax that was being sent through the mail. Anthrax was just one more thing that I didn't know anything about. Still, I was fascinated that someone could hate anyone or anything so much that they would want to send a poison through the mail. In our situation, with the delicate balance of life right before us, it was impossible to fathom such disregard for other human beings. Why couldn't I gain control over Jake's situation? It seemed as though, since September 11th, life had turned into a confusing riddle, and I was simply standing on the sidelines, watching and complaining.

I took a healthy gulp of the beer and clicked the television into oblivion. I all but ran up the stairs to the computer and typed in the words mediastinal tumor. I wanted to gain a small degree of control, and I figured that studying the bad guys might help me a little bit.

A mediastinal tumor, as I soon found out after accessing a medical site, was defined as a tumor in the cavity that separates the lungs and contains the heart, the large blood vessels, the trachea, the thymus, and connective tissues. The tumors are common in the posterior mediastinum.

"What does that mean?" I whispered to the computer screen. I took another sip of beer and read the account of a giant mediastinal cystic hygroma discovered in a three-year-old female. The words smashed into my brain, one by one, like bugs on a windshield. I figured that I understood about a quarter of them.

The left margins of the mass were inseparable from the pericardial surface of the heart, which was displaced to the left. The chest was opened via a right antero-lateral thoracotomy through the bed of the 5th rib. There was a large tumor that was fixed and infiltrating into the anterior chest wall. The posterior part of the tumor was firm, but the anterior part was friable and soft. There was a possibility of teratoma or lymphoma, and a large biopsy was taken. Histology revealed a vascular tumor made up of various sizes of vascular channels lined by endothelium. The stroma was edematous and myxoid, containing spindle and stellate cells with mild nuclear pleomorphism and no mitosis. The stroma contained a diffuse infiltrate of lymphonuclear cells and neutrophils. A fibrous capsule was seen with a few thick fibrous septa. The diagnosis of cystic lymphangioma was made. The patient continued to be symptomatic. The chest was re-explored and near complete excision of the mass was done, leaving only small fragments that were densely adherent to the hilum of the lung. The cysts near the hilum of the lung and adherent to the pulmonary vessels were deroofed, and as much of the capsule as possible was excised. Postoperatively, the patient did well, and a chest radiograph showed clear lung fields.

"What're you reading?" Kathy asked.

I hadn't even noticed her approach. She had two towels wrapped around her, and she peered over my shoulder. I clicked the information off the screen.

"How'd I get so stupid?" I asked. "I never even knew these words existed. I don't even know if what I was reading has anything to do with what Jake has."

"I know," Kathy said.

"Doctors are something," I said. "They have to be the most disciplined, intelligent people in the world. I went to school with a few people that aspired to be doctors. While they were studying their butts off, I was drinking beer."

Kathy touched my right shoulder. I closed my eyes and reached for the rest of my second beer. "Yeah, but I bet you could drink them under the table," she said.

It shouldn't have been funny, but we both laughed. Kathy headed to the bedroom to change for bed. I shut the computer down, and as I let the dogs out into the backyard, I continued my ongoing dialogue with God.

"God, thanks for today," I said to the blackened sky. "I want a million more days like this, but maybe I don't know what I'm talking about. I'm feeling really inadequate tonight, but I do have faith. Help Jacob be good again."

Saturday — October 20, 2001

It had been nearly a full two weeks since I slept past six o'clock in the morning, but hoping that I would be able to sleep longer didn't work. I slipped the covers off at five-thirty. Kathy had already left for work, and thankfully the boys were still asleep.

I quietly poured a hot mug of coffee, grabbed my cellular telephone, and headed to the backyard with Max and Shadow at my heels. Max's paw was showing signs of improvement, and I slipped another pill into his food. I watched as he gobbled the food down, and he chased Shadow to the back lawn.

The patio furniture was still in place, although on any other year I probably would have already stored it for the winter. I sat in a chair at the circular table and studied the early morning sky. There were a few clouds scattered around, but I figured that it probably wouldn't rain. The air was brisk, but it honestly felt good on my bare arms. I punched in the voice mail code on my cellular phone and listened to messages from my father, my brother Jim, and my buddy, Mike Palmer. It was Mike's message that sent me into deep thoughts about my life with Kathy and the boys. Mike had simply said, "This is the most important thing you'll ever battle, buddy. Please remember that my heart is with you through this."

I sipped the coffee thinking hard about the life I built with Kathy. The formulation of a family is a funny thing. Kathy seemed to have a grand design that included three or four children, a few pets, and a house that was large enough to hold all of us comfortably. I didn't have anything against any of it, but, if truth be told, it wasn't all set down in my mind in stone as it was in hers. I was more comfortable living day-to-day and taking things as they came. It was early fall in 1999 when Kathy decided to turn up the heat again. I thought back to our conversation on that day.

"What about another baby?" she asked.

I was tired and still reeling from Jake's first two years of life. I hadn't been prepared for changing diapers, and the insistent crying. I was finally feeling comfortable communicating with Jake and Matthew. I wasn't sure if I had the energy to start all over at ground zero.

"How about we wait six months?" I asked.

I had no way of knowing that Kathy had figured out when she wanted to be pregnant.

"If we wait six months, we have to wait a year. I don't want to carry the child through the summer and be off of work in the winter months. It's either this fall or next fall."

"It's next fall then," I said.

The discussion ended for about a week. The next hurdle was a complete surprise. In early October of 1999, Kathy took the boys to the mall. They played at the game room and then visited the pet shop. That night, all they could talk about was a black Lab that they had already named.

"Can we get Shadow?" Matthew asked.

"Yeah, come on, we want Shadow," Jake said.

"Who the heck is Shadow?" I asked.

"She's a black Lab," Kathy said. "She's absolutely beautiful. It's sad seeing her in that cage."

"No," I said. "No more living things for awhile."

I tried to ignore their disappointment, figuring that the argument was over. I was the king of the castle, and my decision was final. I went out of town on business the very next day, and Kathy called me early in the afternoon. We talked about dinner, how our days were going, and how the children were doing. Just before I hung up, Kathy arrived at the real reason for her telephone call. "Can't we get Shadow? She's just beautiful. You'll love her. The kids want her, and if we get her, I won't bug you about a baby until next year."

"I don't care," I said. "Get her, but Matt and Jake are going to take care of her."

"They will and I'll help them. Thank you."

I smiled at the memory of that day just over two years ago. Surely, I wasn't the king of the castle. Shadow arrived home before I did, and of course she was an absolute horror. I didn't know a lot about black Lab puppies, but suffice it to say that they are a wee bit rambunctious. During the first three weeks of her stay, Shadow grew completely out of favor with Kathy, Jake, and Matthew. She chewed the insides out of our living room couch and messed on every carpet in the house. By early November, Kathy's tone had changed. "We have to get rid of her. That couch was expensive, and I absolutely hate her."

"We can't get rid of her," I said. "What kind of message is that for the boys? They'll think that if they're bad we'll just discard them. Shadow's a part of the family now. I'm going to have to deal with her because you all abandoned her, but your punishment is that she stays."

"She can stay on one condition," Kathy said.

It was incredible, but now I was fighting for the dog. "What's that?" I asked.

"That I get pregnant now."

I guess it would be accurate to say that I lost the argument. Shadow settled in as a member of the family and Salvatore "Sam" Gordon Fazzolari was born on June 25, 2000.

As I sipped my coffee in the cool, fall air, I nearly laughed aloud as I considered my father's theory of division. My family consisted of Kathy, Matthew, Jacob, Sam, Max, and Shadow. I was about 2 percent of the man that I once was. The rest of me consisted of them.

I let the dogs into the house about half an hour later. I watched the sports news reports on television until the boys stirred from their slumber. I spent the entire morning chasing Jake and Sam around the house.

The Yankee game was on in the afternoon, but Seattle pounded them. The game was over so quickly that it didn't provide the distraction I sorely needed. I felt as if I were walking on a treadmill. Time was moving slowly, and everything I thought I knew seemed out of my grasp.

Kathy and I spent the evening hours catering to Matt, Jake, and Sam's every whim and we even took them to Blockbuster to rent games and videos. We didn't have a lot of time to talk about Jake's condition, but when the children went to bed, Kathy and I spent a couple of hours talking. Then I returned to the computer. I needed to know a little more about The Children's Hospital of Buffalo and their pediatric surgery department. I clicked on the hospital's website and sorted through volumes of information. It was hard to believe, but we were mere miles from one of the top twenty children's hospitals in the country. Year after year, The Children's Hospital of Buffalo was cited for its excellent service in pediatric medicine. *U.S. News & World Report* noticed the research and care provided at Children's.

What really startled me was the number of patients treated at Children's every year. Over 28,000 were admitted annually, and more than 123,000 were treated on an outpatient basis. Still, most everyone that came into contact with us at Children's acted as if Jake were the most important patient there. *Thank God that place is here,* I thought.

I sifted through the general information. The hospital was established on September 6, 1892 as the area's first and only hospital dedicated exclusively to children.

I did the math quickly. An average of 150,000 people treated over one hundred and eight years meant that 16,200,000 patients had been treated since the hospital's inception. I wondered what the hospital's founders, Martha Williams and her mother Harriet, would have thought of that.

I scanned the names of the surgeons and physicians in the pediatric department. I had never met associate professor Guy F. Brisseau, MD. Or associate Professor Michael G. Caty, MD, FACS, FAAP. I didn't even have a clue what the initials stood for!

I searched for Marc Levitt, MD, and found him listed alongside Joy Graf, MD, and Scott Boulanger, MD. I recognized the name of the pediatric nurse practitioner, Karen Iacono, MSN, PNP, but they were all virtual strangers. What sort of grace were they blessed with to take my ailing son to their hearts?

The surgeon-in-chief was listed as Phillip L. Glick, MD, FACS, FAAP, FSCCM, and under his name was Joseph K. McIntosh, MD.

I wanted each and every one of the available doctors to work on Jake. I don't know what made me do it, but I plugged in the keyword *doctor* and stumbled upon the International Code of Medical Ethics. It's a good thing I didn't know what I was looking for or I might have missed the driving force behind the dedication of the people at The Children's Hospital of Buffalo.

"A doctor must always maintain the highest standards of professional conduct...A doctor must practice his profession uninfluenced by motives of profit...A doctor must always bear in mind the obligation of preserving human life...."

I drifted off to sleep on Saturday, October 20, 2001 with renewed confidence. I wasn't thinking about the Yankee heroes past or present. For the first time in my life, I was in awe of people that were actually making a difference in the world for 16,200,000 patients — and counting.

Chapter Ten

Sunday — October 21, 2001

Typically, Sundays were reserved for the trip to North Collins to visit my parents, but we understood that even a slight cold could tip the scales out of Jake's favor. Perhaps we were being a bit over-protective, but we decided to stay in the house. Jake's breathing was excellent, and his stamina had seemed to improve. His naps weren't quite so long, and his mood was fantastic. Still, I continued to walk around in a fog. How was it possible for life to change so quickly?

I thought of a day less than three months ago. It was a lesson learned that I didn't recall until that very morning.

I had been to the grocery store three times on that Saturday. Yet, just after dinner, Kathy informed me that we were out of formula for Sam. I complained about it for a few moments, but eventually I decided that I would return the beer and pop cans that had accumulated in the basement. If I had to go to the store again, I might as well make it a productive trip.

I pulled into the parking lot of the grocery store. It had been a bright, sunshine-filled day and the evening sky was bright orange. I had opened the latch on the back gate of my truck and had begun putting the cans into a cart when I heard what sounded like an animal grunt coming from the car right next to me. The passenger side window came down, and a huge man grunted again. I turned to him when I realized that he was trying to say hello.

"Hi," I said.

"Beer cans?" he answered.

Immediately I realized that the man was mentally ill. I wondered about the person that had driven him to the store. How could they just leave him sitting in the parking lot?

"Yeah, I got a few beer cans," I said. "We had a party."

"I used to like Beck's beer," he said.

It was a strange comment, but I just let it pass. How did he know about Beck's beer?

"You got pop cans too," he said.

"The kids like pop."

"How many kids you got?"

The last thing I needed was a long conversation, but something made me stay and talk.

"Three boys," I said.

He laughed real hard and smacked his hand on the side door panel.

"I have five boys," he said. "Always remember to love your kids."

Now, I was really intrigued. I moved closer to him. "My name is Cliff."

"I'm Fred," he said. "Do you work at the Ford plant?"

"No," I said.

"I used too," he said. "How old are you?"

"Thirty-six," I answered.

Fred looked as if he were trying to figure something out. His face went blank as he searched for the words to his next sentence.

"I was thirty-nine when I had my stroke," he said.

My heart dropped into my stomach. I considered his five children and the tragic turn of events that shaped the remainder of his days.

"I used to make a lot of money," he said. "Do you make a lot of money?"

I noticed the approach of Fred's wife from clear across the parking lot. She was already apologizing for her husband, but I waved her off.

"Fred and I are just catching up a little," I said. I reached into the car and shook Fred's hand.

"It was a beautiful day, wasn't it?" Fred asked.

I wanted to tell him that he had made it a little bit better for me, but his pretty wife was sliding into the driver's side, still apologizing for him.

"Remember what I said about those boys of yours," Fred said.

I watched their car move toward the exit. Fred's eyes never left me, and I stood outside the store watching him, a cart filled with empty cans right in front of me. Why had he asked me if I made a lot of money? How come he kept mentioning loving my children? Was he a walking, talking lesson?

There just aren't any guarantees in life, and I was pretty well aware that a little rain had to fall. Yet Fred seemed to be handling his rainfall all right. He had taken note of the beautiful day, and his mind still allowed him trips back in time to what a beer tasted like and how it felt to love his children. His life had surely changed, but it wasn't over, and he was going to make the most of what was left.

On that Sunday, mere days before Jake's operation, I took my cue from Fred. I got the boys ready for church, and in all of our glory we attended the ten-thirty mass. Sam seemed to enjoy the singing, but Matt and Jake squirmed in their seats as only young children can. When it came time to exchange greetings with the other parishioners, Jake made his way up and down the aisle, shaking everyone's hands. For the first time in a couple of weeks, I felt really alive, and during the course of the day, I saw the same sort of light dancing in Kathy's eyes.

We were beginning to feel mildly confident about Jake's situation. He was running around the house, smiling and acting like a healthy little boy. A number of people had said that kids bounced back in amazing ways, and we were beginning to see a little of that spirit.

The household chores still needed to be carried out, and Kathy and I had always done a decent job of splitting them up. I gathered up the laundry baskets and dumped the mound of clothes on the basement floor. I admit that I didn't sort them as well as Kathy might, but they all got cleaned anyway, and I did not turn a piece of clothing a different color.

I got the tomato sauce started and, while I was cutting up the garlic and onions, I thought of my father performing the same task on countless Sunday mornings. The boys were in their rooms playing video games. I'm not sure what it is, but chopping onions and watching them liquefy in a pan coated with olive oil puts me in a peaceful place. "He's going to be all right," I whispered to the dissolving vegetables.

Max was lying at my feet, and he perked his ears up at the sound of my voice. When I bent down toward him, he instinctively hid his sore paw.

"Let me see it," I said.

He sort of resigned himself to the fact that he was being examined, and I looked at the paw without hassling him too much. The swelling was definitely down, and the skin no longer looked bloodied. I patted Max on the head, and I couldn't help but feel relieved that he was on the mend.

Of course, Max's presence in our family also came with a story. I had just purchased a home and, while I was dating Kathy, I was still a firmly entrenched bachelor. We'd always had dogs growing up, and I had missed having one during my years of apartment living. So I stopped by the ASPCA to look at the dogs.

I scanned the cages of the abandoned dogs with an extremely heavy heart. I really did want to take each and every one of those sad pooches home with me. An elderly man with ASPCA stenciled on his shirt passed me in the hall. "See any you like?" he asked.

"All of them," I said.

He grabbed me by the sleeve of my shirt and looked around as though we were being watched. His voice dropped an octave. "The best dog in this place is the one in the very last cage," he said. He was pointing down the hallway. "The shame of it is he's going to be extinguished tomorrow."

"Extinguished?"

"You know, sent to the big kennel. We can't keep them forever. There are too many of them. I just hate to see Max go that way, though. He's a great dog, but he's had a tough life. His previous owners abused him something awful."

The man had certainly gained my attention. I followed him down to the cage where Max was being held. "Isn't he beautiful?" the man whispered. "He's a yellow Lab and Golden Retriever mix. I'd love to find the man that was beating him."

Max's belly was shaved, but that hadn't affected his spirits. He reared up against the cage door, almost begging me to notice him.

"They burned his groin area, and he took a tremendous number of kicks and punches."

That did it. Max was as good as in the car. I petted his head, and he leaned his substantial body against the cage. "What sort of a man would burn an animal?"

"Not much of one," the old man said. "You want him?"

"Yeah, I do."

The old man did something that will stick with me until the day I leave this world. He grabbed me so quickly that I didn't have time to react and his hug was real solid. "That's the best seventy bucks you'll ever spend."

As I dropped Max's paw and petted his head once more, I couldn't help but realize that the man had been right. I never did get my question answered, though. What sort of man could burn, punch, or kick a dog?

* * *

The Yankees continued their unbelievable march as they beat Seattle to take a three to one lead in the series. Kathy and I watched the game together after the kids went to bed, and although we discussed the pitch counts and the clutch hits, we never got too far from Jake's situation.

"I'm starting to feel better about it," I said as I turned off the television. "I don't know what might make me draw such a parallel, but Jake is feeling better and the Yankees are winning. It's almost like the Yankees and Jake are connected somehow."

"I don't know about that. I'm still so scared," Kathy said.

"Yeah, me too," I said, "but faith is rewarded, isn't it?"

"Not every time," Kathy said.

I thought about Fred and the stroke that cut him down in the prime of his life. I thought about his children and how they reacted to their father's dulled motor skills. Bad things do happen to good people — there was no doubt about it. "I'm telling you, I'm starting to feel confident."

I had hardly considered work, but I was due to return in the morning. The game ended shortly after midnight, and I set the alarm for six o'clock. I probably would have been functional if I'd fallen right to sleep, but I wasn't feeling *that* confident. I worked my way through the rosary one more time with the words, "faith is rewarded" swimming through my brain.

Monday — October 22, 2001

Since the days of my childhood, I have clipped and saved quotes from the world's greatest writers, philosophers, or comedians. Occasionally, I use some of the lines on a day-to-day basis to motivate myself to make it through the day.

I was returning to work for the first time since Jacob's illness. I was well aware that I would need to be productive, even though I wasn't feeling up to par. I had slept about three hours, and my sleep had been troubled at best. At the sound of the alarm, I forced myself out of bed and headed for the shower, but I stopped by my office for a moment. I turned on the computer and searched for the file where I kept a folder of my favorite quotations. I was looking for a specific paragraph, and when I found it, I read it quickly.

"Generations come and go, but it makes no difference. The sun rises and sets and hurries around to rise again. The wind blows south and north, here and there, twisting back and forth, getting nowhere. The rivers run into the sea, but the sea is never full; and the water returns again to the rivers, and flows again to the sea...

Everything is unutterably weary and tiresome. No matter how much we see, we are never satisfied; no matter how much we hear, we are not content. So I saw that there is nothing better for men than that they should be happy in their work, for that is what they are here for, and no one can bring them back to life to enjoy what will be in the future. So let them enjoy it now". — Ecclesiastes —

I'm not sure that the quote truly motivated me this morning as much as it made me feel comfortable and reminded me of my responsibility. No matter what was happening, I was being paid to perform a service for a group of individuals that counted on me to do just that. I breathed deeply and vowed to enjoy the day in front of me.

I kissed the boys goodbye and headed to my truck. The sun was trying desperately to break through a heavy layer of clouds. Kathy had returned to work last week. She had explained how difficult it was to leave the house, but I didn't truly appreciate the gnawing ache of separation until I backed the truck out of the driveway. What if something happened to Jake while I was gone? What if he simply missed me? I didn't want to leave, but deep down, I knew that I had to.

I drove the half hour to the office with an ache in my heart and an acidic sensation rising from the pit of my stomach. I kept the radio off and prayed over and over, but the words to my prayers were jumbled and inexplicably, I thought of Frosty the Snowman and the locked greenhouse.

At the main office of Scott Danahy Naylon, my co-workers gathered around me, asking me the details of Jacob's care. Of course, they offered their support, and their questions were shrouded in concern, but I found that telling the story, time and time again, intensified the pain in my heart. I decided that my day's work would be better served in a more comfortable environment. I headed out to a few construction sites with a heart that weighed approximately fifty pounds. Before I made it to my car, I passed Tim Danahy, one of the partners that owned the business.

"It's good to have you back," Tim said. "Just remember, this isn't 1970. They can take your heart out, put it on the table, and ask you how you're feeling. Jake is going to be fine."

As we parted company, his words resonated in my brain and filled me with hope. I carried them with me every day for the next few months. It was by far one of the most comforting sentences ever spoken to me.

After experiencing the collapse of my cozy world, it was strange to realize that the rest of the world was pretty much exactly the way I had left it. I visited a number of jobsites in an effort to ensure that our contractors were performing their work safely. The rules and regulations came back to me quickly, but I was always just around the corner from my next thought of Jake. The feeling of confidence that I had found just the day before was slipping away. I was sure that I wouldn't be able to do any of this if things didn't work out the way that I needed them to. I called Kathy about halfway through the morning.

"How's it feel to be back at work?" she asked.

"I feel ridiculous," I said. "None of this matters."

"I know. I went through the same thing, but you'll come around. We need to do this. We can't just sit in a circle around Jake. Remember, we need to show the kids normalcy."

"I'm depressed," I said. "I watched Bugs with him this morning, and he didn't even flinch when I kissed him goodbye. He doesn't even know what's happening."

We talked for a couple of minutes more and I shared Tim's words of comfort, hoping that they would lift Kathy's spirits a bit.

"We're getting through it," she said simply.

My final lesson of that first day back to work came straight from the mouth of one of the most ignorant men that I've ever had the misfortune of mentioning Jake's illness to. The man was a laborer in one of the work crews, and he was on the fringe of a group that was asking me about the details of Jacob's care. I'd never actually spoken directly to the man and wasn't asking his opinion, but he extended it anyway.

"That's why I don't live with my kids," he said.

"What?" I asked.

He was a scraggly looking fellow with wild hair and an unshaven face. His eyes were on the verge of being bloodshot, which made me wonder if he'd had a couple of beers at lunch. "If you live with them, they just get sick and crap. You have to admit that they're annoying."

"You've got to be kidding," I said. "They're wonderful."

The man laughed as though I was the one without a clue. "Remember how easy life was without kids? All your money was yours, and you didn't get woken up in the middle of the night. I'm glad I don't have to put up with it. They're my ex-wife's problem now."

"Yeah, well ... I'm just hoping my kid gets the chance to grow up," I said.

I hurried away from Mister Ignorant. I didn't care where I was going; I just had to get away. A member of the work crew caught up with me just as I reached my truck. "He's an idiot," he said.

"So I gathered," I said. "That's pretty sad, isn't it?" I felt sorry for the ignorant man and anyone else that took having children for granted. I was angry that anyone could simply look at life in such a pathetic manner, and it pained me to think that some children are forced to live with parents that don't give a damn.

"It takes all kinds to make the world go around."

That night, I just reveled in the chance to be with my family. Jake and I played the Scooby-Doo video game for more than three hours. I danced with Sam as the rhino sang his happy songs, and I held Kathy just a little bit tighter when we had a few minutes alone.

After we tucked the children into their beds, Kathy and I sat in front of the television set and watched the Yankees emphatically close out the Mariners. The game was actually over by the middle innings, and I spent a couple of minutes daydreaming about their fourth straight championship. The one thing that bothered me was that the World Series wasn't set to begin until Saturday, and I was a little worried about how I'd occupy my mind until then every night after the children went to bed. Kathy was right by my side, but we needed a distraction.

"I keep imagining him on the operating table," Kathy said.

"Don't do that," I said.

"This waiting is horrible."

"That's our lesson," I said. "We don't control things."

The game ended just before midnight. I knew that I was headed for at least one more hour of driving myself crazy before I slipped off to sleep.

"I can't help comparing the Yankees in the playoffs to how we're doing getting through this," I said. "When Jake went into the hospital, and things seemed bleak, the Yankees were down two games to Oakland. As Jake's breathing improved, the Yankees started winning, and they eliminated Oakland on the day Jake was released from the hospital. Now, he's doing wonderfully, and the Yankees are just marching. The way I have it figured, the Yankees are going to win the World Series on the day the tumor comes out."

Kathy smiled brightly. I could tell that the Yankees win didn't mean exactly the same thing to her, but her shining eyes led me to believe that she was thrilled that I was attaching symbols to it all. "We need to find hope to make it through the day," she said. "If you want to pin your hopes on the Yankees, I guess that isn't such a bad way to go."

I kissed Kathy good-night and headed for the stairs. "For the record," Kathy said. "I do think the Yankees will win the World Series, and I know in my heart that Jake will be fine."

Tuesday — October 23, 2001

The weather in western New York is surely an adventure. Buffalo has a reputation as one of the snowiest cities in the country, and it is a reputation that is truly deserved. Snow is expected anytime after October 1, and the winter can stretch straight on through to May. Still, the city does deserve credit, because the snow very rarely cripples the efforts of a hardworking community.

My down mood would have been better served by an early season snowstorm, but the weather was still relatively warm, and I had to settle for rain. My lack of sleep was surely getting to me. I couldn't stop yawning, and every bone in my body seemed to be aching for more rest. Like Kathy, I often felt as if I were operating on automatic pilot.

That morning, I headed to a job about a half-hour south of the city of Buffalo. The drive allowed me time to stew on everything about Jake's condition, and I actually experienced moments when I had to convince myself that this nightmare really was happening to us. The mind is a tricky tool, and mine sometimes tried to urge me to pretend that the tumor didn't exist.

I listened to Bruce Springsteen all the way out to the job. I concentrated on the lyrics to a song called "*Land of Hopes and Dreams*" and it served as my prayer for the day. In the song, the protagonist looks death and despair right in the eyes and believes with his whole heart that he will, somehow, triumph.

I pulled into my usual spot in front of the construction trailer and had to force myself out of the car. My heart just wasn't in my work, and I felt as if I were simply going through the motions of actually living. I completed the inspection in the usual amount of time and left the site. The rain pelted the windshield as I made my way back toward Buffalo. I called the house and checked on Jake. Kathy's mother explained that he was breathing fine, but was a little cranky. As I clicked off the phone, I realized that I needed to talk with someone. I decided to take a detour and visit my parents in North Collins.

My mother and father's house was on the top of the hill, and I felt comfortable as I angled into the drive. I thought of the warmth and security of living in such a happy home, and I realized that I was an unbelievably lucky child. I grew up in a wonderful home with five brothers and sisters who are still my closest friends. My parents worked hard to make sure we had a good start in life. I stood in front of the door for a moment, looking out toward the backyard where I had played countless baseball games with my brothers and our friends. Mom and Dad had built the house and filled it with love. It was a home that they were proud of and had every right to be.

I unlocked the door and announced my arrival, and my father apparently asked the first question that came to his mind. "Are you hungry?"

"No, I'm all right."

Mom and Dad sat at the kitchen table, and I avoided their eyes as I petted their dog, a yellow Lab, Jeter, who was named after Yankee shortstop Derek Jeter. "Jake's doing well," I said. "You really should hear how much easier he's breathing."

"That's good," Mom said, but I could tell that she was fighting back tears and trying not to vocalize her fears. My father jumped in to help her voice her concern.

"Does that mean he has cancer?" he said. "Does that mean it shrunk?"

"They aren't sure if it shrunk at all," I said. "Maybe he had an infection that was cleared up by the chemo."

Mom was looking at the floor. I was having a hard time looking Mom in the eyes.

"Everyone is praying for him," Dad said. "We've always been lucky as a family. We haven't had a lot of serious illness."

I wasn't sure what Dad was trying to say. I needed to try and calm my parents' fears.

"We're doing fine," I said. "They cure cancer a lot more often these days, and if that's what we have to face, we will. It'll work out all right."

Mom's face had turned dark red, and she was biting her lip to hold back her tears. She nodded along with me as I wrapped her up in a quick, powerful hug.

"We're going to be okay," I said. "He looks so good. Besides, God will get us through this."

"He will," Mom said.

For the very first time, I felt real awkward in the presence of my parents. It surely was odd to see them so unsure of life's events. I had continually looked to them for guidance and support, and while they were right there for me, it felt like they were out of answers.

"Do you need money?" Dad asked.

"No," I said. "We're doing okay."

Dad patted me on the shoulder. I smiled and nodded. "Mom and Dad, you've already given me everything that I need to get through this."

I hugged them both good-bye and escaped out the front door of the house that was always so comfortable to me. I slipped in behind the wheel and turned up the volume on the Bruce Springsteen compact disc.

Wednesday — October 24, 2001

Once again, I slipped out of bed well before seven o'clock. Kathy was already a couple of hours into her shift at work, and the boys were still sleeping soundly. Mindlessly, I flipped through yesterday's newspaper and a rather disturbing story caught my eye. A story about an abused child is unfortunately just a variation of a common theme. Every once in a while a story creeps across the wire that attacks every sensibility of every parent in the world. A couple in Texas was being accused of locking their eight-year-old daughter in a lice-infested closet for days at a time. The story alleged that the child weighed just twenty-five pounds when the authorities rescued her. The parents were also being accused of forcing the child to remain naked as she watched the rest of the family eat their meals. The girl was allowed to eat only her own waste.

In the very same edition of the newspaper was a story about a garbage truck driver who had found a live, newborn baby buried in two feet of garbage. The driver had saved her life by just paying attention and being human.

What twisted person is capable of harming their own flesh and blood? Yet it happens day in and day out, and probably always will. These weren't the kind of stories that I was hoping to read at this time in my life. I folded the newspaper over and stuffed it into the garbage can.

Jake was out of bed a little after seven o'clock. His smile was already in place, and I instinctively asked him how he felt.

"Why does everybody keep asking me that?" he asked. "I'm fine." He crawled up onto the couch, dragging his blanket behind him, and the small plastic tube that had been set to administer the meds forced its way out of his shirtsleeve. I pulled him up onto my lap and switched from the morning news to the cartoon station. Bugs Bunny was chasing Elmer Fudd through the woods.

"This is the duck season one!" Jake yelled.

Together, we watched the cartoon. We laughed together and soon began playing the roles of Bugs and Daffy Duck. Of course, I was the one that always screwed up and got blasted by Elmer Fudd's imaginary gun, and it occurred to me that constantly watching cartoons was making me feel slightly unsettled. I thought of Frosty the Snowman once more, and the mental image of the pool of water inside the greenhouse sent a shiver up my spine.

"Are you staying home?" Jake asked.

"I have to go to work," I said. "Just three more days and then I'll be home for a couple of days. Grandma and Mom will be here, and the nurse is coming by today to change your dressing. We can go to the arcade or something if you do well."

"I'm not doing it!" Jake cried. "It hurts when they take the tape off! That nurse is stupid! Don't make me do it!"

I trapped him in my arms and tickled him. He kicked and screamed for a moment, but soon he was laughing through his tears.

"The nurse only has to come over a couple more times," I said. "Mom will be home. She won't let anyone hurt you."

"Then we can go to the arcade?" he asked. Tears still glistened in his big, brown eyes.

"For as long as you want," I said. I tried to tickle those tears away, and the sound of his laughter made my heart sing. "Hey, we need to take our temperatures. I'm going to beat you this time."

We had made a game out of the placing the thermometer under our arms. One of the biggest risks was a high temperature, and between Kathy and me we probably took Jake's temperature ten times a day. Thankfully, it was always close to normal.

Jake ran into the kitchen to retrieve the thermometer. It made my heart ache to see him run, knowing that the exertion would cause his breathing to be labored for a moment, but I couldn't bring myself to ask him not to be a kid. He wasn't going to just collapse. He'd lived with this affliction for a long time.

He eagerly waited for the thermometer to beep as I held it under my arm. It beeped, and I pretended that I didn't hear it.

"Dad, it's beeping. Why do I have to tell you every time?"

I slapped at my forehead as though I were the dumbest man on the planet. His eyes were wide with anticipation, and I held the thermometer up to read the figures. "Who won?" he asked.

I did my best to feign disappointment as I declared him the winner. "96.5."

"Why do I beat you in everything? You even stink at getting your temperature taken."

I rubbed his head, and he threw a few punches into my mid-section as he giggled as only a child can. I kissed the top of his head. I was just so happy that his hair hadn't fallen out. I silently thanked God that it was one of the little things that we had been spared. I had no way of knowing that it was another river out there, waiting to be crossed.

Kathy's mother arrived at seven-thirty. Carolyn smiled at me as though everything was completely normal, and Jake ran toward his grandmother. I bent down to kiss Jake good-bye, and the best I could do was land a glancing blow on the top of his head. "Be good," I whispered.

As I slipped in behind the wheel I felt completely empty. My father had once explained that one of the hardest things about being a parent was leaving your children from time to time. I was going to know exactly what he was talking about, as I was scheduled to make a trip to my biggest client in Syracuse, New York, two hundred miles away. On Wednesday morning, I had no idea how I was going to pull off such a long absence.

I took a couple of deep breaths and decided that the best thing I could do for myself was to get distracted in my work. I did my best to concentrate on the work, and for the most part, I was able to keep my despair at arm's length. A lot of people in Buffalo asked me about Jake's condition, and I did my best to put a positive spin on it. I told them all about Jake's love for Bugs Bunny and how great Jake looked. It occurred to me that men who had been simply business acquaintances a little over two weeks ago were now my good friends.

But my mind kept shifting back to the poor child that was forced to live in a closet. I couldn't figure out why Kathy and I were dealing with a seriously ill child while that mother was handed a perfectly healthy child that she felt compelled to abuse. Even animals in the wild protect their children, but some human beings hated themselves enough to torture their own kids. I prayed to the interior of my car.

"God, please help those children. Help the parents break the cycle of abuse. Do something, God, because it's driving me crazy today."

Kathy telephoned me just before lunch. She had spent an hour at home with Jake and the nurse, Terri. They battled their way through the changing of Jake's bandage and the flushing of the picc line. Even though I knew that it wasn't painful to Jake, I can't say that I was sorry that I missed it. "He screamed bloody murder all the way through," Kathy said, "but Terri gave him a dollar for the arcade. Terri is a wonderful nurse, but I just can't imagine having a job treating screaming children every day."

While I was appreciative of the nurses and doctors who were working so hard to help Jake, I was still a little leery of basking in complete admiration of their efforts. "Remember the doctors and nurses who looked at him before this? They're the reason why we're in this predicament."

"I thought we weren't going to dwell on that," Kathy said.

She was right. We wanted to focus our energies positively. "We'll have a nice, quiet night at home, and you'll feel better," Kathy said. She truly had a way of calming me down.

"I'll be positive," I said.

In the evening, there was dinner to cook and diapers to change, but Kathy and I found a moment for a long embrace in the center of the kitchen.

"Aw, geez, there they go again," Matthew called out as he ran by us and down the hall. "Jake! Mom and Dad are kissing again."

Jake joined Matthew, and they circled us, singing a song meant to mock us. "Mommy and Daddy sitting in a tree, K-I-S-S-I-N-G. First comes love, and then comes marriage, and then comes Sammy in a baby carriage."

The more they sang, the longer we kissed. I wouldn't have minded if the song went on for the rest of the evening. I was happy just to be with my family, and in the middle of a day when I desperately needed to be hugged, Kathy was there for me.

* * *

The trip to the arcade was fairly typical. We played games with bad guys battling good guys as the bells and whistles sounded all around us. I ran through ten dollars in about a half an hour, but Jake didn't press for more. He looked a little tired, so we walked back to the car, talking about the fun we had. I lifted him in my arms and carried him across the parking lot.

"Why are you carrying me?" he asked.

"Because you're my buddy," I said, "and this is what a daddy is supposed to do. Besides, when baseball players do really well in a game their buddies carry them on their shoulders."

I thought of that child trapped in the closet and the baby dumped inside the dumpster. Jake was resting his head on my right shoulder as we walked across the darkened parking lot.

"There are a lot of stars out," Jake said.

Like me, Jake was enamored of the tremendous sky, and he already knew approximately where God was supposed to live. "Can God see us from way up there?"

"I hope so," I said. "He's got pretty good eyes, though."

"Maybe God has a television with all of our pictures on it," Jake said.

I smiled at his sense of understanding, and his face took on a quizzical look. "Do you think God sees us right now?" Jake asked.

"God definitely sees us," I said, and I was real confident that I was speaking the truth.

Thursday — October 25, 2001

As I opened my eyes a wave of panic surged through my veins. I had dreamed that I was running through a cornfield. Once again, something had been chasing me, and although I was running as fast as I could, whatever was behind me had closed in so quickly that I felt the hot breath of pursuit on the back of my neck. I threw the covers off me, onto the floor, as the reality of Jake's illness blasted to the front of my mind. I put my feet on the floor and shook the remnants of the dream from my mind. It was becoming painfully apparent that I was going to have to change my attitude. I needed to shake the pain from my heart as we were still at least a week away from Jake undergoing the operation that would set him on the road to recovery.

"Please, God, give me some balance," I whispered. "I have to leave home for thirty-six hours, and I need at least a small degree of sanity."

I had no idea of knowing how I could possibly go a day and a half without knowing that Jake was breathing fine every minute. How would I even accomplish getting my work done without slipping off into an emotional abyss?

I drank two cups of coffee waiting for the boys to get out of bed, but Jake and Sam slept soundly until my mother-in-law arrived. Matthew was getting ready for school, and I knocked softly on his bedroom door.

"What?" Matt asked. He was struggling to loop his belt through his pants, and I reached out to help him. "I got it," he said.

I backed off a step. "Of course you do. You're a big boy. You're the man of the house while I'm gone, too. Do me a favor and help your mother with Jake and Sam."

"I will," he said.

I wanted to kiss him good-bye, but Matt was old enough to be a little uncomfortable with shows of affection from his parents. I rubbed his head and he cringed. "See you later," he said.

I entered Sam's room slowly. I surely didn't want to wake him up from a sound sleep, but I leaned my head into the crib. He was askew in the crib with a blanket on his right cheek. I moved the blanket and kissed him. He stirred a bit, but remained asleep.

Jake was also soundly asleep, and I took a few steps into the room and made a conscious effort to listen to his breathing. His breathing was definitely less labored, and it crossed my mind that the medicine had done something to help him. I edged closer to the bed, and although I was as quiet as a church mouse, he turned over and opened his eyes.

"Hey, buddy," I said. "I have to go."

A disappointed look crossed his face, but he replaced it with a smile. "See you later, alligator."

I kissed him goodbye and tickled his stomach. "Turn the cartoons on for me before you leave."

"Okay, but you have to be good for Mom," I said.

He frowned as though it was the most ridiculous request he had ever received. "I will."

It was raining lightly. I looked to the sky for a moment and whispered to the heavens. "Remember, I need a little balance. Please let me feel happy for a moment, too." As I backed out of the driveway, a feeling of absolute hopelessness enveloped me. "Just thirty-six hours," I said.

I hit the road, and the solitude of the highway smacked me right between the eyes. The rain was pounding the windshield, and I couldn't get the wipers to clear it fast enough. I didn't beat the storm, but fifty minutes into the trip I had driven out of it. The clouds hung low, and the rain slowed to a drizzle and then stopped all together. I was nearing Rochester on Interstate 90 when I started scanning the sky for a rainbow. My mind shifted to a day long ago when a rainbow had settled my heart.

Over twenty years ago I had become a member of the Lions slow-pitch softball team. It was a team built on friendship, and although we usually made a decent run at winning the title, we didn't base the success of the team on winning a championship. In fact, it took us nearly twenty years before we won our first one.

I was nearing the end of my athletic career. The arrival of the children had cut down my free time and I was running even slower than usual. I didn't want to risk an injury that would cost me time away from work. In May of 1999, at our annual team meeting, I sat with John Cataldo, Scott Hemer, Jeff Renaldo, and Frank Montaldi and explained that it would be my final year of playing alongside them. It wasn't a dramatic retirement announcement, but they had played on the same field with me since we were fourteen. I was sad to see it end. We decided to make it the best Lions season ever, and in the first game of the year we looked prophetic. I hit well and we won big. The only guy on the team to have a better night was Jeff Renaldo, and I begrudgingly awarded him the first beer at the bar afterwards as player of the game. The next day, Jeff was burned on over seventy percent of his body in a work-related accident. The doctors weren't real sure how his recovery would proceed, and Jeff was still in rough shape when the Lions next scheduled game was to be played.

"I can't play," I told Jeff's wife, Kathleen. "I can't step on the field without him. He's always been beside me for every game, and it'll hurt too much to play a game without him."

Kathleen looked me right in the eye. "You better play," she said. "If he hears you skipped a game, he'll kick your ass, burned or not."

I played miserably in the next game, yet something happened in that game that will stay with me for the rest of my life. Just as the umpire called, "Play Ball", I looked out to right field and saw a perfect rainbow. It hung in the sky like a neon sign from Heaven that my buddy would be fine. Less than four months later, Jeff stood at home plate and lined a single into left field.

Almost two years later, I was pleading with God again. "You gave me a rainbow then," I said. "Come on, God, give me one now."

I drove for two and a half hours. My eyes hardly ever left the sky, but there wasn't a trace of a rainbow to be found. I knew that it was a lot to ask to receive a sign from God, but I couldn't help but feel disgusted as I arrived in Syracuse. "All right, God, I guess there's no deal."

I pulled into the lot of Raulli & Sons, Inc., a steel fabricating and erecting company in Syracuse. Raulli is my favorite safety client, and, like any good relationship, ours is based on friendship and trust. My first stop is always at Raulli's main office, where I spend a few minutes talking with Debby, Jeannette, and Emma. They are the purchasing, billing, and receptionist departments, all rolled into one, and they always need to see each and every picture of my children. They had called me when Jake went into the hospital, and not a day went by that I didn't hear from someone at their office. Still, I was absolutely dreading seeing them this morning. I hadn't seen the rainbow, after all, and my attitude adjustment hadn't gone too well.

As soon as I walked in, everyone in the office surrounded me. I told the story of Jake's care quickly, feeling a pain in my chest as I related how tough the next week was going to be.

"Don't worry about servicing us during this," Tom Raulli said. "Your family is the most important thing. Take care of your boy."

Instantly, I felt extremely grateful. Just then the company safety coordinator, Dave Nichols, entered the office. Dave has five kids of his own. He looked at me sympathetically for a moment, but then he smiled. "Jake is going to be fine," Dave said "I just know he will."

I gathered up my notebook and hardhat. "Are we ready to hit the jobsite?" I asked.

Dave drove out to a job about thirty miles south of Syracuse. We spent over an hour on the job, and as we headed back to the truck for our return trip to Syracuse, Dave pointed toward the sky. "What the hell? It hasn't been raining."

I looked up and saw a magnificent rainbow arching across the horizon in all its glory. I'm sure that if I had tried to speak I would have sobbed all over that truck. Instead, I fixed my eyes on the sky like a madman. I didn't hear a word that Dave had to say about the job that we just visited.

As I continued to work, I couldn't get the image of the rainbow out of my mind. I kept thinking back to the crude demands that I had been making of God. So far, every demand had been met. I checked into a hotel, and I couldn't wait to call Kathy. She answered on the first ring, and I heard the boys squealing with delight as they played in the background. I told her the entire rainbow story. She was every bit as excited as I had been. "You got a letter from your friend, Al DeCarlo," she said. "He sent a great story. I'll read it to you, but first Jake wants to say hello."

"Hey, Dad," Jake said. "I'm kissing your wife!"

The sound of his laughter picked up my mood one hundredfold. I tried to yell at him, but he was off the line, laughing happily over his ability to freely kiss Kathy.

"Listen to this," Kathy said, and began reading.

All for the Good

In India there once lived a Maharajah with vast wealth and servants to serve him. It came to pass one day as the Maharajah was walking through his palace that he was approached by one of his servants. "Maharajah, I'm sorry, but I bring bad news. One of your favorite vases has been broken and lies in pieces on the floor."

Infuriated, the Maharajah scolded him and said, "You failed in the job I gave you. You are banned to the dungeon!" The Maharajah's head servant was with him at the time and responded to the situation by saying, "But, master, this is all for the good." Hearing this the Maharajah shook his head and replied, "You don't know, go away."

Some time passed. The Maharajah was admiring his beautiful garden when another servant interrupted him. "Maharajah, I apologize, but I bring bad news: your favorite camel has died."

"What?" shouted the Maharajah. "You are responsible for this and shall be banned to the dungeon!" Again the head servant said, "But, Master, you don't understand. This is all for the good." Very agitated the Maharajah responded, "You better watch out because if you say that one more time I'll ban you to the dungeon too."

Days later the Maharajah was attending to his favorite hobby of carving. As he carved away, the Maharajah's mind wandered to other things, and in taking his eyes off his work, he severed his right thumb. The Maharajah immediately screamed in shock and agony as his servants ran every which-way in panic to try and figure out what to do. They knew that the Maharajah would blame someone. In the chaos the Maharajah received a cloth and began to apply pressure to the wound. It was at this time the head servant calmly approached the Maharajah claiming, "Master, this is all for the good." Outraged, the Maharajah cried out, "That is enough. I warned you, but now you are banned to the dungeon forever!"

One year passed and found the servant still in the dungeon, while the Maharajah was on a caravan. One evening the caravan was suddenly attacked and captured by an enemy tribe. That night during a ceremony, the captives were to be offered as sacrifices. When it was time for the Maharajah to be offered, at the last moment the Head Tribesman stopped the ceremony and asked to see the Maharajah's hands. The Maharajah showed him his hands while the Tribesmen studied him. Noticing the missing thumb he said, "Imperfect sacrifice. Release him," and the Maharajah was set free.

Immediately upon his return, he had the head servant cleaned up and brought to him. Ashamed and guilt stricken by what he had done, he told the servant of his experience and said to him, "How can you forgive me? You saw something that I never saw. You tried to impart wisdom in my life in saying things work for good, and I punished you wrongly. Name it and anything in my kingdom shall be yours."

Pleased with his offer, the Maharajah waited for a response. "No, Master, that is okay. I am satisfied with everything I have. Besides it was all for the good."

Perplexed by his servant's answer the Maharajah continued, "I unjustly ban you to the dungeon for a year, and you say it's all for the good? How can that be good? I don't understand!"

"Master," said the servant, "If you did not send me to the dungeon, I would have been on that caravan with you. Look at my hands." Curiously the Maharajah looked at his servant's hands. "Don't you see? I have all my fingers. I am the perfect sacrifice. It was all for the good."

The story stuck in my head all through the night. I spoke with Kathy and the boys three more times on the telephone, and slowly but surely, I felt some of the negative thoughts escaping me. I had asked God to send me a sign that Jake would be okay, and I had been answered in spades. The companionship offered by Raulli & Sons, the story sent along by a wonderful friend, and a rainbow as bright as day in a sky that had been mocking me all day.

I turned off the television, lay on the bed, and tried to make sense of everything that had happened in the last couple of weeks. I heard a train whistle in the distance and a couple of voices out in the hallway, but more than anything else, I was completely alone with my thoughts.

"God, I know there's a reason for this, and I might never know what it is, but maybe it is all for the good. Maybe there is something I truly need to learn." The words to Jake's prayer stuck in my head, and I whispered them at eight-thirty, the same time that I imagined Jake saying them at home. *God Bless Mommy and Daddy, Matt, Jake, and Sam, Max, Shadow and Nobody, Grandma and Grandpa Foutz, Grandma Spiffy and Poppa John, aunts, uncles, and cousins. Make me be a good boy, God. Amen.*

I said the rosary as I drifted toward sleep. The sound of Jake's laughter, as he kissed Kathy, was still ringing in my ears. "Thank you, God," I whispered.

Chapter Eleven

Friday — October 26, 2001

I spent the early morning hours in the hotel room reading about The Children's Hospital of Buffalo. When I stumbled across a mission statement from 1999, I felt a powerful sense of respect stirring in my heart.

Children's Hospital serves as a center of excellence for pediatric and maternal health-care. Children's Hospital promotes and advances the health and well-being of infants, children, adolescents, and their families. Children's Hospital provides the full spectrum of primary and specialty pediatric services, health education, outreach programs, and pre-natal and preventative care. Children's Hospital provides a superior base for education of the next generation of pediatric and obstetric care providers, educators, and researchers. Children's Hospital advances the knowledge of children's health, the diseases that affect them, and the means by which children's health can be improved. The Children's Hospital of Buffalo maintains an ongoing commitment to caring for children and women regardless of the severity of the illness or injury or their ability to pay.

I sighed in admiration. The talented men and women at Children's weren't just working for a paycheck. Their work wasn't performed with one eye on the clock or for the love and appreciation of the masses. I'm certain that most of the professionals working on Jake wouldn't have cared about doing an interview about their performances. The sole mission of the organization was to put forth the best care in the world. Kathy and I were lucky in one respect; Jake was stricken with this affliction in Buffalo, and The Children's Hospital was ready for him.

I spent the day in Syracuse, but time seemed to be standing still. Dave Nichols arranged a lunch date with two good friends, Donna Haley and Scott Schrilla. The four of us met at a chain restaurant on the east side of Syracuse, and it soon became apparent just why the lunch had been arranged. Dave and Scott sprinkled their concern for Jake with just enough humor to make me wonder if it was okay to laugh. Donna shared an appreciation for life by telling stories about her children and constantly smiling. During that lunch hour I remembered what it felt like to laugh.

"The best part of this," Donna said, "is that, after it's over, you're going to see life in a whole new light. Everything you appreciate now, as you think about what you could lose, should stay with you forever. When this is over, life is going to be better than you could have ever imagined."

I wasn't sure if what she was saying were true, but it helped to know Donna's husband had been critically ill and had made a complete recovery. "Faith is a magical thing," Donna said. "Just have the faith, and you'll reap the benefits."

I can't even remember what I ate, but that was one of the best lunches of my life. I walked out of the restaurant feeling uplifted and inspired, and I shook hands with each of my friends, knowing that oftentimes I felt rushed by life. It occurred to me that one of the greatest lessons to come of Jake's illness was that I wasn't going to take my friendships for granted anymore.

I started the drive home in the middle of the afternoon. I was still trying to improve my attitude, so I turned the radio down and said the rosary aloud. I asked God to fill my heart with the faith that Donna had spoken about, but I was more than a little doubtful that I was worthy of that faith. My cell phone rang, and I noticed my home telephone number on the display.

"His hair is falling out," Kathy whispered.

"Damn!" My heart sank a little more. I hadn't expected to hear that. I knew losing his hair was a possibility, but in my heart I believed that God had spared us that particular pain. "How much?"

"It's coming out in clumps," Kathy said, "and he's not taking it very well."

"Put him on the phone," I said.

"He's in his room crying," Kathy said. "It's freaking me out, too."

I thought back to the cut sheets on the chemo medicine. The hair loss was the least critical of all of the potential problems, but demoralizing nonetheless. "Will it all fall out?"

"It looks that way," Kathy said. "I hope you got him a present."

"I can pick something up," I said.

I heard Jake's voice in the background, a loud agonized shriek that made me swallow hard.

"I'll be there soon," I said. "Tell him I'll shave my hair tonight if that'll make him feel better."

"I'll get the clippers ready," Kathy said grimly. "I'm willing to try anything."

Kathy clicked off the line, and I fingered the rosary. The more anxious I became, the faster I prayed. "Come on, God, give me the faith. Be in my mind, on my lips, and in my heart. I have a boy with his hair falling out. If faith is in me now, bring it out. Please!"

I covered the one hundred fifty miles in a little over two hours. At Toys-R-Us I grabbed the biggest Power Ranger I could find, planted a smile on my face, and headed for the check-out line. A girl about seven years old was standing directly in front of me, holding tightly to her mother's leg. The girl looked at the Power Ranger I was holding and smiled brightly. "I love the Power Rangers," she said.

I held the action figure out so she could inspect it. "The Red Ranger is my son's favorite."

"I like the pink one. I got a new Power Ranger doll because I got an A on my spelling test."

The girl's mother smiled and glanced at me with pride in her eyes. "She's going to get a lot of mileage out of her good grades."

"That's how it should be," I said.

I was at least a little jealous of that perfectly healthy child and her beaming mother. I stepped up in line, and the clerk spent three long minutes trying to scan the package. "Do you know how much this is?" she asked.

I shrugged, and the girl groaned as if I was the reason why the toy didn't have a price tag on it. She made a hurried announcement over the loudspeaker, and a couple of minutes later, a young kid rushed to the front of the store. The impatient girl handed him the Power Ranger, and he headed back toward the Power Ranger display.

I wondered how bad Jake's hair really looked. Perhaps Kathy had exaggerated. Maybe it was just a few strands that had fallen out.

"This sucks," the girl muttered under her breath.

I wanted to tell her to just slow down and not worry about it, and suddenly it occurred to me that I wasn't feeling anxious. The telephone beside her cash register rang, and she picked it up quickly. She punched in the price, $19.99, before even hanging up the phone. She tossed the Red Ranger in the bag and sort of pushed the bag toward my hand.

I knew that she had no way of knowing that I was buying the toy for a sick child. "Try to have a good night," I said.

"Yeah, fat chance," she answered.

I drove the final mile toward home with tears running down my cheeks. I couldn't understand how Jake, a mere child, was expected to be tough enough to battle through this illness. It just didn't seem fair. I didn't know why any of us lived life in a rush. Why couldn't that cashier have smiled at me? Was that too much to ask?

I pulled slowly into the driveway, taking a couple of deep breaths as I angled the truck into my usual parking spot. A couple of the kids' toys had been left out in the side yard, and on a normal day, that would have driven me crazy. Tonight, I was willing to let it go.

I turned the door knob and took another deep gasp for air before entering the house. "Hello!" I shouted, but no one answered, except the dogs, who came running. The television was blaring, and I immediately recognized Tom Brokaw's voice intoning about the anthrax scare. I quickly searched the kitchen and living room, but there was no one around. It suddenly occurred to me that maybe Kathy had to rush Jake to the hospital. I practically jumped over the protective child gate, running toward the back bedrooms with the Power Ranger clutched to my chest. I felt a truly odd mix of panic and control, knowing the scales could tip one way or another in a hurry.

I entered Jake's room, and immediately a wave of relief surged through my heart and mind. There were three lumps under the covers of Jake's bed. Kathy was standing in the corner of the room, trying to stifle a laugh. Her eyes were red, though, and I knew that she was feeling anything but playful. I smiled, but she shook her head as if to say that the hair loss was unbelievably traumatic.

"Now, where did everyone go?" I shouted.

Just then, the covers went flying off the bed and onto the floor as everyone screamed, "Boo!"

I jumped back screaming, and the boys were in a full-fledged laughing fit. As my gaze settled on Jake's head, my terror became real. His hair was an absolute mess, and I couldn't keep my gaze from going to it. The hair at the center of his head was completely gone. Clumps of hair on the sides made it look as if he'd received a bad haircut from a drunken barber.

"I'm going bald, like you!" Jake screamed.

I ran across the room and scooped him up in my arms. I wasn't sure what Kathy had done to change his mood, but for a moment, he seemed all right with his new looks. I ran a hand through my thinning hair. "You have a lot more hair than I do."

"Yeah, and Mom said that if my hair falls out, it'll grow back. Yours isn't ever growing back."

"I want my hair to grow back too," I said. I grabbed him around the waist and pulled him close. I kissed him so many times that he started punching me in an effort to get away.

"I brought you a present," I said.

His eyes grew wide. He rubbed his right hand through his hair and another few strands floated to the floor. "Did you get Matt and Sammy presents too?" he asked.

I glanced at Kathy, and she smiled. Here he was, his hair was falling out, mere seconds away from another present, and he was thinking about his brothers.

"No, but I'll take them out to get something," I said. I looked at Matt. He shrugged his shoulders as if he understood why just Jake was getting a present. Sam was too young to be concerned with any of it.

Jake considered this compromise for a moment. I wasn't sure if he was going to find it acceptable, but he turned it over and over in his mind. "Maybe just I should get a present," he said. "They didn't lose their hair. I hope it's a Power Ranger!" Jake cried.

I pumped my hand in celebration. I had picked right! I handed Jake the Power Ranger action figure with Donna's words still ringing in my ears. When this was over, we were going to have a life that was better than anything we had imagined. I pulled Kathy close and kissed her quickly. "Good job," I whispered.

"Thanks," she said, her voice trembling. She opened her arms to me, and I stepped in and hugged her tightly.

Saturday — October 27, 2001

I opened my eyes at six-fifteen in the morning, and I immediately closed them again in prayer. Jake's hair loss sent me headlong into thoughts of cancer, and I was simply scared out of my mind. I have no idea how people stricken with cancer battle through the day-to-day treatment of the disease. Millions of people across this land have heard the awful news that cancer has invaded their bodies. I'm not sure if there is a lonelier battle that can possibly be fought. In many cases, cancer results in suffering and death, and although there have been wonderful advancements made, it is still a horrible predicament.

I struggled out of bed and down the stairs, and within an hour, Kathy, Matt, Jake, and Sam all woke up. Jake came out into the kitchen dragging his blanket behind him, and the sight of my partially bald son was absolutely heartbreaking. Kathy's face was a picture of despair.

"Good morning, buddy," I said to Jake.

His left hand went to the top of his head, and a few more strands of hair drifted to his shoulder and down to the floor. "I hate losing my hair!" he cried.

I motioned for him to join me at the kitchen table, but he shook me off and ran down the hall toward his bedroom.

"I can give him one of my Yankee hats," Matt offered.

"That's a good idea," I said.

Matt headed to his bedroom, and a moment later he emerged with a Yankee hat from the last World Series. "Here, Jake," Matt said.

"Get out! I don't want it!" Jake screamed.

I glanced across the table at Kathy. She thumbed through the dictionary in an effort to find a word to fill her latest crossword puzzle. It was beginning to seem like the more frantic things were around the house, the more engrossed in the puzzle she became. "I still can't even get close to finishing one of these," she whispered.

Matt returned with the Yankee cap. He handed it to me. "Maybe you can get him to take it."

"Thanks for trying, Matt, that was very nice."

I traced my finger along the interlocking NY on the cap. It had been so long since the Yankees were my first thought of the day. "Hey," I said to Kathy, "Do you think there's a Power Ranger hat out there anywhere?"

Kathy didn't even look up from the puzzle. "I'll call my mother, maybe she can look for one."

Later in the morning, I sat in the kitchen chair and Kathy ran the clippers through my hair. Jake watched from afar, but having a partner in baldness didn't do anything to cheer him up. I left just enough hair on my head to cover my scalp, but my appearance was the least of my worries. I couldn't get a simple question out of my mind. Why was God allowing this to happen?

I headed for the grocery store, knowing that the wonderful thoughts of faith that had controlled me yesterday were completely missing from my heart. Maybe a better man than me would be able to handle a child's illness without questioning God's plan, but despair just kept bubbling to the surface. I couldn't shake the idea that God and I would be fighting for the rest of my life if this didn't work out right.

I stood in line at the store. The woman in front of me screamed at her child for at least five solid minutes. The boy, who was no older than six or seven, was clamoring for a candy bar, and the mother was answering his cries with loud screams of reprimand. The kid told her that he hated her, and she stooped even lower. "Then I hate you too," she said.

The kid was bashing his head off the side of the grocery cart. The mother glanced at me, and she must have read the look of disbelief in my eyes because she dropped her head in shame. The last thing in the world that the kid deserved was a candy bar, but maybe his mother had gone too far. I wanted to explain what was happening with my boy. I almost told her to enjoy every moment of the catastrophe of child rearing, but it wasn't any of my business. Mother and son battled through the checkout procedure, across the front of the store, and out the door.

"That kid is tough," the young cashier said as I stepped into my place in front of her.

"I have three boys," I said. "Some days are better than others. Some times it feels really good to get out to the grocery store for an hour or so, and some times I miss them badly."

It was probably way more than the acne-faced girl wanted to hear, and she actually grunted as though that was an acceptable answer. To be honest, I don't know what I expected her to say. She finished tallying up my order. "Thank you," I whispered.

I arrived home and put the groceries away just moments before the nurse stopped over. I greeted Terri at the door as Kathy broke the news to Jake about his bandage change.

"Get her out of here!" Jake screamed. "I hate that stupid lady!"

I cringed at his angry words, but Terri smiled right through the tirade. "I'll calm him down."

"He lost his hair," I said. "He's not doing so well today. In fact, none of us are."

"I'm sorry," Terri whispered. "Let's go in there real enthusiastic. Maybe we can turn his mood around."

I followed Terri into the back bedroom. Kathy had her arm around Jake's right shoulder. They were sitting on Jake's bed, and as Kathy whispered into Jake's ear, he couldn't stop a smile from creeping across his face. He looked Terri straight in the eye and said, "I'm ready to get my bandage changed. Just don't rip the tape off real fast."

Kathy smiled, and I looked at her in utter amazement. "How did you settle him down?"

"I told him you'd buy him another present," Kathy said.

I started laughing. "The hospital bills aren't going to be the problem. The bill for Jake's presents is going to put us in the poor house."

After Terri left, Kathy spent a few minutes getting Sam and Jake prepared for their afternoon nap. There was a soft knock on the front door, and I opened it, wondering who was attempting to spoil nap time. It was the mailman, who handed me a package and the rest of my mail. The package was another gift from Yvonne and Tony Conza, and there were at least three cards addressed to Jake. As I opened a card from one of our neighbors, a typed letter slipped from my hand and drifted toward the floor.

A Father's Prayer

Dear God, my little boy of three, he said his nightly prayer to Thee.
Before his eyes were closed in sleep, he asked that Thou his soul would keep.
And I, still kneeling at his bed, my hand upon his tousled head,
Do ask with deep humility, that Thou, Dear Lord, remember me.
Make me kind, Lord, a worthy dad, that I may lead this little lad.
In pathways ever fair and bright, that I may keep his steps aright.
O God, his trust must never be destroyed or marred by me.
So for the simple things he prayed with childish voice, so unafraid —
I, trembling, ask the same from Thee,
Dear Lord, Kind Lord, remember me.
— Author Unknown —

I was still considering the letter when my mother-in-law stepped through the door. She was holding a knit cap with a Power Rangers emblem on the front and a baseball cap decorated with the image of the Red Ranger.

"Where did you find those?" I asked. It felt as if my heart did a little leap in my chest.

"I went to a couple of stores," Carolyn said. "Actually, I took the emblem off another knit cap and sewed it onto the plain baseball cap."

"You sewed it on this morning?" I asked.

There were tears glistening in her eyes. I hoped that she didn't see that I was about to start sobbing. I imagined her with needle and thread, all morning long, tears rolling down her face.

"I feel so bad for him," she said.

I led the way up the stairs. Jake was lying on his bed, and it was evident that his mood hadn't improved much. His hair was almost completely gone, and he wasn't about to let Kathy try to straighten out what was left. Carolyn showed him the baseball cap, and his eyes brightened immediately. Where was God? The short answer is that God was guiding Carolyn's hand as she stitched the emblem on Jake's new hat.

After dinner, Kathy practically pushed me out the front door. The Yankees and Diamondbacks were meeting for game one of the World Series, and Kathy had decided that I needed to be away for a little while. My brother Jeff invited me over to watch the game and have a couple of beers, and I begrudgingly accepted the invitation.

"You can't just sit in the house trying to protect the boys," Kathy said. "Relax a little."

I stopped at the store and picked up a twelve pack of beer and a couple of bags of chips. I was wearing my blue baseball cap with the white NY on the front. The cashier at the store had checked out my groceries a hundred times over the past year. She was well aware of my affection for the Yankees.

"You probably haven't slept in days," she said. "Geez, the Yankees are only in the World Series but once a year." She laughed, and I laughed along with her. I didn't have the heart to tell her that this year it was completely different.

The Yankees were soundly trashed in that first game. I sipped a few beers and spent the night talking to my brother. Jeff was fairly confident that everything would work out just fine. As it became apparent that it wasn't New York's night, we talked about Jake for a few moments.

"I don't know how you and Kathy are handling having a sick child," Jeff said. Jeff's wife Lynn was seven months pregnant with their first child. "I'm praying so hard for a healthy baby, and here you are, with a seemingly healthy boy, fighting for his life."

"Are you trying to cheer me up?" I asked.

"I'm sorry," Jeff said. "I just don't know what the right thing to say is."

"Me neither," I said. "I don't even feel like I'm alive right now. This has got to be what purgatory is like. I don't know if I'm going up or down."

"Yeah, but what do you believe?" Jeff asked.

I knew it was a rhetorical question. Jeff was trying to get me to acknowledge my faith.

"This is the last time I watch a game over here," I said.

"Do you actually think the Yanks will lose the series?" Jeff asked. "They believe that they'll win, and that's why they do."

I understood his analogy but I was too tired to entertain it any longer. "You're reaching. Thanks for having me over. Maybe we can watch Game Two at my house."

Jeff followed me to the front door. "Hang in there," he said. "You watch, Jake will be fine and the Yanks will win the series."

As I drove home, I kept reminding myself that the Yankees were only playing a game. It truly didn't matter if they lost, but for some reason, on a day when Jake was adjusting to his sudden hair loss, the Yankees had performed very badly. Every time that Jake had a bad day, the Yanks had a worse one. It was maddening.

Sunday — October 28, 2001

In the morning, Kathy and I worked together to get the children settled so that we could spend a few moments drinking coffee at the kitchen table. Kathy poured the coffee, and I grabbed the Sunday paper. As I scanned the sports page, Kathy got her first look at the headlines, and ultimately, the crossword puzzle.

"Still not finishing the puzzle?" I teased.

"Are you still dreaming about Frosty?"

We both laughed. Our minds were playing tricks on us that just weren't funny.

"What are your thoughts about Halloween?" Kathy asked.

"I don't have any," I said, and I wouldn't have even given Halloween a second thought, but I suppose that is why God created mothers. Kathy had marked the biopsy on the calendar as though she were noting one of Matthew's hockey games. I hadn't even noticed that it fell on the 31st.

"He can't go trick or treating the night of the biopsy. In fact, Doctor Levitt said they need to keep him overnight. Maybe we can take him out on the night before, on Tuesday. I can walk through the neighborhood and explain the situation."

"Whatever," I said.

"He's really looking forward to wearing his *Scream* mask costume."

"It's a good idea if you feel comfortable talking to all of the neighbors," I said. "Everyone in the neighborhood understands that Jake is sick, so there probably won't be a lot of resistance."

"I just can't see asking Jake to give up Halloween," Kathy said. I was getting used to seeing the tears in her eyes, but that didn't make it any easier on me.

After breakfast, I tossed a ball with the boys as Kathy canvassed the neighborhood. She made the trip up and down our street, receiving a lot of hugs, dedication of prayers, and a solemn promise to make it the best Halloween ever. Jake's best friends in the neighborhood, Colt and Savannah, promised to go along with him. Jake's other buddies, Brett and Bradley, followed Kathy home and presented Jake with a huge rescue hero's action figure. Jake played with the present until it was time for all of us to go to church.

It was difficult to concentrate on the mass with three boys squirming beside me and horrible thoughts circling my brain. I had memorized the father's prayer, and I said it time and again. On the way home, Matthew asked about Jake's hair loss.

"That happens with the medicine," Kathy said. "It'll grow back."

"You aren't going to let him go to pre-school looking like that, are you?" Matt asked. "The kids will laugh at him."

"He'll be okay," I said. I was a little hurt that Matt was embarrassed by all of this. I wanted to tell him that it didn't matter if Jake looked strange for a while. All that really mattered was that Jake was healthy. It pained me to think that Matt was being selfish about it, but what could I say?

"If someone laughed at my brother, I'd have to punch them," Matthew said.

I felt a smile work its way across my face. I didn't want Matt punching anyone, but the idea that he'd protect Jake was enough to make me proud.

"It's going to be fine," Kathy said. "You won't have to punch anyone."

That afternoon, as Jake played with Matt and Sam, he seemed to be pretty much over the loss of his hair. Whoever first mentioned that kids bounce back fast from disaster was right on the money. While an adult might dwell on misfortune for years, a child is usually able to process it all fairly quickly and move on.

As I tucked Jake into bed for his midday nap, he addressed the issue once more. "We're both bald, right, Dad?" Jake asked.

"Yeah, but yours will grow back," I said.

"It's not bad being bald, is it?" Jake asked.

"Nah. You know what my grandpa used to say?"

Jake rubbed his hand across his bare scalp, shrugged and smiled.

"My grandpa's name was Clifford," I said, "and he was bald too. Whenever someone said something about it, he'd tell them, 'You can't have hair and brains too.'"

Jake thought it was a great line, and he promised to try it out on Matthew right after nap. I kissed him on the top of his mostly bald head, and he closed his eyes with a huge smile adorning his face.

I headed to the kitchen to start the sauce. I cut up the garlic and onions, thinking of my Grandpa Clifford Schryver. It had been years since my grandfather's death, but I still thought of him quite often. As I prepared the sauce, my mind floated back to the days of my youth, and my earliest contemplations of death.

As a teenager without a driver's license, I often walked the neighborhood with my friends, Tom Rybak, Dave Lauber, and Jeff Renaldo. My brother John was usually with us too, so we formed quite a pack. My parents' home was about a mile from the village of North Collins, and sometimes we'd cut the walk short by heading into the woods behind Dave's house and walking up to the railroad tracks. If I was walking with Jeff Renaldo I would meet him in the cemetery at the end of Shirley Road, and we'd head to the tracks from there.

Being a teenager is a real dicey proposition, but it is the time when a lot of back philosophies are formed. I can remember that it was a beautiful day in '81. I was waiting in the cemetery for Jeff, and for some reason my eye caught the markings on a headstone. The man's name was Peter Randazzo, and he had walked the earth from 1891 through 1944. Under the dates inscribed for his birth and death were the words, *To a great husband and father — He will be sorely missed.*

I didn't say anything to Jeff about it that day, and to be honest, I never mentioned it to anyone. But I spent a lot of time thinking about Peter Randazzo and the family he left behind. Around the same time, there was another man who walked the village streets. I never knew his name, but I knew that he had a wife and a few children. His days were spent with a whiskey bottle, and word on the street was that he had completely lost his mind. Considering Peter Randazzo and the village drunk, I came to the conclusion that we're given one shot at life and how we live it goes a long way to how we'll be remembered.

I wonder if Peter Randazzo is still missed some fifty-seven years after his death. It didn't hit me at all at the age of sixteen, but Peter Randazzo's gravesite became sort of a hangout for me as I waited for Jeff to walk with me. I didn't try to imagine the man's life, but once in awhile I would pick the weeds and mention that he hadn't been forgotten. As I think back on it some twenty years later, I realize that I was just trying to make sense of the sweeping curve of life. Gazing into the mystery of life through the eyes of a teenager is troublesome at best, but as an adult with three children living under my roof, I am not sure I understand life or death any better. Thoughts of my grandfather, years after his death, lent me an understanding of sorts. Clifford Schryver was still sorely missed as a husband and a father. Maybe somehow, through stories passed down from generation to generation, Peter Randazzo is still missed by someone. Maybe that is all we can really hope for. On that Sunday, a little more than a week away from Jake's operation, I knew that I would never truly grasp the full meaning of my grandfather's life.

That night, Kathy and I put the children to bed and settled in front of the television to watch the Yankees play Arizona. Neither one of us vocalized it, but we were expecting the Yankees to play well. I wasn't sure if Kathy felt as strongly as I did about the connection between the Yankees success and Jake's ability to overcome the illness, but my hopes were quickly dashed. Arizona jumped out to a lead and held on through the late innings. As the game ended, the telephone rang.

"Are you worried?" my brother Jeff asked.

"Not about the Yankees," I answered.

"It's going to be fine," Jeff said. I don't think he was talking about the Yankees either.

Chapter Twelve

Monday — October 29, 2001

My first thought of the day was centered on the idea that the time was finally at hand. We had an early morning appointment for the CT-scan that would tell us, once and for all, if the chemo had shrunk the tumor. We spent most of the morning trying to convince Jake that going to the hospital wasn't a big deal and he put on a brave face for awhile. He watched cartoons in his room, and Kathy sat beside me as we choked down a couple of cups of coffee.

"I still don't know what I'm rooting for," Kathy said. "It must have shrunk a little, huh?"

"I don't know," I said. "Is it possible that he had an infection and that whatever medicine they gave him with the chemo cleared it up?"

"I was thinking that," Kathy said. "He might have got an antibiotic. I guess we'll find out." Kathy didn't look tired. In fact, I was amazed at how well she had held up. Every task in her life was centered on the children. She nurtured them every step of the way, and she would have been the first to proclaim that Jake's illness was her worst nightmare come true. "So, we're rooting against it shrinking, right?" she asked.

"I am. I don't want him to have to deal with cancer. I want the doctors at Children's to take it out and throw it in the garbage. I want it to be over now." I crossed the kitchen and poured the last of the coffee into the sink and watched it circle the drain.

"We have about ten minutes before we have to leave for the hospital," Kathy said. "Mom's coming for Sam. Have the dogs been fed?"

I placed my coffee cup in the dishwasher. Kathy came up behind me and tapped me lightly on the shoulder. I hugged her tightly. We didn't have to talk about it anymore to realize that the results of the CT-scan could change our lives forever.

When we broke the embrace I headed to the basement to take care of Max and Shadow. I had fed the dogs, but all at once I remembered Max's medicine. I let the dogs in, and they jumped on me. I grabbed hold of Max's paw. He had a few more days of medication left, but it was hard to tell that he'd ever been hurting. His paw was completely healed. I grabbed him and kissed him on the head. "Thanks for getting better, Max." He must have thought I was out of my mind.

Kathy helped Jake into the backseat of the truck. I slipped in behind the steering wheel, and I traveled the skyway into downtown Buffalo, listening to Jake and Kathy's conversation. The workday was just getting underway, and there were people lined up at every corner, waiting for the light to cross. I edged my way down Delaware Avenue.

"I don't have to stay overnight?" Jake asked.

"Nope," Kathy said. "They'll take a couple of pictures, and then we're going right home."

"They don't have to do a blood test?" Jake asked.

"Nope, just a couple of pictures," I said as I turned left into the parking ramp on Hodge Street just across from the hospital.

"I get to go home for a lot of days?"

"We have to come back soon," Kathy said.

Jake groaned, and I groaned right along with him. I left Kathy and Jake off at the emergency room door, and I slowed down to take a ticket before driving up the parking ramp. The words to a prayer my sister Carrie sent along entered my brain, and I rushed through them as I parked.

Heavenly Father

In the name of God, I call on you right now in a special way. I know, Father, that it is through your power that Jacob was created. Every breath he takes, every morning he wakes, and every moment of every hour, he lives under your power. Father, I pray now that you will reach down from the heavens and give Jake a touch of that same power. For if you created him from nothing, Dear Lord, you can certainly recreate him. Dear God, please fill Jake with the healing power of your spirit. I pray, Dear God, that you will remove the tumor that has invaded Jake's body. Rid him of any inflammation and cleanse any infection. Lord, from the top of his head to the tips of his toes, cast out anything that should not be in him. Mend what is broken. Please, Lord, root out every diseased and unproductive cell. Open any blocked artery or vein, and rebuild every damaged area. Almighty God, let the warmth of your healing love pass through Jake's body and make new every unhealthy area so that his body will function the way that you created it to function. God, restore Jake to full health in mind and body so that he may serve you the rest of his life. I ask this through God. Amen.

By the time I finished the prayer I had met Jake and Kathy in the X-ray room. We were just hours away from knowing if the tumor had shrunk or not.

I was quite aware of what my role would be during the CT-scan. Kathy grabbed Jake's hand as he sat on the table, and I stood directly in front of him, distracting him with funny faces. Fortunately, the technicians assigned to Jake's case were familiar and well-schooled in his potential to have a tantrum. It probably didn't vary much from child to child, but that was the beauty of The Children's Hospital of Buffalo. I couldn't imagine the trouble we'd have been in had Jake's care been in the hands of professionals used to dealing only with adult patients.

"We have a whole bowl full of lollipops," the technician said. "All we need to do is take a few pictures, and then you can have all of the lollipops you want."

It wasn't going to be quite as easy as the technician had explained. The biggest problem, of course, was that Jake was going to be stuck with a needle after the first set of pictures because they were going to inject dye for the second set of pictures in order to get a contrast. Of course, Kathy sat on the table, holding Jake tightly and whispering words of encouragement.

I slipped into the room with the computer just a few feet away. I could still see Jake, on the table, through the glass, but I could also see the computer screen where the scanned images were being presented. The nurse in front of the computer flashed a smile that was filled with pity. I wanted to spill my guts to her and explain that Jake was doing wonderfully, but I was sure that she was well aware of the seriousness of his condition. Jake screamed loudly, and I bowed my head, knowing that I did deserve the smile of pity.

They performed the first CT-scan of his chest, and I pretended that I could actually interpret what was on the screen. I knew that I was painfully ill-prepared to read even a simple X-ray, but I did try to read the scan, hoping that somewhere along the line I had picked up such knowledge. Jake was repositioned, and he screamed loudly again as the needle entered his small arm. They attempted to add the dye, but moments later, the nurse whispered something to Kathy.

"What happened?" I asked.

"They have to stick him again," the nurse said. "The first needle stick probably wasn't good."

Jake screamed every bit as loudly, and Kathy spoke harshly to the nurse at the bedside. I sighed heavily as I considered the no-win situation that the nurse was in. Sometimes it was necessary to try to find another vein, but it was impossible to explain this to a child patient or an emotional mother. To be honest, dear old Dad wasn't taking it very well either. I cupped my hands over my ears in an effort to muffle Jake's cries. Yet, in a matter of moments, the ordeal was over. The images on the computer screen changed a few times, and I was clueless as to their meaning. The technician who administered the scan entered the room and stood in front of the computer screen.

"Did it change?" I asked him.

The technician considered the question for a moment. I knew right then and there that he had some idea, but he didn't let on. "They'll read it downstairs."

I hustled back into the room and helped wipe a few of Jake's tears away. There was a basket filled with lollipops on a small table near the door. I grabbed three or four of the red ones to soothe my aching child. I scooped him up to my arms, handed him the lollipop, and headed for the door. He stopped crying almost as soon as the lollipop touched his tongue.

"Did you see anything?" Kathy asked.

I felt completely incompetent again. I shrugged and looked at the floor.

"That's okay; Doctor Levitt will call this afternoon."

"Can we go now?" Jake asked. "I don't have to stay here, do I?"

Finally, I had some good news. I carried him out the door, into the elevator, and across the parking lot. "We're going to the toy store," I whispered. "You can pick out another present."

The handbook that the hospital had given to us during Jake's first visit stated that a parent should try and refrain from buying too many presents so that the child did not become spoiled by their illness. But Kathy and I were more than willing to take a second mortgage if that's what we needed to keep him in presents. We felt that Jake was working really hard to try to get through each of the tasks that were presented to him, and more than anything else, we wanted him to be happy. Neither Kathy nor I felt that we were spoiling Jake. We were trying to make him comfortable, and we've always known that that is our number one job.

After the CT-scan I dropped Kathy and Jake off at home so they could take a well-deserved afternoon nap. Doctor Levitt was due to call with the results in the late afternoon, but I returned to work for a couple of hours so that I wouldn't be just sitting by the telephone waiting for the call. I visited a couple of clients on three different jobsites and actually sat down and wrote reports. I was doing anything to keep my mind off Jake's scan, but I was also building a game plan. I didn't think that the tumor was malignant. Call it blind faith or eternal optimism, but I just didn't think that Jake had cancer. Yet I also believed that the tumor had somehow changed and that Jake would go under the knife and the surgery would cure it. The one thing that was nagging at me was the biopsy. Doctor Levitt had explained that they would do a biopsy before the operation, and I couldn't figure out why were they going to put him under twice. Couldn't they just perform the operation and get it over with? The question haunted me until the late afternoon. I pulled the truck into the driveway and ran into the house.

Kathy, Sam, and Jake were just getting up from their nap.

"Has the doctor called yet?" I asked.

Kathy lit a cigarette, shook her head and looked at the phone. "Should I call them?"

"Give them half an hour," I said. "I'll start dinner. Is there anything you feel like eating?"

"Absolutely nothing," she said.

I headed down to the freezer in the basement. My head was in the freezer, searching for something that I could serve without too much of a hassle. I never heard the telephone ring. When I returned upstairs, Kathy was seated on the couch, holding the telephone to her left ear. The tears in her eyes told me that it wasn't exactly the conversation she was looking for. I listened to her end of it with one ear attuned to Jake and Sam, who were playing in their rooms.

"I don't want to hear that he might die," Kathy said.

I put my arm around her shoulder, and her body quaked under my touch.

"You've done this sort of operation before, right?" Kathy choked out.

I rubbed her shoulders as she listened to Doctor Levitt's answer.

"Did you ever lose a child?" she asked. "No, I understand that."

Kathy looked at me and shook her head. I felt like hot tar was running through my veins. What the hell was he telling her?

"Do you have any questions for the doctor?" she asked me.

I honestly didn't have a coherent thought in my head. I wanted to ask her to confirm the time for the CT-scan and the biopsy, but the words wouldn't come.

"All right, thank you," Kathy said.

"He's done this operation before, right?" I asked.

"About ten times."

I strained for a breath of air. It felt as if I had swallowed something and my own airways were being cut off.

"Has anyone ever died?" I asked.

Kathy was dabbing at tears. She shook her head. "But this is a big one. He told me straight out that Jake could die from the operation."

It was the first time that the words were actually out there for consideration. I should have grabbed hold of Kathy and squeezed her tightly, but neither of us moved. We just stared at one another in utter disbelief. I wasn't sure how to comfort her, and every word of her conversation with Doctor Levitt, was like a dagger.

Sam screamed out, and the sound of his cry cleared my mind a little. I finally went to Kathy, pulling her close. We cried together as Sam's screams became increasingly louder. Kathy sighed heavily and filled me in on the rest of Doctor Levitt's words as we headed down the stairs toward Sam. She lifted Sam into her arms and rocked him softly as she spoke. "Doctor Levitt said that the fact that it didn't shrink is good news and bad news. The good news is that it didn't respond to chemotherapy, meaning that it is most likely benign. The bad news is that it is a very large operation. Doctor Levitt asked me if you and I wanted him to proceed."

"What else would we do?" I asked.

"Exactly. I told him, yes. Doctor Levitt also said that there's no reason to take a biopsy as there has been no change in the size of the tumor despite the chemotherapy. Doctor Levitt told me that there's a chance of nerve and vocal chord damage. There are going to be a team of doctors in the operating room, and they'll put him on a bypass machine should his airways collapse."

Sam was trying to grab Kathy's nose. She continued to rock him on her hip as tears flowed down her face. "The sentence I can't get out of my head is Doctor Levitt explaining that there's a chance Jake might not make it through the operation."

"He'll be all right," I said lamely. I turned away from Kathy's eyes. I didn't want her to see how scared I was.

For the rest of the day, I walked around in a virtual fog. I couldn't help but think that life had always been a challenge. I had attended the funerals of grandparents and dear friends. I had pledged eternal love for Kathy, Matt, Jake, and Sam and I always believed that we could get through anything as a family. Yet Doctor Levitt's words, repeated by my wife, hung in the air, and it was the absolute worst evening of my life. Unfortunately, it was an evening that was about to give way to even more challenging times.

Tuesday — October 30, 2001

I was out of bed and in front of the computer by five-thirty in the morning. I concentrated on the web page devoted to The Children's Hospital of Buffalo, and the more research I did, the more evident it was becoming that we were dealing with a healthcare dynamo.

I studied the web page for a little over an hour, and then I headed to the kitchen to have a cup of coffee with Kathy. She immediately voiced a concern about the surgical team. "They say that the doctors at Children's are the best, but are they?"

"We have to trust someone. I'm not going to work on him. I can't change the oil in my car."

My answer didn't knock her off course, and she barely smiled. "I want the best surgeon in the world. We can borrow money. Let's take him to the very best surgeon."

"I don't know who that is," I said. "It might be Doctor Levitt for all we know. Besides, this is a nationally ranked hospital. We can meet Doctor Levitt before the surgery, right?"

"He offered to see us on Friday afternoon. Do you want to go?"

The look of absolute fear on Kathy's face was enough to rattle my own confidence.

"Yes, we should meet with him. We're entrusting everything to him."

"What about the Cleveland Clinic or Strong Memorial Hospital in Rochester?" Kathy asked.

I didn't know exactly what I was speaking about, but I shook her off. "This hospital is one of the best children's hospitals in the world. I'll look into it a little more, but Jake's in good hands. Wait right here for a minute."

I took the stairs to my bedroom two at a time, and I printed off a cut sheet of information that I had read in the wee hours of the morning.

"Listen to this," I said to Kathy when I returned to the kitchen. She lit another cigarette, took another gulp of coffee and stared at me through tear-stained eyes.

Did you know that The Children's Hospital of Buffalo was established in 1892 as a 12-bed child-care facility? Today The Children's Hospital of Buffalo diagnoses approximately 95% of all children with cancer-related illnesses in Western New York and every year an average of 70 new patients are diagnosed with some form of cancer. Did you know that The Children's Hospital of Buffalo is the only freestanding pediatric and maternal health care facility in New York State; has 313 beds — 174 pediatric, 67 adult OB/GYN and 72 critical care; Serves patients from the eight county regions of Western New York, northeastern PA, eastern Ohio and Ontario, Canada; Provides $1-2 million in unreimbursed healthcare annually; Treats over 28,000 patients in the hospital annually; Sees over 123,000 outpatients in the emergency room or one of the forty-five subspecialty clinics; plays host to over two thousand medical, nursing and allied health students annually; is one of the few hospitals in the country with full service OB/GYN and pediatrics in one specialty hospital.

I was reading quickly, but I had Kathy's complete attention.

Did you know that three thousand infants, the majority of which are high risk, are delivered annually, and the intensive care unit, which they call the Alfiero Family Pediatric Intensive Care Unit, was renovated and expanded in 1995? It holds eighteen beds in the unit to treat 1,000 children each year. They treat the most critically ill and injured infants and adolescents, and they have the ECMO (Extra Corporeal Membrane Oxygenation) unit that allows the heart and lungs of an infant to rest while healing.

Kathy digested the information quickly. I couldn't tell if she was more impressed by the hospital or the fact that I had searched for the information.

"This is the best place for us to be right now," I said. "Let's just focus on bringing Jake to them as healthy as he can possibly be."

"He's not healthy though," Kathy cried.

I hugged her tightly and kissed her on each cheek. "I'm sorry that we're going through this," I said, "but this is the right decision. He has to have the operation and Doctor Levitt will study the case from top to bottom. I know he will."

"We have to pray for Doctor Levitt," Kathy said.

"He won't be the only guy in there. They'll have everyone involved."

"Then I'll pray for everyone," Kathy said.

We parted company to head out to jobs that seemed horribly insignificant. Why was I even going to work with my son's life hanging in the balance? Why were we putting up this tremendous facade when it all might come tumbling down in less than a week?

I drove twenty minutes east toward the main office of Scott Danahy Naylon. Once again, I was surrounded by my co-workers. One of them, Eileen Coleman, greeted me with a worried smile covering her face.

"I don't know if you know this, but my daughter, Kelly, is a cancer survivor. She was treated at Roswell Park. I know what you're going through, but Jake will be fine, you'll see."

"Thank you, I appreciate hearing that," I said. "The thing that's driving me crazy is that we're trusting doctors that we don't even know."

"Don't worry so much," Eileen said. "The doctors at Children's are wonderful people." Eileen touched me lightly on the shoulder. "Remember, they're talented too. Let them do what they feel is right."

I hugged Eileen quickly. She had read my fears and helped me immensely.

I spent the day at a construction site. It was certainly strange, but one of my thoughts throughout the day was that our friends seemed afraid to call. Our parents and siblings were constantly on the line, but our close friends were allowing us to battle through our ordeal without much interference. I was appreciative of their efforts while Jake was in the hospital the first time, but I felt lonely all day. I wished I had someone to talk to about my pain.

I returned home in the late afternoon, knowing that the cancelled biopsy didn't change our plans to go trick-or-treating a day early. Jake greeted me at the door in his Power Ranger costume. "Boo!" he screamed.

I screamed and jumped backwards with my hand over my heart.

"It's only me," Jake said, lifting the mask.

"You scared me!" I said. I grabbed him around the waist and lifted him high above me.

I prepared hot dogs and macaroni and cheese. It was a fast food type of dinner, but the kids were thrilled with the menu and ate quickly. Just as dinner ended, the doorbell rang. I looked quizzically at Kathy.

"That's Colt and Savannah," Kathy said. "They're going trick-or-treating with us."

For the first time in a couple of weeks, Jake was real excited. He jumped around like a normal, healthy child. I followed him toward the front door. "Let me scare them," Jake said.

I opened the door and was greeted by a vampire — Colt — and a witch — Savannah. They both screamed, and Jake screamed back at them. I feigned absolute terror and they all lifted their masks. Colt, who is a couple of years older than Jake, smiled at me. He was missing a couple of teeth. I reached out and rubbed his brush-cut head.

"What's up, Cliffy?" Colt turned toward Jake. "Dude, what happened to your hair?"

Jake started laughing, and he threw a couple of punches at Colt's midsection.

"You look awesome," Colt said. "I want to do my hair like that."

I took a few photos. Suddenly the door sprang open, and Kathy's mom entered. She had watched the children all day, but she had returned for the Halloween festivities.

"You can't stay away from here, can you?" I asked.

"I don't want to," Carolyn said.

The assembly of costumed kids moved to the front door, holding bags for the anticipated candy. I slapped Jake a high-five before he stepped out the door. "I'll bring you some candy, Dad," Jake said.

"Where's Matthew?" I asked Kathy.

"He doesn't want to go," she whispered.

"He should go," I said.

Kathy held a finger to her lips, and I knew that for some reason, Matt was upset. When I stepped into his bedroom, he looked away from me.

"What's up?" I asked.

"I didn't feel like going," Matt said.

I glanced at the cartoon flashing across the television screen. "That's okay," I said. Matthew's room was a mess. There were video game cartridges all over the floor, and his school clothes were rolled in a ball and had been tossed in the general direction of his hamper. Matt was in bed sulking, and he turned back toward the cartoon.

"Will Jake be all right?" Matt asked. I knew that Kathy and Jack had discussed Jake's illness with Matt, but I was getting the feeling that he needed to hear it from me.

"They have to operate," I said, leaning into his bed, just inches from his face. "They're going to cut his chest open and take the tumor out, but Jake thinks they're going to do magic; so just let him think that, okay?"

Matthew sat up. His face contorted with worry. "It sounds easy. They open him up, take it out, and close him up, right?"

"It'll be pretty easy," I said.

Without further warning, Matthew burst into tears. "He's going to die, isn't he?"

"Of course not," I said. "The doctors are smart. They've done this before."

I sat on the bed as Matt battled tears. He looked at me with eyes longing for comfort.

"Thanks for letting Jake have your *Scream* costume from last year," I said.

"I'm glad he likes it," Matt answered.

"You're a good brother," I said.

Matt finally forced a smile. He was wearing a brave mask to hide the pain in his heart.

"Are you going to go trick-or-treating dressed like a cheerleader this year?"

Matt pushed me playfully and I fell off the edge of the bed and rolled on the floor.

"I don't feel like wearing a costume this year," Matt said.

I rolled onto my back and looked up at him. "It's okay to be worried about Jake," I said. "But he's going to be just fine."

"I know," Matt said. He rubbed away the tears. "I'm going to pray for him."

"That's a good idea," I said. "That is exactly what a good brother has to do."

The trick-or-treating lasted a little over an hour, and Kathy returned with the costumed brood and buckets filled with candy. Jake sat at the kitchen table, flanked by his two brothers, and he shared the candy bars and lollipops. It had been a truly happy day for him, and it clicked in my mind that a good day for Jake usually meant a good night for the Yankees.

Kathy tucked the boys into bed. I watched the pre-game show and then headed to the boys' bedrooms to say good-night. I went to Matt's room first. "How are you doing, pal?"

"Better," Matt said. "Did the baseball game start yet?"

"In a couple of minutes," I said.

Matt turned away from me toward the wall. "Don't worry. The Yankees will win."

"They have to win tonight, or they're in trouble."

I headed to the door, and Jake's bedroom. Matt's voice pierced the darkness. "If Arizona wins, it isn't the end of the world. Nobody wins all the time."

I couldn't help it. I carried that statement with me all through the night. After kissing Jake good-night and listening to his prayers, I settled in, with Kathy at my right side, and watched the Yankees take an early lead and then hang on for dear life.

──────Chapter Thirteen──────

Wednesday — October 31, 2001

I am blessed. I've always felt a strong connection with my family, and I have developed lifelong friendships that have sustained me for years. Better yet, every time I've needed a swift kick in the pants there has been someone whom I least suspected right behind me with a poised foot.

Take Mary Flanigen, for example. Over the course of the last two years, I worked out of The Gateway Building on Route 5 just outside of Buffalo. The receptionist, Mary, became a great friend, and we have discussed everything from the death penalty to changing my children's diapers. Six months ago, my company moved out of the building, but I still swung by the desk to shoot the breeze with Mary, who has a heart of gold.

I woke up thinking about Mary, and I decided I would pay her an early morning visit. Before leaving the house, I looked in on Jake. He was still sleeping, but I said a prayer as I watched him sleep. It was almost as if I couldn't stop praying, but the prayers weren't easing my mind. I closed his bedroom door, feeling miserable. I left the house at a little after seven. I had a few jobsites to visit, but I pictured Mary in my mind. I knew that her eyes would fill with tears as I broke the news of Jake's tumor, and I was a little ashamed that I hadn't talked to her about it earlier.

I parked in front of The Gateway Building. It was a cold morning, and as I swung the front door open and the building heat slammed me right between the eyes. Mary glanced up, away from her morning crossword, and shouted my name across the lobby. I felt better already. I made my way to the desk, and she must have seen something odd in my expression.

"What's wrong?" she asked, her eyes filled with worry.

"Jake has a tumor," I said and explained it as best I could.

"He's going to be fine," she said. "God will watch out for you."

I shrugged and rolled my eyes.

"Don't even tell me that you're having doubts," she said. "You have a wonderful faith and this is the time when you need it. God is a healer. All you have to do is ask."

"I know," I said. "I do believe God is there for me, but I'm just so scared."

"All of those doubts are just the devil talking," Mary said.

I looked into her eyes to see if she really believed what she was saying, and the truth of the matter is that I had never seen eyes so filled with conviction.

"We all face things in life that will test us and define our relationship with God. You can't make sense of it now, but this is just a mountain for you to climb. Don't let the devil in. Satan is battling God right now for time in your head. It's up to you to keep Satan out."

I wasn't sure that I was completely buying into the thought of a fight between Good and Evil going on in my brain, since I was certain that I wasn't worthy of that much consideration. "I'm just a guy trying to live a happy life," I said.

"Then you know what to do," Mary said. "I'm serious. When you have doubts about how Jake will do, make a conscious effort to drive the devil's words out. When you start thinking that the worst is going to happen, denounce the works of Satan, and say a prayer. Think about doing that."

I spent another half-hour sharing my misery with Mary, and she told me time and again to drive negative thoughts far from my mind. "There's a true peace in talking to God. This is when you need to find it most of all."

I promised her that I would try, and I gave her a big hug before I headed back out into the cold. It was truly phenomenal, but I felt as though I had received a swift kick in the pants. I had needed to hear Mary's words, and as the day went on, I felt comforted by the simplicity of God in, Devil out. Each and every time that I considered the worst, I chased the devil from my mind with The Lord's Prayer. I couldn't get the thought out of my head that perhaps God had sent a message to me through a truly dear friend.

* * *

We had comfortably slipped back into our family routine. The children were playing video games after dinner, and Kathy and I watched a sitcom in an effort to unwind. I told Kathy about my meeting with Mary, and she promised to try to battle the negative thoughts that were creeping into her own mind.

"We have to be distracted a little," I said.

"Thank God we have the Yankees," she said.

That night, we shared the pleasure of putting the children to bed. Kathy and I stood at their bedsides as Jake and Matt whispered their prayers. Jake's voice resonated in my head long after he was asleep.

God Bless Mommy and Daddy, Matt, Jake, and Sam, Max, Shadow, and Nobody, Grandma and Grandpa Foutz, Grandma Spiffy and Poppa John, aunts, uncles, and cousins. Make me be a good boy, God, and help the doctors get rid of my tumor. Amen.

Our family members called one after another as we settled in to watch Game 4 of the series. It had been such an up and down day that I didn't have any concrete thoughts about New York's chances. I talked with my sister Corinne for quite a while, and hung up just before the first pitch.

The Yankees fell behind early, and their offense was non-existent through the first six innings. I sat on one couch, and Kathy sat on the other. The dogs were at our feet, and I don't know about Kathy, but my mind drifted toward the surgery with the break after every pitch. The announcers were squarely behind the Diamondbacks, saying that the Yankees were too old and too overmatched to compete. After the first couple of innings, I started taking my frustrations out on the announcers. As the eighth inning started, I was arguing with every close pitch and the inane comments coming from the announcers' mouths. The Yankees were down by two runs in the bottom of the ninth, and when they got down to their final out, I hit the mute button and went to the refrigerator for a beer.

"I'm glad you turned the volume down. They were getting on my nerves too," Kathy said.

I kept telling myself it didn't matter if they won, and Matt's words ricocheted through my head; "Nobody wins all the time." But as I faced the possibility that the Yankees would go down three games to one, I couldn't help but think that someone was piling it on my head.

The room was deathly quiet. The Yanks got a runner on. I sipped the beer and wallowed in my self-pity.

"I can't believe they're losing to this crap team," I said.

"They won't lose," Kathy said. "Tino Martinez is going to hit a homer; have faith"

I just couldn't see it happening. I've watched thousands of Yankee games in my life, and although they usually came through for me, it just wasn't in the cards tonight. Arizona's pitcher reared back and threw, and with the mute button still engaged to silence the announcers we did not hear the crack of the bat or cheer of the crowd. We didn't hear the announcer's call. The outfielder drifted back as though he might have a play.

"There it goes! It's a home run!" Kathy said.

My mouth literally dropped open. I yelled out, causing Max to jump.

"I told you to have faith," Kathy said.

I thought of Mary's words earlier in the afternoon. A baseball game wasn't life. The Yankees march toward the title didn't have anything to do with Jake's beating the tumor, but it was hard not to draw a parallel. The Yanks won the game in extra innings, and for the first time in a long while, I went to bed happy. I didn't get to sleep, of course, but for a few moments Tino and the boys had made me feel elated. I thought of the people who had lost loved ones in the September 11th disaster. Hopefully, the entire city of New York had a little reason to smile. We were one day closer to the surgery.

When I closed my eyes, I envisioned Jake on the operating table. It was an image that I just didn't need. I thought of the devil trying to edge his way into my mind. "You won't win, you bastard," I said. I visualized a huge wall protecting my home and my heart. I also thought about Frosty the Snowman melting in the greenhouse, and for the first time, I actually saw Santa Claus leaning down over the puddle of water and placing the hat into the water to miraculously bring Frosty back to life.

Kathy had asked me if I had faith. "I have faith, God," I cried. "I really do."

Thursday — November 1, 2001

As impractical as it sounds, my first order of business for the day was a scheduling meeting at the office. I guess that I didn't look so good because the head of the department insisted that after the meeting I take the rest of the day off to get some sleep. I wasn't about to argue the point, and we launched into a discussion of the month ahead. I didn't say too much because I just couldn't fathom the possibility of what could happen to my life. Yet I felt a little better about everything, and it was due to the fact that I was chasing negative thoughts away with a profession of faith. Still, I couldn't get beyond the thought that most of life was a colossal waste of time and effort. It struck me as odd that there is a lot of filler time in life that is made up of some very unproductive moments. I can almost imagine being on my deathbed, praying for a little more time with my family, wondering why I spent so much time watching television or working. That is life, I guess.

* * *

Driving home, as I considered the doctors who would be working on Jake, I thought back to an interview that Fox Sports was doing with a defensive tackle from the Oakland Raiders. The guy's name isn't important, and his philosophy of life is surely lacking; but he said something most alarming. When the interviewer asked him about his most recent drunk-driving arrest, the man said, "Regular people just don't understand the commitment that we make in becoming professional athletes. We have to keep our bodies in form, and sometimes the pressure is too much. We need an outlet, and occasionally that comes in the form of alcohol or chemicals. We deserve the chance to let off a little steam."

The words were shocking and unbelievably short-sighted. Commitment to a goal is not confined to professional athletes, and they surely don't deserve the right to drive drunk just because they play a game in a stadium filled with people. Yet, more than anything else, the comments propelled me into thinking about focus, determination, and commitment. They are words I apply to a doctor or a priest or a firefighter or policeman. These words make sense when applied to a dedicated professional, but they seem out of place when used to describe a thrice-arrested defensive tackle.

I continued to do my homework on The Children's Hospital of Buffalo. I studied the personal profiles of all the doctors involved, and I came away undeniably impressed. I printed off a few sheets of information, and I leaned back in the chair in my home office and went over the careers of the principle doctors that would be in the operating room.

Doctor Marc Levitt began his academic pursuits at the University of Pennsylvania in Philadelphia. He earned a Bachelor of Science degree in May of 1989. I remember graduating from college in 1986, and the very last thing that I wanted to do was to go on studying. Marc Levitt didn't waste much time in continuing his pursuit of excellence. He moved onto Albert Einstein College of Medicine in The Bronx, New York, where he earned his M.D., A.O.A. standings in 1993. Then Levitt became a resident in the Department of Surgery at Mount Sinai Medical Center in New York, New York, where he worked until 1999.

Around the time of Jake's birth, Doctor Marc Levitt was also serving as a research/clinical fellow in pediatric colorectal surgery at Schenider Children's Hospital and in the Division of Pediatric Surgery and Department of Surgery at the Long Island Jewish Medical Center. Somewhere along the line, Marc Levitt made a decision that was crucial to the Fazzolari family. He decided to continue his life's work at The Children's Hospital of Buffalo, and his decision wasn't made because of the quality of life in Buffalo. It wasn't made because of the Buffalo winters, and the success of the Bills and Sabres didn't even cross his mind. Doctor Levitt established a life in Buffalo because it was the best place for him to continue his commitment to a life he chose. He made his decision so that he would be in a position to give life to a child, like Jacob, who was in serious trouble.

After Doctor Levitt arrived in Buffalo, his career surged ahead. He was appointed as a clinical director of The Miniature Access Surgery Center at the Children's Hospital of Buffalo, and in July of 2001, he was appointed to the position of attending pediatric surgeon. It was in this capacity that our paths crossed. I wasn't real certain that Doctor Levitt's career moves would ensure success during Jake's surgery. All I truly cared about was that his hand was steady on Monday morning.

In the middle of the afternoon, I took a break from reading and headed downstairs. Kathy's mother stayed until Sam was in the crib for his afternoon nap, and Jake and I put cartoons on the television and settled down in the living room for our naps.

I drifted toward sleep on the couch with Jake across the living room, on the small sofa. His eyes were on the verge of closing too. The Scooby-Doo movie was on, and I tried my best to block out the voices of the cartoon characters.

"Hey, Dad, can I ask you something?" Jake asked.

"Sure, what's up?" I didn't even open my eyes. I was so tired that I was dizzy.

"Does the magic hurt?" Jake asked.

"Not when they do it," I said. "It might hurt a little afterward, but Mom told you all about it, right?"

Jake turned over, and I opened my eyes a little just to gauge his position on the couch.

"How do they learn how to do it?" he asked.

"They have to study," I said. "You know how you study in school?"

Jake took a moment to digest the information, and then he closed his eyes and smiled. "You mean like coloring?" In his world, excellence in coloring was akin to removing a cantaloupe-sized tumor from the chest of a child. His smile grew broader.

"What're you laughing at?" I asked.

"Close your eyes," he said.

I shut my eyes. He scampered across the floor into his bedroom, then back across the living room. I snuck a peek as he put the burping dinosaur balloon right in front of my face.

"Are you sleeping?" he asked.

I pretended to snore, and he let out a loud burp, followed by a giggling spree as I jumped from the couch.

"Where did he come from?" I shouted.

We played the game a few more minutes, and Jake surprised me as only a child can.

"When I grow up, I want to be a doctor," he said, "and I'll give you and Mom blood tests."

Our nap lasted about an hour. When I opened my eyes the burping dinosaur was inches from my face, and it startled me into a sitting position. I thought Jake would bust a gut from laughing.

After dinner that evening, Kathy, Matt, Jake, Sam and I played together in the living room. After a couple of hours there were blocks, books, balls, and stuffed animals scattered all around. I cleaned up the mess as Kathy prepared the boys for bed. As I was cleaning, it dawned on me that I was happy to do it. Kathy and I had the children in bed by the time the third inning of the fifth game of the World Series started.

The game that night was almost a carbon copy of the previous night's game. It didn't matter how many times I lectured myself on the unimportance of it; I was on the edge of the couch, swearing at the television set as the Diamondbacks carried a lead into the late innings. Kathy was beside me, but she was in much better shape.

"They'll be fine," she said. "Even if they don't win tonight, they can win the next two."

"I don't think so," I said. "Arizona has their two best pitchers scheduled for games six and seven. The Yankees are in a lot of trouble if they lose this one."

I went to the refrigerator for a beer. I sat in the same spot as the night before when Tino Martinez hit his blast. I also hit the mute button. "It worked last night."

Kathy shook her head. It has been about seventy years since a team came back with two outs in the bottom of the ninth. Asking the Yanks to do it two nights in a row was too much. They quickly made the first two outs before getting a runner on base. Their last chance was Scott Brosius, a good hitter, but not a true home run threat. I was just happy that I couldn't hear the announcers because I was sure that they were reveling in the fact that the Yankees were on the verge of defeat. The first pitch was a fastball inside, and Brosius lined it foul.

"That was his pitch," I said. "He loves inside fastballs and everyone knows it. He got one and missed it. They'll never give him another one."

I never saw the placement of the next pitch because it went out as quickly as it came in.

"There it goes!" Kathy screamed. "It's another home run!"

I nearly fell off the couch. I pumped my fist as the ball settled into the stands. The New York fans were on their feet, silently screaming their joy. Kathy turned the sound back on. The announcer talked of the devastation of September 11th and the Yankees' ability to play for the city.

"They're playing for us too," I whispered.

They won the game in extra innings to take a three to two lead.

Friday — November 2, 2001

Once again, I woke up tired. I was getting used to that, but what really concerned me was that I also had a tremendous pain in my chest. I struggled out of bed and the pain subsided a bit. I decided against talking to Kathy about it. She had enough to consider, and I was almost sure it was all stress-related.

Jake was out of bed before seven, and we all sat down together for breakfast. Kathy had the day off work, and I was scheduled to work just a few hours in the morning. Our big appointment of the day was our scheduled consultation with Doctor Levitt.

"What time are we meeting Doctor Levitt?" I asked.

"Doctor Levitt sees patients until noon. He asked that we come down after that so he has enough time to answer all of our questions."

I felt the anxiety pains in my chest once more. I pushed the plate with a half-eaten piece of toast away from me. "Are we bringing Jake?"

"I don't know," Kathy said. "At that time of day he's probably just better off taking a nap."

"I'll meet you at the hospital," I said. I stood up, grabbed my car keys, kissed everyone goodbye, and headed toward the door.

Kathy followed me down the stairs. She tapped me on the right shoulder. "Pick me up here," she said. "We should be together. There's a chance that what Doctor Levitt has to say might not be what we want to hear. We're better off being together if it's unpleasant news."

I struggled to work effectively. I couldn't focus my mind, and the pain in the center of my chest never truly subsided. I returned home at eleven-thirty. Kathy's mother's car was in the driveway, and Kathy was sitting on the front stoop, smoking a cigarette in the cold, November air. She stood up and walked toward my car. Her jaw was set tight in determination, and I truly admired her sense of resolve. Through the early years of child rearing, Kathy was unbelievably over-protective, and although this had to be killing her, she remained completely level-headed.

"Are you ready?" she asked as she slipped in on the passenger side.

"We're going to get this done," I said. "They're going to spell it out for us, and it might not be pretty, but we are on the way to healing him. That's all that matters."

"Is an operation the only way to healing him?" Kathy asked. "Could it be possible that making this decision might lead to his death? I would never forgive myself if we agree to go through with this and it isn't the right decision."

"We don't have a choice," I said. "He can't live with that thing growing inside him."

We traveled to the hospital in silence. It felt eerily similar to watching the baseball game with the mute button on. I angled the truck into the parking ramp across from the hospital. As we crossed the street in the direction of Doctor Levitt's office, Kathy took my hand in hers.

"I love you," she whispered.

"Me too," I answered as I felt tears sting my eyes.

We rode the elevator up to the second floor. Kathy led the way to Doctor Levitt's office. There were cartoon characters painted on the corridor walls. Doctor Levitt's secretary, Joy, sat at a desk behind a window. She smiled through the glass. "Hi, Mr. and Mrs. Fazzolari. Doctor Levitt will be with you in a few minutes. You can sit in the waiting room." She pointed to a large room to the left of her window.

Kathy was still holding tightly to my hand. We sat beside one another in the empty waiting room, and Kathy massaged my hand with tears glistening in her wonderful eyes. "This is going to be the hardest conversation of our lives."

Suddenly, my heart was filled with admiration for her and for our relationship. We had battled through some difficult days, and we always had seemed to agree on what was right for the family that we had built together. We were side by side in the waiting room, and that was how we would come out of it too.

"I can't stop imagining the operation," she said. "I see him on the table, hanging in the balance between life and death, his tiny little chest wide open." Her face was an absolute picture of despair. I gripped her hand a little tighter, and she massaged my fingers.

"We don't have to perform the operation," I said, "and we don't have to imagine it, either. We should be visualizing Jake playing outside on the swing set or running through the house. Every time you think about the operation, imagine him riding his bike or something."

"When I picture him on his bike, I just lose it," Kathy said.

Joy popped her head into the room and asked if we would mind filling out a consent form and a new patient evaluation. We worked together on the evaluation sheet, debating about our family medical histories and trying to pin down the dates of our own medical surgeries. We discussed the preoperative surgery instructions. Jake wasn't allowed to eat or drink anything after three in the morning, and we were due at the hospital by six o'clock on the morning of the fifth.

"You're signing the consent form," Kathy said.

"It's just consent for treatment," I said.

"I'm not signing anything," she said. "I know it's stupid, but maybe I'll feel less responsible for this decision if I don't sign the paperwork."

I scratched my name across the document. Normally I don't have the world's greatest signature, but in this case it was especially shaky.

Joy returned and took the forms from my trembling hand. "Follow me, please."

We entered Doctor Levitt's office, and he extended his hand to me. He was shorter than I imagined he would be. Maybe I was expecting a larger than life character. After all, he was in charge of saving my child. I couldn't help feeling a little intimidated as I shook his hand.

"Please have a seat," Doctor Levitt said. He adjusted his glasses and extended his hand toward the two chairs directly in front of his desk.

There was another man in the room that I recognized as Garret Zallen, a chief resident. He was in a chair beside Doctor Levitt's desk, and we had seen him around Jake's room from the start. I shook Garrett's hand before sitting down. I scanned the room quickly. There were thick books scattered around the room, but Doctor Levitt's desk was immaculate. I don't know why it mattered, but I was glad that the man had a clean desk. I took it as a sign of organization.

Still, it almost felt as though I were waiting to be hanged. The noose felt tight around my neck, and I reached for Kathy's hand.

"I called you in here to discuss the operation," Doctor Levitt began. "First of all, it is a major surgery. You do understand that, right?"

We glanced at each other, then back to Doctor Levitt. We both nodded.

"Jacob is in some danger during this surgery. The tumor is massive, and it hasn't shrunk at all."

"That's kind of good, right?" Kathy asked.

Doctor Levitt leaned back a bit. He was holding a pencil in his hand, and I watched as he twirled it between his fingers. I couldn't help but think about his many talents and how they would all have to be working together to heal our child.

"It is good," Doctor Levitt said, "but it also makes our work a lot harder. The position of the tumor is causing us a lot of problems. Yet, we've discussed it at length with the entire staff, and we also presented Jacob's case file at the American Academy of Pediatrics conference in San Francisco. The doctors in attendance agreed that our course of action is the best one, and I want you to know that this hospital is one of about twenty in the country that can handle an operation of this magnitude."

His last sentence brought a return of the chest pains as I considered that Jake was in probably even more trouble than I had realized. I was also thankful that we were sitting across the desk from this man. His soft tone, confident demeanor, and unwavering professionalism seemed evident. He almost appeared to be studying our faces as he spoke. "We don't have a choice here. The chemotherapy didn't change the mass, and there's no real reason to continue along that vein. We will be well prepared. There will be a full staff working on Jacob. I have a boy about his age, and I promise you that I will treat Jacob as if he were my own child."

Doctor Levitt's proclamation brought tears to my eyes. I stole another look at Kathy and saw that tears were streaming down her face. "Can he live without the operation?" Kathy asked.

Doctor Levitt didn't hesitate. "No."

"What is the biggest risk?" I asked.

"There's a chance that when we put him under anesthesia, his airways will collapse, but we have precautions in place. We will be prepared to use ECMO and rigid bronchoscopy, but there is a bleeding risk. As I've said, the anaesthesiologist will be crucial to what we are trying to do. I'm working together with Doctor Michael Caty on this operation, and we have a very capable staff assembled. We have been preparing for this operation since we received the results of the CT-scan. All of the doctors in the unit will be available. There is also a risk of vocal cord paralysis and phrenic nerve paralysis. We'll do everything in our power to ensure that Jacob is not damaged in any way, but there are risks, and I have to present them to you."

An awkward silence followed, and I was chasing questions around in my brain. I was powerless to articulate them as the room was dancing around me in a dizzying spin.

"So, he can die. That's what you're telling us," Kathy said. She was absolutely sobbing. I squeezed her hand as we waited for the answer.

"Yes, there is that risk, but I believe in the abilities of our staff. I predict that we will open him up, it will be sitting right there, and we can remove it slowly, but surely. We will have to take our time and work it out, but we'll be deliberate and precise; if everything goes right we'll be able to clean it out."

I couldn't help but study the man's face. He looked determined and almost angry that Jake was afflicted with a tumor. I knew right then and there that Doctor Marc Levitt was the man that I wanted in charge of saving Jacob's life because he looked as determined as I might have been.

"Is it attached to anything?" I asked.

"We won't know for sure, but the preliminary evidence is that it isn't. We haven't had a biopsy, so we aren't exactly sure what we are dealing with. But we have a lot of talented people working here, and we all agree on what we think it is. I predict that it is a mostly benign tumor, and chances are good that it might be one hundred percent benign."

"Where did it come from?" I asked. "We heard something about it being a twin that went bad."

Doctor Levitt shrugged. He didn't appear to be concerned with the past. He was focused on the task at hand, and I appreciated that too. He tapped the pencil eraser on the desk as he considered the question. "A tumor is a wild growth. I don't know what accelerated the growth, but it has to come out. That's what we are up against on Monday. This is going to be a crucial week for all of us. We all need to take the weekend to put some sleep in the bank. The operation may last anywhere from six to sixteen hours, and the recovery period will be rough on all of us. We need to be rested and ready. Also, this might be a good time to say a few prayers."

"It's already been done," Kathy said. "Everyone in the county is praying for him."

Doctor Levitt looked us straight in the eye. He offered a smile that said he would do his best to help us out of this predicament, but I can't say that smile eased all of our pain.

"You plan on getting some rest too, right?" I asked. "No big parties planned for the weekend?"

"We'll be ready," Doctor Levitt said.

I felt even more nervous shaking his hand at the end the discussion. I wasn't smart enough to ask all the right questions, and my heart felt like it was about to explode. I wrapped my arm around Kathy's shoulder, and we walked out of the office, knowing that we weren't the same people who had walked in. Life felt different already. We had been forced to consider that our child could be taken from us, and it was a realization that threatened the rest of our days. We were in for the fight of our lives, and we were putting all of our faith in the hands of a man we met one time and a God that we knew was on our side.

All the way home we discussed what we might say to our parents. We agreed that we should spare them the details, but we felt that we needed to prepare them for the absolute worst news. We took turns crying and comforting one another.

"What did you think of Doctor Levitt?" Kathy asked.

"He has toenails smarter than me and he'll be prepared for every event. He isn't doing this alone, and he predicted what he thinks will happen. He wouldn't say those things if he didn't believe them. He has to tell us the risks, though, and we have to face them."

We didn't talk for a long time. We were less than seventy-two hours away from the operation and a moment that could shatter our lives.

"I believe in my heart that he will be fine," Kathy said.

"Me too," I said. "That's what faith is about."

I pulled into the driveway of our home and leaned across the seat to hold Kathy for a moment. She cried into my right shoulder, and I ran my hand through her hair. "We'll get through it," I whispered.

Kathy's mother was in the living room with Jake and Sam. Carolyn sent the boys away and immediately asked what the doctor had said. Kathy pretty much froze up. I really couldn't blame Kathy, and at first I couldn't find the words either. "He explained the operation," I said. "Doctor Levitt is confident that he can get the tumor out without a complication, but he told us that if anything goes wrong, Jake could be in trouble."

I didn't know how else to phrase it, and even though I thought I framed it all right, Carolyn nearly fell to the ground and screamed out in terror. Kathy wrapped her mother in her arms, and I came up behind both of them and joined them in a long hug. Jake was in the back bedroom, oblivious to the discussion, and I wished we were all oblivious to it.

"He can't be in trouble," Carolyn said. "He's such a beautiful boy."

"He'll be okay," I whispered.

"I know he will," Carolyn said, "but I'm so sorry that you two have to go through this."

We stood embracing each other in the center of the kitchen, and there wasn't a lot more that we could say. I left Kathy hugging Carolyn, and I ran into the back room to tickle Jake. If he was facing trouble on Monday, I was going to make sure he had the best hours of his life in the next couple of days.

Jake was sitting on his bed, leafing through a Spiderman comic book. He pointed to a green monster with tentacles shooting out of its back. "Is this what the tumor looks like?"

I leaned in over his shoulder. The character on the page wasn't nearly as gruesome as I imagined the tumor to be. "Something like that," I whispered.

"Then I want them to take it out and throw it away," he said.

I ran my hand over his completely bald head. I can't say that I was even close to being comfortable with the way he looked. It tore at my heart, and Jake must have sensed it. "Remember, my hair is going to grow back," he said.

I left the room with a smile on my face, but when I returned to the kitchen, I had to turn away from the sight of Carolyn wiping tears from her eyes.

"You better call your parents," Kathy said.

The very last thing that I needed to hear was the sound my mother made when I told her of the visit with Doctor Levitt. She cried as though I had physically attacked her.

"I'm sorry, Mom," I said, and I was. It was the absolute worst thing that I ever had to tell her, and it hurt me to cause her such pain.

I walked from the kitchen with the portable telephone pressed to my ear. My mother was reassuring me, but she wasn't totally convincing. I'm not sure how that conversation ended, but there weren't many more conversations that stayed in my head over the next couple of days. Every solitary thought that I had was centered on Doctor Levitt's words.

That night, I stood in the backyard for twenty minutes. My words to God weren't a prayer. Instead, I begged God to leave my family intact. The wind whistled through the pine trees lining the fence behind the swing set where Jake spent hours on countless summer days.

"God, please, don't do this to us. We came too far to have it taken away now. Jake is such a beautiful boy. Why would you give us such a wonderful child and then take him away from us? Please, I'm begging you to help the doctors make Jake right. I can't live without him. God, this will ruin my beautiful family. Kathy is so full of love, and Mom and Dad, and Carolyn and John and Matthew and Sammy…we'll never make it through this."

I swept my eyes across the sky, but saw no evidence of being heard. There wasn't a face in the moon or a star spiraling toward earth. The wind didn't stop blowing, and I didn't hear a voice from above trying to calm me. I was going to have to find my own peace in the middle of chaos. "At the very least, give me the strength to be a husband and a father. Help me walk like a man."

Shadow leaped up, and I caught her and hugged her to me. She was standing on her hind legs at hip level. "Jake's in trouble," I cried. "My beautiful boy is in trouble."

Shadow bit playfully at my arms. I patted her head as tears flowed down my cheeks. It almost seemed like Shadow was doing her best to comfort me, and in a small way she was. "Please, God, don't do this to us."

Chapter Fourteen

Saturday — November 3, 2001

It's amazing how many times a child can watch a cartoon or movie. When Matthew was young, we saw the movie *Balto* about a hundred times, and it got to the point where I found myself rooting against the canine protagonist. Scooby Doo was another real problem, as I had memorized the dialogue for every episode. I can remember nearly pulling my hair out over one too many Barney episodes one Sunday morning, only to have Kathy, who had noticed my discomfort, ask me to just block it out. I told her that Barney's name was going to wind up all over my suicide note. I even ended up singing the stupid theme song in the shower.

Whenever a new movie arrived in stores, we rushed out to get a copy, and that day was no exception. *Shrek* was making its long-awaited debut on video, and we headed to the video store five minutes before it actually opened.

Jake's physical appearance was in sharp contrast to what we knew he was up against, since he was breathing easier than he had at any other time in his life. We had nearly completed our job of ensuring that he was as healthy as he could be for the surgery.

"How many times can I watch *Shrek*, Dad?" Jake asked. He was holding the movie up close to his face, and his excitement was actually contagious.

"As many as you want," I said.

"Will you watch it with me?" Jake asked.

"Yep, as many times as you need to see it."

The movie was unbelievably entertaining. Perhaps it wouldn't have been on any other day, but Jake sat on my lap, and we replayed all the funny parts. We put it in for a second go-around when a brilliant idea hit me like a ton of bricks. "Why don't we go to the theater? We can see *Monsters Inc.* if you want."

Jake actually jumped for joy, and Kathy searched the paper for the next showing. We decided on the noon show, and Jake started *Shrek* over again as I headed for the telephone. I had one very important call to make, as I wanted to attempt to set up Jake's ICU nurse for the day of the surgery. There wasn't much that we could do in way of preparation, but I figured that perhaps Susan Mazurchuk was available to be Jake's nurse when he returned to the ICU after surgery. We were comfortable with how she had attended to Jake, and if securing Susan to be his nurse was all I could do, then I had to at least try.

Janine Cross is a nurse in the ICU at The Children's Hospital of Buffalo. Janine and her husband, Neil, have been personal friends for well over a decade, and before Jake and I headed to the theatre, I telephoned Janine to see if she could help me to schedule Susan for the day of the surgery. Janine answered on the first ring, and I quickly explained the situation.

"I'm sure Susan would like to be there when Jake comes out of surgery," Janine said. "God, I would like to be there myself, but we've been friends so long that I don't know if I could help."

"I understand," I said. "It's just that I feel so helpless right now, and the only thing I can think of doing is requesting Susan."

"Jake's in good hands," Janine said. "Doctor Levitt is an excellent surgeon, and he'll have help in there. Have you ever heard of Doctor Graf or Doctor Caty?"

"To tell you the truth, I don't know. We've met so many doctors. I can't remember."

"Well, these are pretty impressive doctors. They will do everything they can to make Jake well. Children's Hospital is an amazing place."

We talked for quite some time, and Janine answered a lot of questions about the procedure. I thanked her and hung up just as Jake ran into the kitchen to tell me that Shrek was passing gas during the very first scene of the movie. We laughed hard and rewound it at least three times. The movie played right up until the moment that we left for the theater, but I can't say that I was able to concentrate on that second viewing. I was thinking about the doctors that would work on Jake, and just as I had marveled at the commitment and dedication of Doctor Levitt, I found myself doing the same for Doctor Michael Caty and Doctor Joy Graf. I decided that I would do additional research at night, but first, I was taking Jake to the movie.

We arrived at the theater just moments before the show started, and we wound up sitting in the front row. Jake stood in front of my chair, eating popcorn and candy and drinking soda as the furry characters in *Monsters, Inc.* danced across the screen. My neck was sore from staring straight up at the screen, and a child of about seven threw a little chocolate ball that hit me on the left shoulder. "Sorry," the boy said, "I was trying to hit the kid behind you."

I just smiled. How I could possibly get angry? All I could think about was seeing Jake grow into a man. He deserved the chance to grow up. He was entitled to make mistakes and enjoy success and battle failure. Even though I would frown upon such a thing, Jake deserved the right to plug another boy's father with a chocolate ball.

"This is a great movie, isn't it, Dad?" Jake screamed at one exciting point in the show.

I couldn't help but run my hand over the top of his bald head. I pulled him close and kissed him on the left cheek. "It's the best movie I ever saw."

After the show ended, I carried Jake to the car, and he thanked me at least seven times for taking him. When we returned home, I stapled the ticket stub to the wall in my office, and I promised myself that I would glance at that ticket when the world seemed to be spinning too fast. I would never forget the way that I felt in that theater with my boy, enjoying every minute of the experience.

That night, the Yankees were soundly thrashed as the Diamondbacks forced a seventh game. The announcers kept talking about a do-or-die situation, and I wanted to bash in the television screen. I didn't see much of the game though, as I spent the early part of the evening in the back bedroom playing video games with Matthew, Jake, and Sam. We didn't even bother to enforce the usual bedtime regimen; our only rule was that each kid had to kiss at least one of us every half hour. By ten-thirty we were all ready for bed.

When the kids were finally asleep, Kathy and I settled in front of the television. I grew so tired of the announcers talking about how important the baseball game was that I decided to head up to the computer to once more go over the credentials of the surgeons. I hesitated at the stairs, and Kathy called out to me. "One more day," she said, but she shook the thought from her head. "That's not what I meant."

"He's going to have fifty-thousand more days," I said.

Kathy met me at the foot of the stairs, and I hugged her tightly.

"Sorry about the Yanks," Kathy said.

"It's all right," I said. "They're supposed to clinch the World Series the night before the surgery. That's the way it's gone all along. No one said it would be easy."

Kathy returned to a seat on the couch, and I headed to the computer to continue researching The Children's Hospital of Buffalo. I punched in the website address as I considered that it was becoming unbelievably apparent that the men and women that would be working on my son would be bringing years of blood, sweat, and tears into the operating room with them. These were healthcare professionals that studied throughout the world to bring the best possible pediatric care to Buffalo, New York. I began my research by reading about Doctor Graf who took the west coast route to The Children's Hospital of Buffalo. Her academic resume included the University of San Francisco, San Francisco State University, the University of California at Berkeley, and the University of California, Davis. She joined the staff at Children's in 1999 and was appointed as a pediatric surgical fellow in 2000.

Just as Doctor Levitt had, Doctor Graf dedicated her life to medicine and healing children. She was honored throughout her career, including an award for excellence in surgery. Doctor Graf had an impressive listing of writing credits, including book chapters, published abstracts, and journal publications.

Both Janine and Doctor Levitt had mentioned Doctor Michael Caty, and I was in awe as I considered his accomplishments. Doctor Caty earned a

Bachelor of Science degree from Boston College, then moved on to the University of Massachusetts Medical School, earning his MD degree in 1985. Doctor Caty completed his general surgery residency at the University of Michigan Hospitals, earning a slew of honors and awards along the way. Anyone that has ever uttered the phrase, "I don't have enough time" should glance at Doctor Caty's unbelievable professional credentials. Doctor Caty was invited for presentations ranging from "Congenital Diaphragmatic Hernia" as presented in September, 1994 to the "Clinical Problem Solving Session" on October 19, 2001 (where Jacob's information was reviewed).

Additionally, Doctor Caty researched and wrote about a wide range of serious issues, including working with Doctor Levitt on the *Handbook of Pediatric Surgery*. Doctor Caty had been honored on a list of *Best Doctors in America* and was also listed in *Who's Who in America*. Yet it was evident that Doctors Levitt, Caty, and Graf had dedicated their lives to much more than monetary pursuits and personal accolades. One of Doctor Levitt's sentences in particular kept coming back to comfort me: "I will treat Jacob as if he is my own child."

Maybe that is exactly what it takes to dedicate your life to saving children.

Sunday — November 4, 2001

I woke up believing that my chest pains would be gone. Although we were mere hours from the operation, I had slept a little more soundly and felt as if I deserved a break. Yet the pain was much more pronounced, and I didn't know if I was imagining it or not. I felt as if my left arm were tingling a little bit. I decided against mentioning it to anyone. I didn't know many thirty-seven year old men that suffered a heart attack, and I had more on my mind than my own health.

We worked hard to frame the morning as just a typical Sunday. I played video games with Matthew and Jake, and Kathy attended to Sam's every whimper. The one huge goal of the day was to keep everyone awake and alert so that we could attend ten-thirty mass as a family. After breakfast, we made the short trip to the church.

"We should light a candle," Kathy whispered.

I had already thought of it but was too scared to mention it. I nodded, and Matthew chimed in from the backseat. "Why are we lighting a candle?" he asked. He was usually quite involved in every conversation.

"So God watches over Jake tomorrow," Kathy said.

"I'm going to say some prayers," Matthew said. "We said prayers at school too. My teacher said that God heals sick kids if you ask."

"I'm not sick," Jake said.

We took a pew in the center of the church. Kathy was carrying Sam, and I was walking with Matthew and Jake on either side. We stood before the candles, and I reached for a wick when I saw an usher moving fast in our direction.

"I'll light the candle for you," he whispered. He took the wick from my hand, and together we scanned the hundreds of candles flickering in front of us. "Unbelievable," he said. "They're all lit. Sorry, but we don't have one available to light."

I glanced over my shoulder at Kathy. In her eyes I saw a moment of despair, and I could almost read her mind. Did the success of the surgery depend upon lighting a candle? We moved the kids along, and over the course of the next hour we commanded the attention of everyone around us. Jake was giggling, fighting, talking loudly, eating crackers, and distributing the books. He shook everyone's hand when it was time to exchange signs of peace, and the only thought in my head was that God had to know that Jake was there. He giggled and joked all through mass. In a setting where Kathy and I would usually demand quiet, we allowed Jake a little extra space.

After mass I made the sauce for Sunday dinner. My mother and father called to say they'd stop by, and I invited my brothers and sisters. My brother Jeff and sister-in-law Lynn said they could make it for dinner, and my brother John, sister-in-law Dana, and my nieces Andrea and Nicole would be by in the late afternoon. Kathy's family showed up throughout the course of the day. I understood that we were lucky to be facing the operation surrounded by such a loving family.

"Why are we having a party?" Matt asked.

"It isn't a party," I said. "Everyone just wants to stop by to wish Jake luck. Everyone just wants to let us know that they are thinking about us. That's what families do."

The dinner was awkward at best. Jake was weary of the attention, and he barely came out of his bedroom. We ate macaroni and made feeble attempts at small talk, but the discussion always swung back in the direction of what tomorrow might bring. We didn't entertain negative thoughts, and to be honest, there was almost a sense of calm. It was hard to look at my parents, though, because I knew that their hearts were aching.

The telephone rang every three minutes all day long. John, Dana, and the girls stopped by with gifts, cookies, and a few wrestling moves to try out on the boys. John is just a year older than me and, as we grew to adulthood, he passed the time by pummeling me every chance that he got. Yet we are close in every way. His eyes misted over as we stood at the front door.

"I'll be there in the morning," he said. "He's going to be better than ever."

"I know," I said.

"And the Yanks are going to win too," Dana added. "Jake's tough; don't worry."

"We're just around the corner from the light of day," I said, which was a line from a Springsteen song. Dana smiled. They must have kissed the boys a hundred times.

* * *

The chest pains wouldn't subside. I took a couple of aspirin, then helped Kathy gather items for Matt and Sam to take with them. Matthew was going to stay at Jack's parents, and Sam was headed to his home away from home at Kathy's parents' house.

Jake and I watched cartoons, and it was hard to imagine that I would ever miss an inning of the seventh game of the World Series, but Bugs was definitely the choice. When the show went to commercial, I led Jake into the bathroom. He stepped up on the stool that my sister Corinne made for him and watched as I dabbed toothpaste on his Scooby brush.

"I don't want to go to the hospital," he said. "I want to keep my tumor."

We'd been through it a thousand times, but I knew he was scared. I couldn't blame him. "It'll be easy," I said. "Those doctors are going to do their magic and you'll never have to go back again. Remember, the tumor is a bad guy."

He ran the brush across his teeth a few times, then smiled wide. "How do they look?"

I couldn't help it. I pulled him close to my chest, squeezed real hard, and kissed the side of his face. He took it for a minute, but I never saw the punch coming. His tiny fist struck me just under the chin, and I rolled onto my back with my eyes closed.

"Do you want a piece of me?" he roared.

"That's what I get for leaving you alone with Uncle John," I said, rubbing my jaw.

I carried Jake into bed and Kathy joined us. I stood off to one side with my eyes closed as Kathy sat on the edge of the bed. Jake blessed himself and began his prayers. *God Bless Mommy and Daddy, Matt, Jake, and Sam, Max, Shadow, and Nobody, Grandma and Grandpa Foutz, Grandma Spiffy and Poppa John, aunts, uncles, and cousins. Make me be a good boy, God, and help Dr. Levitt do his magic and get rid of my tumor. Amen.*

Kathy and I sat together on the couch, watching the Yankees battle Arizona for the championship of baseball. I kept massaging the area over my heart, and it didn't matter that it was one of the best pitched ballgames that I had ever seen; I couldn't concentrate on what was happening. Kathy and I traded questions back and forth, and I was proud of her for being strong enough to guide us through the weeks of waiting.

"I'm still so damn scared," she whispered.

"Me too," I said.

Alfonso Soriano hit a long home run to give the Yankees the lead in the late innings. I felt a sense of relief surge through my body. The Yankees have the best relief pitcher in baseball; it was just a matter of time before the celebration began. I went to the kitchen for a bottle of beer and Kathy looked in on Jake before the bottom of the ninth inning. The Yanks held a two to one lead, and Mariano Rivera was popping the glove.

Kathy sat down close, and I offered her a sip of beer, which she took with a smile of relief crossing her face. I could sense that she had also equated the Yankees success with the anticipated success of the operation.

Arizona got a couple of runners on base, and although I slid forward on the couch in my anxiety, I wasn't seriously worried. The Yankees were our symbol. They would be fine — except they weren't.

Luis Gonzalez hit a soft fly into centerfield as the runner on second raced toward the plate. A sign flashed on the screen declaring the Diamondbacks the new world champions.

"Oh, my God!" Kathy screamed. "The Yankees lost!"

I grabbed her by the shoulders. "It doesn't mean anything. The Yankees don't have anything to do with Jake."

Kathy was nearly inconsolable. Tears threatened her eyes, and I reached out to grab her.

"They can't lose! They're our lucky charm! The Yankees lost! What's going to happen to us?"

We watched the Arizona players celebrating in the middle of the diamond, and the Yankee players displayed the agony of defeat.

"It doesn't mean a thing," I whispered.

"We aren't supposed to lose either," Kathy said. "But what if we do? What if we do?"

"We won't," I said. "I read all about those doctors. They will get rid of the tumor. They will throw it in the garbage!"

"You better be right," Kathy cried.

We held each other on the couch for a long while. But as I climbed the stairs, I thought of the failed attempt to light the candle and the stunning World Series loss. The bedroom seemed a little darker, and I held the rosary on my thumb. "I have the faith," I whispered. The words of the Lord's Prayer flashed across my mind. I didn't give the Yankee game another thought for a full three weeks.

Chapter Fifteen

The day was cold and damp. We left the house in darkness, and all three of us were still wiping sleep from our eyes. Kathy was partially through her caffeine and nicotine fix, and Jake's eyes seemed to be rolling from a lack of sleep. I can't say that I felt as if I had, "sleep in the bank," as Doctor Levitt had prescribed, but adrenalin was definitely surging through my veins. I despised the idea that I would have to make the daily trek to The Children's Hospital of Buffalo, but I could only pray that I would be making it every day for the next week or so.

"Who is the best surgeon in the world?" Kathy asked. She had asked this question before, but it was especially unsettling this morning.

"I don't know," I whispered.

"Don't you think he deserves to have the best surgeon in the world working on him?"

"Of course he does," I said. "Come on, don't do this. You know the reputation of Children's Hospital. This is where we want to be. Besides, who's to say that these doctors aren't the best at this sort of operation?"

"I just want to be able to say that we did the best we could," she whispered.

I refused to resign myself to such dark thoughts. My mind shifted to prayer as I put a John Mellencamp CD into the drive and turned it up a little.

We walked hand-in-hand through the emergency room doors. Jake hadn't said a word, and I wondered if he was upset at all. Kathy knew right where to go, and within a few minutes we were standing in front of the desk at admissions. Jake was all signed in, but the wall clock showed that it was just ten minutes after six. Surgery wasn't scheduled until seven-thirty. What would we possibly do for all that time? Still, I wasn't in any position to wish even a minute away. We were shuffled to a large waiting room with an extensive selection of toys, including a Pokemon video machine. Even though Jake wasn't much into the characters, he headed for the machine.

"Are there bad guys to fight?" Jake asked.

"I don't know, let's see," I said.

I hoisted him up, and he studied the screen. I wasn't exactly sure what to do to turn the machine on, and Jake pounded at a couple of the buttons. Kathy was getting the rest of the paperwork in order, but she was watching us out of the corner of her eye. I was as worried about her as I was about Jake. As a mother, her heart had been breaking for the better part of a month. She would be a basket case in a matter of hours.

"I'm really tired," Jake said. He yawned big and wide, and I rubbed his bald head.

"Why don't we play with your battling robots?" I asked.

Jake received seven of the large, plastic, multi-colored robots during his first hospital visit, and John and Dana delivered the eighth the night before. We set the robots up on a small, wooden coffee table in the center of the room and used the remote controls attached to each robot to smash them together. There were a few other people in the waiting room, and their eyes were drawn to our battle. I had to be real careful not to knock Jake's robot over, and after he beat me five or six times, he asked for Kathy.

"Dad, why don't you let Mom battle for awhile? You aren't very good at this."

I gave up my spot at the table so Kathy could take a turn at getting beat and acting upset. Every once in a while, Kathy looked at me, and I could see the sheer terror in her eyes. I just knew that, like me, lightning was running through her veins. We were both on the absolute brink of an emotional meltdown, and we were playing battling robots.

After what seemed like an eternity, we were shuffled to the surgical waiting room. We lost the Pokemon machine, but another set of toys and books was waiting for us. I read a couple of books and showed Jake the pictures of a few large animals. He couldn't stop yawning, and he complained a couple of times about being hungry.

"The doctors are going to do their magic, and when you wake up you can have whatever you want." I wasn't sure he'd be able to eat for quite some time, but I was trying hard to comfort him.

Jake was well aware that he was going to sleep through the magic act. "Will you be here when I wake up?" Jake asked.

"Absolutely," I said. I kissed him a few times, and Kathy couldn't resist the urge to join in. For almost half an hour we passed him back and forth like a tiny baby, kissing and hugging him. Jake giggled through most of it, but he also kissed us back.

Doctor Levitt stopped by a few minutes after eight o'clock. We had expected the surgery to start earlier, but we were glad to see Doctor Levitt, who appeared alert and centered.

"We're almost ready," he said, and rubbed Jake's head in a friendly way.

"Are you doing the magic?" Jake asked.

Doctor Levitt smiled. "Not yet." He bent down and whispered something to Jake. I stole a look at Kathy, who offered me a nervous smile.

"Wow, he's asymptomatic. I was expecting his breathing to be a little more labored," Doctor Levitt said. "This can go very well."

He turned to the door, and, as the words sunk into my brain, tears filled my eyes. I wanted to share the moment with Kathy, and this time her smile was much brighter.

"It might be a long day," Doctor Levitt said, "but we'll be getting started soon. We're setting up the ECMO team."

Doctor Caty had explained to us earlier that the ECMO is similar in principle to a cardiopulmonary bypass that is done to allow cardiac surgeons to operate on the non-beating heart. Doctor Caty had been trained at the University of Michigan by Doctor Robert Bartlett, the man credited with inventing ECMO in the 1970s. The ECMO team involved an attendant from the intensive care unit, a nurse, an ECMO specialist, and a pediatric surgeon to place the catheters in the blood vessels. "I hope they don't have to use that ECMO thing," Kathy said.

"I'm glad they have it if they need it," I said.

Jake was visibly agitated. He was alternating between biting his fingernails and kicking his feet against the chair bottom. It was amazing that his instincts were so sharp. He had little idea about what he was facing, but he was becoming more scared by the minute. He complained about being tired and hungry, and I wanted to scoop him up in my arms and carry him home. Nonetheless, we spent another fifty minutes waiting for the preparation work to be completed.

I have little recollection of who actually took Jake from Kathy's arms into the waiting room, but his cries of terror will stay with me until the day I leave this earth. "Dad, I don't want to go! Mom, I'm not ready yet!"

We kissed his beautiful face about a hundred times inside of two minutes. The tears streamed down our faces while the attendant waited patiently. "It's magic, Jake," I told him. "You'll be all right. Just do good, buddy. I love you!"

Kathy followed Jake and the attendant to the operating room door, nearly doubled over in grief. When she turned back to me, I held her tightly as we cried together without restraint.

"He's got to be all right," she sobbed over and over.

"It's up to God and these people," I said. "We did our jobs. We got him here, and we showed him love every minute of his life."

* * *

We were all too aware that the most pivotal moment of the surgery would take place when the anesthesiologists did their work. The men placed in charge of Jake's care were Doctor Doron Feldman and Doctor James Foster. Doctor Bradley Fuhrman, the director of the ICU, was also crucial to the success of the operation, as he organized the activities. Properly regulating anesthesia is important in all operations, and it is particularly tricky for children. Additionally, Jake was a special case, as his breathing was compromised by the tumor. My prayers during that first fifteen minutes of the operation were centered on Doctor Feldman, Doctor Fuhrman, and Doctor Foster.

I felt absolutely helpless as Kathy and I headed to the surgical waiting room on the second floor. Our family was waiting for us there; John was sitting against the back wall next to Kathy's sister Lori and my sister Corinne. We were well prepared for a long day of waiting, since Corinne brought enough food to feed everyone in the waiting room and the surgical team. Her thoughtfulness and unbelievable compassion warmed my heart.

I sat beside Lori, and she grabbed my hand. We are good buddies and usually find one another at all the family parties. We've shared hundreds of laughs, and yet Lori felt a lot like a sister as she worked to comfort me. "I just know he'll be fine," Lori said.

"This first half-hour is the important part," I said. "If he goes under okay, we'll be halfway through the battle."

"He's a tough little boy," Lori said.

As Lori said the words, I felt an overwhelming sense of grief. I had often told Kathy not to imagine Jake on the operating table, but I couldn't help but picture it in my mind. I thought of Frosty the Snowman melting in the greenhouse behind the locked door, and I began to shake. Kathy handed me a coffee, and I sipped it with a quivering lower lip. "Come on, God," I whispered.

The wall clock was moving especially slowly. Kathy's hand was coupled with mine and Corinne, John, and Lori were whispering words of encouragement.

"This is the worst day of our lives," Kathy whispered.

"It's going to be the best day," I said.

At twenty minutes to ten — just forty minutes after the start of surgery — a member of the anesthesiology team opened the door.

"He's under just fine," she whispered. "Doctor Levitt wanted me to let you know. Jake's left lung is doing all the work, and he's real comfortable."

I pumped my fist and hugged my brother. Corinne was holding Kathy, and Lori was waiting for someone to grab onto. We were a long way from being out of the woods, but we had passed the first test.

The minutes crawled by. My mother and father joined the gathering, and their presence made my heart ache even more. Kathy left the room a couple of times to call her parents on my cell phone. They were at their house watching Sam, and I couldn't even imagine what they were going through. I drank a huge cup of coffee, and when I was done John offered me a can of chewing tobacco, which I gladly accepted. My heart was under tremendous strain, and the pain radiating up and down my left arm was much more pronounced. I must have looked pale because Lori offered me something to eat.

Kathy was passing around a plate of pastries, but I shook her off. I was in the middle of the rosary again. Lori edged to the table in the corner of the room. She reached into a bag and pulled out a deck of cards. Before long, a lifeless game of scat was in full swing. John, Lori, Corinne, and Kathy tossed the cards out, always keeping an eye on the door and the ticking clock.

"I need to go for a walk," I said. The clock read 10:15, and I blinked away thoughts of Jake lying on that operating room table. I headed down the hall to the rest room just around the corner, where I splashed water on my face and cried at my reflection in the mirror. "Come on, God."

As I stepped from the room, I immediately recognized Doctor Grossi walking with two other men, removing masks from their faces. Doctor Grossi had been the first doctor to talk to us after the discovery of Jake's tumor. Behind the masks were ear-to-ear grins. When Doctor Grossi recognized me, his smile grew even wider.

"He's doing wonderful," Doctor Grossi said. "They opened him up, and it's sitting right there."

"It's a piece of cake," one of the other doctors said.

My heart jumped into my throat. I did all I could to stop myself from dropping to my knees. I took a deep breath and hurried back to the waiting room to make the announcement. I spent the next twenty minutes hugging and kissing my family.

Kathy, Lori, John, and Corinne were still playing scat at the front of the room. My mother and father paced the floor nervously, sipping coffee at a record pace. Finally, out of sheer frustration from everyone telling me to eat something, I headed to a small table in the back corner of the room to make a sandwich. I glanced at the wall clock: it was fifteen minutes after twelve. Jake had been in surgery for two and a half hours.

As I put the mustard on the bread, I heard the door swing open. Then I saw Doctor Caty approaching Kathy, and my world started to spin too fast. It was too early. Doctor Caty was supposed to be in the operating room. What was he doing out here?

"He wants to talk to us," Kathy said without raising her voice.

I pulled back away from the table, and the bread hit the floor at my feet. I didn't even bother to pick it up. I hurried to the patient-doctor conference room adjacent to the waiting area. Doctor Caty entered and took a seat. "You can all come in," Doctor Caty said. "It went well."

Mom and Dad rushed in right behind us. I felt my father's hand on my right shoulder and realized that it has been there for all the important moments of my life. Corinne, John, and Lori grabbed a place behind me, and Kathy sat across the table on the other side of Doctor Caty.

"We were able to get it out without complication. Doctor Levitt is closing him up, and it went real well. He's a strong kid," Doctor Caty said.

I don't know what it was about Doctor Caty, but he seemed to be as mentally spent as I felt. I could feel tears gather in my eyes, and I expected those. What surprised me was to see that Doctor Caty was on the verge of tears too.

"When we put him under, his left lung held on and carried him through the operation. The anesthesiologists did a fantastic job throughout, and we didn't have to use the ECMO unit." Doctor Caty paused for a long moment. "It went as well as could be expected."

I'm not sure how Doctor Caty felt at that moment, but I knew what was racing through my heart and soul. "Somebody better hug this guy," I said to anyone that might listen. Doctor Caty flashed a relaxed smile, though tears glistened in his eyes. Everyone in the room looked too stunned to move. "I'm going to do it then," I said and stood up. So did Doctor Caty. I threw my arms around his shoulders and hugged him tightly. "Thank you," I said.

"We're glad we could do it," he murmured.

The dam was broken. Kathy and Lori also hugged Doctor Caty. I'm not sure if he went through hugs on a daily basis, but he took it well. "Doctor Levitt will be out in a little while and he'll break it all down for you. I was just helping out in there."

I couldn't believe that he was so humble, but the entire hospital staff had performed their jobs in such a manner. Each doctor deferred to the other, and the work on Jake's case seemed to be equally divided with only one true goal; to send him home healthy and happy.

After Doctor Caty left, we spent the next ten minutes crying in each other's arms. It felt so good to hug my mother, who wept tears of joy. "I knew God wouldn't let me down," I said. "You taught me to pray to God and I've talked to him all my life." My voice broke as I searched for the right words. "I talked to God about everything and he was there for us. Thank you, Mom, for teaching me faith."

Mom cried even harder, but I had to break away from her for a moment. I found Kathy just a few feet away. She was wrapped in Corinne's embrace. I tapped Corinne on the shoulder and said, "I need to see my wife for a second." Corinne gladly stepped aside, and I pulled my wonderful wife close to me.

"Jake did it!" I cried. "Our beautiful boy is going to be all right!"

It seemed that everything that happened in my entire life led up to that very moment. Kathy cried into my right shoulder, and I kissed her face over and over. "I love you for helping me through this," I said. "I love you for having faith."

Kathy and I cried together as our family looked on.

* * *

At 1:15, Doctor Levitt led us into the same patient conference room, his eyes alive with his success. He was as thrilled as we were. "Jacob did very well," he said. "We were able to go in and do our work, and he's stable. We got every piece of it, and from the looks of it, it is most likely a benign tumor. We will send it to the lab, and they'll take it apart and study it. There was hair and bone in it, and I predict that it is benign."

It was the second piece of wonderful news that we'd heard in just over an hour. Kathy's hand felt warm in mine, and the smile on her face made her tears inconsequential.

"When he comes out of the operating room, he'll be heavily sedated, and he's going to look a little puffed up. He'll have tubes in a lot of different places; don't be alarmed, that's what he's supposed to look like after an operation like this. Slowly but surely, we'll remove the tubes and give him back to you as good as new. Does anyone have any questions?"

"When will you know if the tumor is benign?" Kathy asked.

"In about three to five days," Doctor Levitt said. "First things first, though. Let's not worry about that unless we have to. Like I said, it sure looked benign." His smile was as bright as day.

I glanced around the table. "Are you guys going to make me hug him first?" I asked.

This time there was a line to hug the doctor. My admiration for the man who saved Jake's life was threatening to turn me into a babbling idiot. "Thank you, thank you, thank you," I whispered as I hugged him.

"I was glad to do it," Doctor Levitt said.

* * *

We stood in the hallway awaiting the appearance of Jake's gurney. I just wanted to see his wonderful face, although I knew that it wouldn't look very pretty at first glance. He was coming out alive, and that's all I needed to know. I was by Kathy's side, and we hugged for the hundredth time as the doors swung open. Kathy gasped. I strained to see his face. There was tape over his eyes, and that was the one thing that alarmed me. Doctor Feldman was at my side in a flash. I didn't say anything, but he read the look on my face. "Don't worry about the tape," he whispered. "They'll get it off as soon as he gets into ICU. He'll never know it was on."

I suddenly realized that Doctor Feldman had played an integral part in the operation. "You don't get away without a hug," I said. I think I caught him by complete surprise because he actually stumbled backwards as I grabbed him in an embrace. Corinne saw the entire scene, and her laughter made my heart sing. Doctor Feldman smiled brightly as he headed on down the hall.

Our sense of relief was as draining as our sense of fear had been. Jake was moved to a room in the Intensive Care Ward. One of the nurses greeted us at the entrance of ICU. "It will be about half an hour before you can visit his room, and only two at a time," she said. "You can wait in the ICU waiting room just down the hall, and I'll call you when it's okay to see him."

We went to the ICU waiting room, all by ourselves. We resumed the card game and spent the next hour seeing who had the biggest smile. I couldn't stop kissing Kathy. "I'm proud of you," I said.

About twenty minutes later, the telephone on the wall near the door rang. Kathy ran toward the phone and picked it up breathlessly. "We can go in," she said.

Kathy and I hurried to the Intensive Care Unit. Jake's bed was in room number four, directly across from the nurse's station. We entered the room slowly, holding hands tightly. The tape had been removed from Jake's eyes, but he was on a ventilator, three chest drains, a blood pressure line, and a line to check his heart rate. Although his face was swollen, it looked absolutely wonderful to me. I leaned close to his right ear. "You did it, pal. You kicked that tumor's butt. That bad guy is heading for the garbage where he belongs."

Kathy was at his left side. She kissed his forehead and whispered her own words of praise.

"I'm still scared," I said.

"Not me," Kathy said. "I'm just real happy now." She came around the bed and touched me on the arm. "Frosty the Snowman came back to life."

I smiled and kissed her again, but something was still bothering me, and I couldn't put my finger on it. My sense of relief had been tremendously short-lived. I was flat-out frightened out of my mind. What if Jake had an infection? What if his chest didn't drain properly or his heart rate suddenly dropped? How could I handle a turn for the worse after riding the top of the clouds for most of the morning?

"He did it," Kathy said. "These doctors and nurses saved our baby's life. Now it just gets better by the minute."

Chapter Sixteen

was alone in the waiting room, as Corinne, John and my parents had headed back to their lives and Kathy and Lori were taking a walk outside. A young black man entered the ICU waiting room in the middle of the afternoon. His eyes showed signs of wear and tear, and I nodded at him as he took a seat in front of the television set. I wanted to share my joy with someone, but the somber look on his face told me that he had his own problems and that his news wasn't probably as good. Every parent in the hospital was fighting extreme sorrow and despair, and we were all better off fighting our battles alone.

I dug into the bag of food that Corinne had left behind and began making a sandwich, recalling that my last attempt ended up on the floor of the surgical waiting room. The man glanced over at me. I don't know what made me do it, but I spoke up. "Have you eaten?"

"I'm okay," he said.

"Seriously, I have a ton of lunchmeat here. Help yourself." I pushed the food toward an open chair across from me, and the man smiled and headed over.

"Was that your boy with the tumor?" he asked.

"Yeah," I said. "He's doing great."

"That's awesome," the man said. I reached across the table and shook his hand. "My daughter is in here. She was badly burned." I sighed, and he bowed his head. "It was a faulty showerhead, and I checked the water before I put her in."

I struggled for the next breath of air as I imagined the guilt this poor man was feeling.

"She just has to be all right," he said as a stray tear worked its way down his right cheek.

"This is the place to be," I said. "These doctors will fix her up."

"Amen to that," he said.

He reached across the table, grabbed a couple of pieces of rye bread and some turkey and assembled his sandwich. We ate in silence, just two fathers trapped in worry over our children.

"I'll say a prayer for her," I said.

"I'm already praying for your boy," he said.

* * *

Kathy and I were at Jake's bedside. Kathy was doing a crossword puzzle, and I was simply staring at Jake under the covers. It was a little after eight o'clock at night. The nurse, Ellen, had explained that Jake was well sedated. He wouldn't be awake until the morning.

"You aren't going to believe this, but I'm going to finish this puzzle," Kathy said. She scribbled furiously as the answers came to her one after another.

"It's good to see things getting back to normal," I said.

All at once, Jake started thrashing around. I stood up quickly, and Kathy ran into the hall screaming Ellen's name. I moved closer to the bed and placed my hand on Jake's right arm. He was struggling to open his eyes, and it seemed to me like he was trying to talk. Three nurses were in the room in a flash, and I moved to one side as they focused in on his movements. From my vantage point at the foot of the bed it looked like a classic Jake temper tantrum, complete with a swinging fist.

"He may be having a seizure," one of the nurses said.

I knew enough not to say anything, but I was fairly confident that it wasn't a seizure at all. He was just mad, and he wanted to let all of us know.

"He was heavily sedated," the nurse whispered. "He must be as strong as an ox."

Kathy was at the front desk talking with Margie, the receptionist. Kathy was shaken but unbowed. "Is he all right? I couldn't watch."

"He's fine," I said. "He's fighting back already."

Kathy and I sat at Jake's bedside until eleven o'clock. We held hands and smiled at one another as we watched Jake rest. I was still real scared that Jake could have a relapse or something, but Kathy was completely at ease.

"You should get some rest," she whispered. "I'm going to get to sleep soon. Why don't you go home?"

I didn't want to leave, but I wasn't doing much good sitting in the chair. I stood up slowly, and Kathy rose out of her chair. She wrapped her arms around my waist, and we hugged for a long moment. "You were right," she said, "this was the best day of our lives."

I walked down the empty hallway and out the side door near the emergency room. The night was quiet and my eyes found the cloudy sky. "Thank you, God, thank you."

I don't know why, maybe it was from fatigue, but I was crying when I entered the parking ramp on Hodge Street. The ramp was quiet except for a couple of people talking in low tones in the corner by the elevator. When I turned the corner, I nearly ran smack into Doctor Levitt. I guessed he was going home for the evening, and he gave me a huge smile.

"I don't even know how to begin to thank you," I said.

He waved me off and said something that sums up the dedication of every pediatrician at The Children's Hospital of Buffalo. "Don't be ridiculous.

I was just doing my job. You have one spunky boy there."

"Jake's a beautiful boy," I said. "He has a wonderful personality."

"It's good that I'll have the chance to know him," Doctor Levitt said.

He shook my hand again. He had no idea how lucky he was to get away without another hug.

I slept rough that first night after the operation, but the next day brought us one day closer to a full recovery. The plan was to remove the ventilator early in the morning, and the nurse explained that they had reduced Jake's sedative a bit, as the doctors wanted him semi-alert when it happened. I was dreading the fact that he might feel pain, but it was important to start removing some of the machines that were doing the work for him. The doctors actually delayed the procedure for a little while, so I stepped out into the hall to call work. When I returned, the ventilator was history, and Jake was sleeping soundly. Kathy had stood by the side of the bed to watch the procedure.

"How was it?" I asked.

"He thrashed around a little. They say he may come around a little later on. I'm just so relieved," she said.

We shared a long hug, and this time I was battling tears of relief. "You know, this is the first time in a month that I've actually felt hungry," I said.

"I was thinking about lunch too," Kathy said. "Maybe I'll run down to the pizza joint."

"Yeah, bring lots of food back."

I don't think I had even settled into the chair before Jake groaned. I edged real close to the bed, and he tried to open his eyes. "Hey, buddy, you beat the bad guys," I whispered.

"Did they do the magic?" he croaked out.

"Yes. There were a lot of bad guys in there, but you beat them." I was laughing and crying all in the same voice. Jake's eyes closed again, and he almost seemed to smile. He started to say something and stopped. I leaned in closer. "You fight 'em next time," he whispered.

I kissed his cheek, and he slipped back to sleep. I wanted to tell him that I was fighting right beside him, but I wasn't. He had battled through it himself. An amazing wave of adrenalin surged through my veins. I thought of the years gone past, and they all felt like one long day. Everything about my life had brought me to this point in time. I felt born anew in my Catholic faith and in humanity because of the wonderful work of the medical team at The Children's Hospital of Buffalo. I only wished that Kathy had been there at that moment.

"I love you, pal," I whispered. "Thank you, God. You made us whole again."

Kathy and I shared a pizza in the room beside the bed. Jake was in and out of sleep for most of the day, and he didn't say much when his eyes were open. I could only imagine what was going on in his mind, and it hurt me to know that he was probably in pain.

In the early evening, Doctor Levitt stopped by. He opened the door slowly and smiled brightly when he saw Kathy. There was something in his manner that showed me that surgery was much more than a job.

"How's he doing?" I asked.

"Wonderfully," he said. "Come on, I'll show you."

I glanced back at Jake, who was still resting comfortably. I followed Kathy and Doctor Levitt out the door toward a computer screen in the middle of the ICU nursing station.

"You remember his X-ray from a month ago, right?" Doctor Levitt asked.

"We'll never forget it," Kathy said.

"Well, let me show you his new one so that you know that we actually did something in there yesterday." Doctor Levitt put the X-ray up on the screen. "See those nice, expanded lungs and the perfect little four-year-old body?"

We all stared at the wonderful image and my heart was just plain singing.

"There is one thing," Doctor Levitt said. He must have noted my concern because he smiled. "When Jake is eighty and needs open heart surgery, you're going to have to let the doctor know that he had this little procedure."

"I don't think I'll be around when he's eighty, but if I am, okay," I said.

Doctor Levitt touched Kathy on the shoulder and headed on down the hall.

"How can we ever thank him?" Kathy asked.

"I don't know," I said. "He probably knows how grateful we are."

"It doesn't seem like enough though," Kathy said.

I struggled with the thought for a long time. There wasn't any way that we could properly express our gratitude. Suffice it to say that we are just eternally thankful to all of the people that worked on Jake's behalf.

Every day passed quicker than the last. Slowly but surely the staff at The Children's Hospital of Buffalo worked to remove the remaining tubes from Jake's body. He came to life before our eyes, almost as if he were being born again. He sipped a little water on that first day and immediately asked for a bag of potato chips. He never once complained of pain and was soon taken off all painkillers. Kathy actually ordered a pain killer for him once because she couldn't believe that he wasn't hurting.

"Geez, remember what a baby you were when you tore your Achilles?" Kathy asked me.

"I'll never complain about anything ever again," I said, which made Kathy smile. "Seriously," I said. "Life will never be the same for any of us."

"I know I appreciate everything more," Kathy said. "We always put the children's welfare before our own, but even that hardly seems like enough. We learned a lot about love and faith, didn't we?"

I couldn't exactly put my finger on it, but I did know one thing — I was happy that I felt eternally grateful. Love had seemed to explode in my heart, and with every second that passed, my love seemed to grow. To equate it to another cartoon, I felt a little like *The Grinch Who Stole Christmas*. My heart was expanding to a thousand times its normal size. I knew right then and there that there really is no limit on how much I could love. If that was the lesson I needed to learn, then I had learned it well.

Over the next few days, Kathy and I remained at Jake's bedside. We became used to the routine X-rays and the words of encouragement from the ICU nurses. Behind the scenes, the doctors monitored Jake's progress, and while we couldn't be sure of the technical aspects of Jake's recovery, our evidence of the staff's competence was in the bed under the covers. Jake was coming back to life.

Jake spent three days in the intensive care unit. While he was in and out of sleep on the first day, he was wide awake by Tuesday morning. The drains were on the floor beside his bed, and the nurses and doctors checked them regularly. Slowly but surely, Jake's appetite and sense of humor returned. Doctor Brecher, Doctor Grossi, Doctor Graf, and Doctor Caty all looked in on Jake, and their lightened moods made it apparent that they were happy with their work. Of course, Doctor Levitt was by at least twice a day. Kathy and I were simply overwhelmed by our own feelings of gratitude.

On Thursday, November 8th, just three short days after the operation, Jake was transferred out of the intensive care unit. We gathered all of his items and moved to the 9th floor, knowing that the move up was one step away from the move out. All of the nurses on duty stopped by Jake's room to wish us well.

Still, one moment of absolute horror still awaited me. After we had moved Jake and his bed upstairs, I returned to the intensive care unit to grab the food left behind in the refrigerator. Jake's spot in room number four of the ICU was already taken, and one of the nurses was yelling for assistance. I stood outside the door watching as the doctors and assistants ran to the bedside of the child in the room. I almost felt guilty because my son was upstairs, on the mend, and another family was going through absolute hell. I saw a man standing off to one side, his head bowed, his shoulders shaking as he sobbed. I thought of what I had been through, and I said a quick prayer asking that the child in that bed would one day be healthy again. As I turned down the hall, I nearly bumped into the man who had shared a sandwich with me on the day of Jake's surgery.

"How's your daughter?" I asked.

"Awesome," he said. "We're moving out of intensive care tonight."

I shook his hand and smiled. "We're already upstairs on nine," I said.

"Oh, thank God!" I was halfway down the hall before his final words reached my ears. "Take care of that wonderful family," he said.

Chapter Seventeen

Our families continued to visit, but now there was a definite feeling of awkwardness as we all got used to the idea that the worst was over and we were actually going home with a cured child. I couldn't help but think of the dear children who suffered for weeks, months, and years. We surely had been through hell, but in all likelihood we were going to soon return to our everyday lives. So why was I feeling so sad?

The dark mood started with Jake. He didn't want to be in bed anymore, but he didn't want to have the final chest drain removed either. "I hate everyone," was how he put it.

We brought in his video games and tried to distract him as we had during his first hospital stay, but he had no stamina; he struggled to watch even a ten minute cartoon. It took a huge St. Bernard dog named Samson to finally bring a smile to Jake's face. Samson was a service dog, ushered through the hospital to visit the sick children. The 200-pound, slobbering beast ran straight to Jake's bedside, thrusting its giant muzzle right up into my son's face. This prompted Jake to ask, "What's his name, Head?"

The dog's enormous head must have weighed thirty pounds, and Jake's question struck me as funny. We all laughed for the better part of ten minutes. It was a laugh of sweet relief, and to this day Jake will look at me and repeat his question whenever things are too quiet for his tastes.

My mother-in-law also stopped by with the best present Jake could have possibly received. She had Sam in her arms, and Matthew stood beside her. When the brothers saw each other their smiles were unbelievably infectious. Matt and Sam's short visit lifted Jake's spirits. We were able to brave the final days with a true sense of purpose and even good humor.

On Friday night, Kathy and I talked with the resident doctor. He explained that Jake's recovery was progressing without complication and that there was an outside chance that we would be home before the end of the weekend. When the final chest drain was removed on Sunday, Kathy hugged me close. "We made it through," she whispered. "I feel like we can handle anything as a family."

"I know we can," I whispered.

Early on Sunday morning, November 11, 2001, I carried a couple of suitcases as Kathy wheeled Jake out of the elevator into the main lobby of The Children's Hospital of Buffalo. "I don't have to come back for a lot of days?" Jake asked.

"Right," Kathy said, her eyes glittering with tears of relief. I touched her right shoulder, and she turned to me. "I've never felt better in my life," she whispered.

The hard air was crisp, and a few snowflakes winged their way past us on a breeze. It was exhilarating to know that we were well on the way to getting our life back. I pulled the car up to the emergency room doors, and Jake had one more surprise for me. "Thanks for staying with me when I was in the hospital," he said.

I lifted him out of the wheelchair and kissed his right cheek. "You're welcome, buddy."

* * *

There still was one more major cause of concern: the nature of Jake's tumor. Once again we waited as the pathologist prepared the report on the tumor. Over the course of the next few days, I readied my mind for the news that cancer cells had been found. I also steeled myself against the reality that I truly didn't have much of a say in some of the more important things in life. I could make sure that my family was protected and safe on a day-to-day basis, but the presence of Jake's tumor taught me that in matters of life and death, I was at the mercy of God.

On the eve of the release of the pathology report, I sat on the couch with my arm around Kathy's shoulder. We were both unbelievably down in the dumps as we awaited the news.

"I don't know what I'll do if they tell us that there are cancer cells in there," I said.

"You'll face it," Kathy said. "We'll face it together."

I caressed her shoulder and kissed her on the cheek. "I suppose we will, but the thing is, we don't control anything about their lives. We're just care-takers, and we're at the mercy of a higher power. We can't stop bad things from happening to the boys."

Kathy considered this for a moment. She leaned away from me, but all at once, her eyes sparkled. "We have to surrender our lives to God," she said. "After this, we know to trust God. No matter how this life works out, our faith will be rewarded."

There are moments of pure love in a marriage, and this was one of ours. When Kathy framed the depth of our faith in such a neat package, I can honestly say that I loved her more than ever. "You're a wonderful mother and woman," I said.

"I know," she answered, and we laughed.

The next day, we received the last bit of great news: The tumor was 100% benign, and Jake's follow-up treatment would consist only of annual check-ups.

* * *

On Thanksgiving morning, just three short weeks after the operation, I sat down at my computer screen and punched up the e-mail option. Kathy and the boys were still asleep. We were planning to visit my parents for Thanksgiving dinner, and given Jake's rapid recovery, we had a lot to be thankful for. I checked my e-mail from my friends and co-workers, and one message captured my heart. They were the words of Abraham Lincoln's 1863 Thanksgiving Proclamation.

"We have been the recipients of the choicest bounties of heaven; we have been preserved these many years in peace and prosperity; we have grown in numbers, wealth, and power as no other nation has ever grown. Intoxicated with unbroken success, we have become too self-sufficient to feel the necessity of redeeming and preserving grace, too proud to pray to the God that made us. It has seemed to me fit and proper that God should be solemnly, reverently, and gratefully acknowledged, as with one heart and one voice, by the whole American people. I do therefore invite my fellow citizens in every part of the United States...to set apart and observe the last Thursday of November as a day of Thanksgiving and praise to our beneficent Father who dwelleth in the heavens."

Later that day, as we settled in for Thanksgiving dinner at my parent's home, the words of Abraham Lincoln's proclamation gnawed at my brain. My mother set the turkey in the center of the table, and she looked directly at me as she said, "We need someone to say a prayer."

For the first time in a lot of years, all of my brothers and sisters were there with their spouses and children. I considered each and every one of them for a moment as my eyes filled with tears. Matthew was seated directly across from me, and his eyes misted over with worry as he considered my tears.

"We have a lot to be thankful for," I whispered. "I wish I knew the right words to the right prayer. All I can tell you is that we faced one of the greatest challenges that we'll ever face, and we really needed each and every one of you. And you all came through for us."

I glanced around the table. My mother was crying, as were both of my sisters. My brother Jeff bowed his head and Kathy wiped tears from her eyes. I searched the room for Jake and I found him sitting beside my brother John. Jake smiled wonderfully.

"Kathy and I always knew that we had terrific families, and no one let us down. Thank you. We also knew that our faith was strong and that God would answer us somehow. Life doesn't always work out the way that we want it to, but this time, our prayers were answered exactly as we needed them to be. Thank you, God."

After dinner, my sisters presented birthday cakes for my brother John and my mother. Jake sat between them, and, as Carrie lit the candles, we all waited for the final test. We sang the birthday song and my mother's eyes filled with tears as Jake dug deep and blew out the candles with a single breath of air. Without question, it was the greatest moment of my life.

Epilogue

June 6, 2002

Our Lady of the Sacred Heart's 2001-2002 Pre-K Class gathered on the stage in the gymnasium. Kathy and I entered hand-in-hand, with Sam, Matt, Kathy's parents, and sister Carilee following close behind. The gym was a bustle of activity as the families of each member of the class milled about, talking and laughing. I spotted Jake up on the stage, and he waved.

"We're lucky to be here tonight," I whispered to Kathy. She squeezed my hand a little tighter.

Jake's Pre-K teacher, Mrs. Matte, grabbed a microphone and addressed the gathering. "This has been a terrific year for me," she said. "I have had the pleasure of meeting all of the wonderful children that made up the Pre-K class, and I have thoroughly enjoyed teaching them this year. Tonight, we have arranged a presentation called Celebrate the Seasons. The children have worked very hard to make this entertaining, and I hope you enjoy the show."

Camera bulbs flashed as one by one the children walked across the stage to recite their lines. Jake was the sixth child to cross the stage. He looked a little nervous as he brought his mouth to the microphone, and I ran across the room in an effort to snap a great photo. Jake hesitated for a moment, and then his voice boomed out as he recited his one line. "Summer's over, now its fall."

I raised the camera to my face, and my heart raced with pride and appreciation as every second of his illness came back to me like a tidal wave. The voice inside my head was screaming out to me. "Thank you, God! A million times over, thank you!"

I lowered the camera and reached out for Kathy's hand. She looked up at me and smiled. "I love you," she said. "I love our family."

The class was singing a song that called for them to slip on a pair of sunglasses. Jake fumbled his glasses and nearly dropped them. He slipped them on his face, all the while screaming out the words at the top of his voice. His unbridled enthusiasm brought tears to my eyes. We were celebrating life, pure and simple, and we were lucky to have such an opportunity.